CAMBRIDGE
UNIVERSITY PRESS

Success

International English Skills

for Cambridge IGCSE™

COURSEBOOK

Frances Reynolds, Ingrid Wisniewska & Marian Barry

CAMBRIDGE
UNIVERSITY PRESS

University Printing House, Cambridge CB2 8BS, United Kingdom

One Liberty Plaza, 20th Floor, New York, NY 10006, USA

477 Williamstown Road, Port Melbourne, VIC 3207, Australia

314–321, 3rd Floor, Plot 3, Splendor Forum, Jasola District Centre, New Delhi – 110025, India

103 Penang Road, #05–06/07, Visioncrest Commercial, Singapore 238467

Cambridge University Press is part of the University of Cambridge.

It furthers the University's mission by disseminating knowledge in the pursuit of education, learning and research at the highest international levels of excellence.

www.cambridge.org
Information on this title: www.cambridge.org/9781009122542 (Paperback)

First published by Georgian Press (Jersey) Limited 1998
Second edition 2005
Reprinted and published by Cambridge University Press, Cambridge 2010
Third edition 2015
Fourth edition 2017
Fifth edition 2022

20 19 18 17 16 15 14 13 12 11 10 9 8 7 6 5 4 3 2

Printed in Malaysia by Vivar Printing

A catalogue record for this publication is available from the British Library

ISBN 978-1-009-12254-2 Paperback with Digital Access (2 Years)
ISBN 978-1-009-11399-1 Digital Coursebook (2 Years)
ISBN 978-1-009-11400-4 eBook

....

DEDICATED TEACHER AWARDS

Teachers play an important part in shaping futures. Our Dedicated Teacher Awards recognise the hard work that teachers put in every day.

Thank you to everyone who nominated this year; we have been inspired and moved by all of your stories. Well done to all of our nominees for your dedication to learning and for inspiring the next generation of thinkers, leaders and innovators.

Congratulations to our incredible winners!

WINNER

Regional Winner	Regional Winner	Regional Winner	Regional Winner	Regional Winner	Regional Winner
Middle East & North Africa	Europe	North & South America	Central & Southern Africa	Australia, New Zealand & South-East Asia	East & South Asia
Annamma Lucy	**Anna Murray**	**Melissa Crosby**	**Nonhlanhla Masina**	**Peggy Pesik**	**Raminder Kaur Mac**
GEMS Our Own English High School, Sharjah - Boys' Branch, UAE	British Council, France	Frankfort High School, USA	African School for Excellence, South Africa	Sekolah Buin Batu, Indonesia	Choithram School, India

For more information about our dedicated teachers and their stories, go to
dedicatedteacher.cambridge.org

CAMBRIDGE
UNIVERSITY PRESS

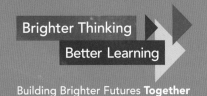

Brighter Thinking
Better Learning

Building Brighter Futures **Together**

〉 Contents

> Contents chart

Language study / grammar spotlight	Vocabulary and spelling	Exam-style questions	Assessment objective focus
Using apostrophes Present simple and continuous	Vocabulary about plans for the future and attitudes to people Spelling words ending in *-ate/-ite* Approaches to spelling Why do we misspell words? Describing people's qualities Negative prefixes Homophones Multi-word verbs	Reading: open response Writing: informal and formal Listening: interview Speaking: interview, short talk and discussion	R2, R3, R4 W1, W3, W4 S1, S2, S3, S4 L2, L3, L4
Compound adjectives with numbers Conditional forms with *if*	Vocabulary for sports and fitness Words in context Adding suffixes to words ending in *–e* Word families	Reading: note-taking Writing: informal and formal Listening: multiple matching Speaking: interview, short talk and discussion	R1, R2, R3, R4 W1, W2, W3 S1, S3, S4 L1, L2
Using the gerund Order of adjectives Passives	Vocabulary about home and for description Prefixes Doubling consonants when adding suffixes	Reading: multiple matching Writing: informal and formal Listening: dialogue Speaking: interview, short talk and discussion	R2, R3, R4 W1, W2, W3, W4 S1, S2, S3, S4 L1, L2, L4
Using connectives to guide the reader Expressing reasons and consequences Further connectives Making predictions	Vocabulary about global warming Euphemisms Spelling patterns with /dʒ/ Vocabulary in context Words often confused	Reading: multiple matching and multiple choice Writing: informal and formal Listening: sentence completion Speaking: interview, short talk and discussion	R1, R2, R3 W1, W2, W3, W4 S1, S2, S3, S4 L1, L2
So . . . that and *such . . . that* Viewpoint and evaluative adverbs Present perfect tense	Vocabulary about films and sounds *So... that* and *such... that* Collocations The letter *c* Words in context The letters *ch* Language for reviews Present perfect tense to talk about experiences	Reading: multiple matching Writing: informal and formal Listening: short extracts and multiple matching Speaking: interview, short talk and discussion	R1, R2, R3, R4 W1, W2, W3, W4 S1, S2, S3, S4 L1, L2, L3

Language study / grammar spotlight	Vocabulary and spelling	Exam-style questions	Assessment objective focus
Using modifiers before adjectives Adverbs as modifiers Adverbs of frequency	Vocabulary about travel, tourism and the weather Adjective collocations Colloquial expressions Adjective suffixes Vocabulary in context Words from names More homophones Spelling adjectives with –y	Reading: note-taking Writing: informal and formal Listening:sentence completion Speaking: interview, short talk and discussion	R1, R2, R3 W1, W3, W4 S1, S2, S3, S4 L1, L2, L3, L4
Giving advice *Should/shouldn't* + *have* + past participle Text speak	Vocabulary about studies and student life Colloquial words and phrases Building nouns from verbs Building adjectives from nouns Silent letters Idiomatic expressions	Reading: open response Writing: informal and formal Listening: dialogue and interview Speaking: interview, short talk and discussion	R1, R2, R3 W1, W2, W3, W4 S1, S2, S3 L1, L2, L3, L4
Narrative tenses Reported speech Defining relative clauses Non-defining relative clauses Adverbs Interrupted past continuous	Vocabulary about adventure and the sea Prefixes *mal-* and *counter-* Adjectives Suffixes *–tion* or *–ion* Adverbs	Reading: multiple matching Writing: informal and formal Listening: short extracts Speaking: interview, short talk and discussion	R1, R3, R4 W1, W2, W3, W4 S1, S2, S3, S4 L1, L2, L3
Prepositions after verbs Adding emphasis Rhetorical questions Past perfect passive	Vocabulary for animals Regular plurals Irregular plurals Words for feelings Collective nouns	Reading: multiple choice Writing: informal and formal Listening: multiple matching Speaking: interview, short talk and discussion	R1, R2, R3, R4 W1, W2, W3, W4 S1, S2, S3, S4 L1, L2, L3, L4
Idioms Similes Phrasal verbs Using apostrophes Superlatives	Vocabulary about work, skills and qualities Approximations Criticising statistics Suffixes: *-able* and *–ible* Superlatives of long and short adjectives Adverbs of degree	Reading: multiple choice Writing: informal and formal Listening: interview Speaking: interview, short talk and discussion	R1, R2, R3, R4 W1, W2, W3, W4 S1, S2, S3, S4 L1, L2, L3, L4

> How to use this series

All the components in the series are designed to work together.

Coursebook with digital access 	The Coursebook is designed for students to use in class with guidance from the teacher. It offers complete coverage of the Cambridge IGCSE and IGCSE (9–1) English as a Second Language syllabuses (0510/0511/0991/0993) for examination from 2024. Ten topic-based units engage students and help them to develop the necessary reading, writing, speaking, listening and grammar skills. Each unit contains opportunities to check progress, with exam-style questions and self-assessment features. A digital version of the Coursebook is included with the print version and available separately. It includes the video and audio as well as simple tools for students to use in class or for self-study.
Workbook with digital access 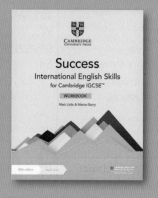	The write-in Workbook provides further reading, writing and listening practice and is ideal for use in class or as homework. A digital version of the Workbook is included with the print version.
Teacher's Resource with digital access 	The Teacher's Resource provides everything teachers need to deliver the course, including suggestions for differentiation and common misconceptions, audioscripts, answers, sample writing answers, a word list, unit tests and a full practice exam-style test. Each Teacher's Resource includes: • a print book with detailed teaching notes for each unit • digital access with all the material from the book in digital form plus extra downloadable resources and audio.

› How to use this book

In this book, there are a variety of features to help you learn.

LEARNING INTENTIONS

These cover what you will learn in the unit.

BEFORE YOU START

An engaging image with questions to help introduce you to the theme of the unit.

INTERNATIONAL OVERVIEW

These are fact files based on the theme, providing an international insight and a chance to learn how to extract information.

GLOSSARY

Definitions are provided for new or difficult words within texts.

GRAMMAR SPOTLIGHT

These focus on key grammatical points from within the unit, linking back to texts and activities, and taking them a bit further.

ADVICE FOR SUCCESS

This will help you to think about how you learn and give you practical advice on how to demonstrate this.

› **Critical thinking** These are questions specifically designed to develop your critical thinking skills as part of your studies.

Videos can be accessed through the Digital Coursebook.

Audio tracks can be accessed through the Digital Coursebook and the Digital Teacher's Resource.

SELF-ASSESSMENT CHECKLIST

Linking back to the learning intentions at the start of the unit, this provides an opportunity to reflect on how confident you feel on each point, and whether you need more practice.

EXAM-STYLE QUESTIONS

Exam-style questions provide practice at answering the type of tasks that appear in examinations.

 Some of the Language focus sections and Language tips are informed by the Cambridge English Corpus – a multi-billion word collection of examples of spoken and written English. We use our corpus to answer questions about English vocabulary, grammar and usage. Along with this, we collect and analyse learner writing. This allows us to clearly see how learners from around the world are similar and different in how they acquire and use language. These insights allow us to provide tailored and comprehensive support to learners at all stages of their learning journey.

> Syllabus overview

The information in this section is taken from the Cambridge IGCSE and IGCSE (9–1) English as a Second Language syllabuses (0510 / 0511 / 0991 / 0993) for examination from 2024. You should always refer to the appropriate syllabus document for the year of your examination to confirm the details and for more information.

The syllabus document is available on the Cambridge International website at www.cambridgeinternational.org.

Reading and Writing

The Reading and Writing paper lasts for 2 hours. There are 60 marks in total. The paper contains four reading exercises based on four different reading texts, and two writing exercises.

Listening

The Listening paper lasts for approximately 50 minutes. There are 40 marks in total. The paper involves listening to several short extracts and longer texts and completing five multiple-choice exercises.

Speaking

The Speaking paper lasts for approximately 10–15 minutes. There are 40 marks in total. After a warm-up conversation, students engage in an 8–11 minute discussion with the examiner on a given topic.

Assessment objectives

Skill	Assessment objectives	
AO1: Reading	R1	demonstrate understanding of specific factual information
	R2	demonstrate understanding of the connections between the ideas, opinions and attitudes
	R3	identify and select details for a specific purpose
	R4	demonstrate understanding of implied meaning
AO2: Writing	W1	communicate information, ideas and opinions
	W2	organise ideas into coherent text using a range of linking devices
	W3	use a range of appropriate grammatical structures and vocabulary
	W4	use appropriate register and style for the given purpose and audience
AO3: Listening	L1	demonstrate understanding of specific information
	L2	demonstrate understanding of speakers' ideas, opinions and attitudes
	L3	demonstrate understanding of the connections between ideas, opinions and attitudes
	L4	demonstrate understanding of what is implied but not directly stated
AO4: Speaking	Candidates will be assessed on their ability to:	
	S1	communicate a range of ideas, facts and opinions
	S2	demonstrate control of a range of vocabulary and grammatical structures
	S3	develop responses and maintain communication
	S4	demonstrate control of pronunciation and intonation

> Introduction

Dear Student,

Success International English Skills for Cambridge IGCSE™ is a course designed to support you as you study the Cambridge IGCSE English as a Second Language syllabus and prepare for your exams.

This Coursebook helps you to develop the skills you will need for success in your studies – whether it is reading and listening comprehension, vocabulary expansion, note-taking or different styles of writing or speaking. This book aims to stretch and challenge you to reach your full potential in all these skills.

Success is topic-based, and you will be practising your language skills while deepening your understanding of a range of contemporary issues. The exercises are thematically linked so you will find it easy to learn and remember new vocabulary and language structures. Each unit of the book focuses on an exciting and thought-provoking theme and challenges you to analyse it in a critical way.

The units help you build up your skills, from the simpler aspects of learning, such as recognising and understanding information, to more challenging ones like understanding people's attitudes. Reading and listening to different views on the topic will help you to develop your own opinions. Discussing them with your classmates will help you to express your ideas so you will learn to communicate clearly and confidently on a range of topics.

Even when you have lots of good ideas, it is sometimes a struggle to get them down on paper. The exercises in *Success International* will help you overcome that kind of frustration because each topic is broken down into small segments. This means you can get each part of an exercise clear in your mind before moving on to the next part. In the end, you will have an overview of a whole topic and will find that you can produce an excellent email or article, or present an impressive talk to your group.

Developing your ability to express yourself in writing is an important goal of the course. Before you start a writing task, you will be given lots of help with vocabulary and the style to use, so when it is your turn to write independently, you'll be able to do so confidently and easily. There are several exercises that show the difference between a simple, basic way of writing and a more developed style, which is appropriate

for a young adult. Improving your writing style means learning to look at your work and others' work with a critical eye. This requires effort and concentration, but it is what will help you become a more effective writer.

This book provides many opportunities for you to share your ideas in English with your group. Discussion is a great way to share ideas with other people, take a concept further or get ready for an interesting listening or reading exercise. Use the photographs in the book to stimulate ideas. Be creative. Be passionate about your own opinions, but listen carefully to others as well. Collaborating with others and getting feedback from them is crucial to improvement. Learning to engage in a conversation or a discussion is an important life skill that will help you in any future study or work context.

Before you start a new unit, remember to check the Contents chart. There, you will see all your learning aims for the unit. You will also see how what you are going to study relates to what you have already done. You should always be clear about what you are learning and how it is going to help you.

At the end of each unit, you will be asked to reflect on what you have learnt. This will help you evaluate your progress, so you can see what you need to do next to keep extending and developing yourself. Learn to identify strengths and areas for improvement. The 'Advice for success' section provides ideas for further practice and building skills. Everyone is different, so mark the 'Advice for success' according to whether the suggestions are a top priority for you or interesting but not a top priority. Write down your personal priorities and make sure you follow them through. Build on your learning in the classroom by finding ways to practise outside class.

Throughout the book, you will be practising skills and tasks that will help you in your future study and work. At the end of each unit, there are exam-style questions for you to practise. You may use them to practise working in a timed setting, or simply as further skills practice. Remember to apply the techniques you have learnt during the course to each of the exam-style questions.

We hope you'll enjoy using the book and will find it a useful tool on your path to success!

Goals and achievements

LEARNING INTENTIONS

In this unit you will:

- Explore the topic of goals, achievements and qualities we admire
- Build awareness of audience, purpose and features of texts
- Learn skills for describing people and their qualities
- Practise listening to understand the speaker's ideas and attitudes
- Write a formal email for a specific purpose and audience

01 Watch the video about goals and achievements in the digital coursebook.

BEFORE YOU START

Look at the photo on this page.

a   Describe what you can see in the photo.

b   How do you think the woman with the glasses feels, and why?

c   Why is this day important in the lives of the young people in the photo?

d   What other 'milestones' in life do we celebrate?

A Our outlook on life

1 Quiz

Our outlook on life is the way that we think about life. Complete this online quiz in pairs to find out about your outlook on life. Make a note of your own and your partner's answers.

1 You are going to watch a film with some friends, and they say it's your turn to pick the film. Do you:
 A Tell someone else to choose – they might not like your choice.
 B Choose a film you love, hoping your friends will enjoy it too.
 C Choose a film you think your friends want to see.

2 All your friends are signing up for a free scuba diving 'taster day'. You've never tried scuba diving before. Do you:
 A Make an excuse – you might not like it.
 B Go along – it might be fun.
 C Go, but only because you don't want to be the odd one out.

3 What do you watch online?
 A Anything – it's a way of killing time.
 B I choose things that interest me, but I limit my viewing time as I have other hobbies too.
 C I mainly watch videos that people have recommended – but I know I ought to be doing something more useful!

4 How do you feel about making new friends?
 A I already have some good friends and that's enough for me.
 B I enjoy getting to know all sorts of people.
 C I think it's important to expand your social circle.

5 A friend texts you 2 minutes before an important family meal: they are very upset about a personal issue. Do you:
 A Ignore the text for now – you'll answer later.
 B Reply straightaway by text explaining you'll call him/her later.
 C Tell your family you'll be late, and call your friend.

6 Do you plan ahead?
 A Not really, I take life as it comes.
 B Making plans gives me a sense of purpose, but I like a few surprises too.
 C Yes, I like to set goals for myself and know that I'm not wasting my time.

7 How do you deal with difficult situations?
 A I avoid the kind of situations that may hurt me.
 B If a situation is upsetting me, I walk away.
 C I try not to let things get me down: I face the difficulty and stay.

8 How do you decide what to wear?
 A I'm not interested in clothes, so I don't give it much thought.
 B I choose the clothes that are most comfortable and practical.
 C I try to be fashionable.

9 You forget to turn up for an important school meeting. How do you feel?
 A Upset that none of your friends reminded you.
 B Disappointed, but next time you'll set a phone reminder.
 C Annoyed with yourself for being so stupid.

10 What motivates you most to do well at school?
 A Future job prospects.
 B Personal satisfaction.
 C Making my family proud.

See the end of Unit 1 for quiz scores.

2 Discussion

Discuss the following with a partner:

1 The quiz talks about knowing what you want in life. Do you think it is possible to live your life entirely in the way that you want? What are the secrets to a happy life?

2 Do you like to set goals for yourself? Why / why not? Do you write down your goals, or are they in your head?

3 Think of an example of a goal that you set for yourself that you achieved. What was it, and how did you feel when you achieved it?

3 New Year resolutions

> **Critical thinking** In many parts of the world, people set New Year resolutions (personal goals) for themselves at the beginning of each year. Do people do this in your country?

Work in a small group to answer the following questions:

1 Look at the list of topics for New Year resolutions. Which do you think are the five most popular? Put them in order 1–5. Give reasons for your chosen order.

- Spend more time with relatives
- Get more sleep
- Change your lifestyle to help the environment
- Travel more
- Take up a new hobby or learn a new skill
- Do more exercise and improve your fitness
- Get a better job
- Do some volunteering or charity work
- Spend less time on social media
- Spend less money and save more
- Eat more healthily
- Work harder

2 Can you think of any resolutions *not* on the list that would be popular in your country?

3 Research shows that most people fail to keep their New Year's resolutions for very long. Why do you think that is?

4 Setting goals for the future

Here are some useful sentence starters for talk about hopes, dreams and plans for the future.

> My goal is to. . .
>
> My dream is to. . .
>
> I hope to. . .
>
> I'd love to . . .
>
> I'm determined (not) to . . .
>
> I'm (not) going to . . .

1 Write one or two sentences expressing your own hopes, dreams and plans about some of the following areas of your life:

- Learning English
- Education in general
- Travel
- Career
- Work–life balance

2 Just for fun, think of a 'pipe dream' for yourself – a dream that you think is completely unrealistic or impossible (e.g. *My dream is to live in the first colony on Mars*).

Share your ideas with a partner.

5 Pre-reading tasks

> **Critical thinking** Think about what you do when you come across a word in a reading text that you don't know.

1 One helpful strategy is to use context clues. With a partner, decide what *plokzack* (not a real word in English) might mean in the following sentences. What clues helped you?

  a She got a *plokzack* for driving the wrong way down a one-way street.

  b Older mobiles tend to *plokzack* more quickly than newer ones.

  c We can assure the public that we have tested our new vaccine *plokzackly* so it's absolutely safe.

2 As you read the text in Section A6 (Reading for gist), underline or note down any unfamiliar words and use context clues to predict their meaning. Don't look them up in a dictionary for now.

6 Reading for gist

Read the text below for the first time to get a general idea, without worrying too much about details. Then answer the questions.

1 Where would you expect to find a text like this? What type of text is it? How can you tell?

2 Who is it written for (the 'audience')?

3 What is its purpose?

4 What sort of person might have written it?

HALEENA K
MAKE EVERY DAY COUNT

HOME   ABOUT ME   CONTACT

Plan your life – or not?

8 January 2022

Some of you have been asking for my tips on how to set goals (yes, it's that time of year!) I find it interesting that, when we were five, our teachers gave us gold stars and smiley face stickers for
5 reaching our targets – and that habit of wanting to 'tick off' our progress on a chart has never really left us! So, let's talk about goal setting.

A cousin of mine set his heart on studying law at a top university – to the surprise of his family as
10 he had never been a high flyer at school. But he worked like crazy, got accepted at the university – and allowed himself one night of celebration before setting himself a new target: a first-class degree. There followed three years of head-down
15 study (with zero social life), then he did a Master's degree and more years of work . . . He had barely received his certificate before he disappeared to volunteer in a stray animal shelter in Malaysia, where he's lived very happily ever since. It took him
20 seven years to admit to himself that he loathed law: he just had to keep pursuing that next goal.

OK, so don't set the wrong goals in the first place – but sometimes it's hard to be sure of what we really want until we get it. There's nothing wrong
25 with having aspirations and taking a few chances, but the secret is not to make the end goal itself the only thing that matters. Make sure you enjoy the process of getting there, and reward yourself for the small milestones you reach along the way.
30 So if it turns out the destination itself isn't what you thought you wanted, you haven't made the journey for nothing.

Another mistake we often make is to focus solely on that one small point on the horizon – our distant
35 goal – without allowing ourselves to see things that unexpectedly enter our peripheral vision. (A bit like a wildlife photographer unsuccessfully scanning the sky all day for eagles and ignoring the rare butterfly that lands on her camera case.) Sometimes
40 happiness comes from unexpected directions: keep your eyes and your mind open to opportunities.

Remember, too, that you may not have the total control over your goals that you think you do. All sorts of obstacles can hold you back (family
45 issues, illness, money), or your schedule may be unrealistic. (If you've never run before, you're not going to complete a marathon next week!) The key here is flexibility – and not to beat yourself up. Be honest with yourself – and move the goalposts.
50 Move them as often as you like!

7 Comprehension check

True or false? Underline the words in the blog that give you the answer.

1   We set goals and tick them off because we learnt to do this at an early age.

2   The writer thinks his cousin was wrong to have a goal.

3   The writer thinks you should break down big goals into smaller sections.

4   The writer thinks it's important to stick with your goals and not change them.

8 Style features

Different types of texts have different features, depending on their audience and purpose.

With a partner, find examples of each of the following in the blog text:

a   direct address to the audience

b   writer making connections with the reader (we/us)

c   writer sharing information about him/herself

d   some informal, conversational language.

9 How helpful is your dictionary?

Predicting the meaning of words in context is a very useful skill – but a dictionary can provide lots of extra information. In pairs, use your dictionaries to answer the following questions about words from the blog text. You can use either an online or print dictionary. (If possible, work with a partner who is using a different dictionary.)

For each question, note down:

•   whether or not the dictionary gives you the information (and how)

•   the answer to the question (if possible).

a   *loathe* (line 20) – How do you pronounce it?

b   *stray* (line 18) – Does it belong to more than one grammatical class (e.g. verb, noun, adjective)?

c   *aspiration* (line 25) – Are there example sentences showing how this word is used? Choose one example to write down.

d   *vision* (line 36) – Is it countable, uncountable, or both?

e   *goalpost* (line 49) – Are there any idiomatic expressions using this word? Choose one example to write down.

f   *beat yourself up* (line 48) – Is this expression formal or informal?

10 Figurative meanings

The blog says the writer's cousin was not a 'high flyer' at school – and she refers to 'moving the goalposts'. The literal meaning of *fly* is to move through the air and *goalposts* are (literally) the vertical parts of a goal in a sport such as football. But the figurative meaning of *high flyer* is someone who is much more successful than other people, and *moving the goalposts* (figuratively) means changing the rules for something. (It is often used as a criticism.) There are lots of figurative uses of words in English: look out for them.

Practice

In each of the following sentences, underline the figurative language. Then discuss its meaning with your partner. Finally, make up sentences of your own to illustrate the meanings. Don't forget to use a dictionary when you need to.

1   When she was offered the chance to work in New York, she jumped at the opportunity.

2   Losing her grandmother's ring broke her heart.

3   We're fighting the authorities who want to close our village school.

4   His face broke into a smile when he heard the good news.

5   I'm tired of battling with staff who refuse to accept different working conditions.

6   When I shop online, I always keep my eye out for a bargain.

7   The hospital helpline was flooded with calls from worried people.

B Facing challenges

1 Discussion

> **Critical thinking** Sometimes we set ourselves goals that really challenge us and we have to overcome obstacles (things that get in our way). With a partner, discuss whether you have ever faced the following kinds of challenges. How did you feel? How hard do you think it is to meet challenges like these? Do you believe it is possible to achieve anything if you 'put your mind to it'?

•   Overcoming a fear (e.g. spiders, the dark, heights, deep water)

•   Giving up a habit (e.g. getting up late, spending too long staring at screens, procrastinating)

•   A hard physical challenge (e.g. swimming/walking/ running a long distance).

2 Expressing fears and reassuring someone

In pairs, read the following dialogue.

A: I've got to recite a poem in front of the whole school.

B: How do you feel about it?

A: To tell you the truth, I'm a bit worried about it.

B: Don't worry. You'll be fine. Everyone thinks you're great!

1   When people want to express fears, they use expressions like these. Select the one(s) that sound most fearful.

☐ I feel sick every time I think about it.

☐ To tell you the truth, I'm a bit scared about it.

☐ I'm not really sure I can cope.

☐ To be honest, I'm not sure I'll be able to do it.

☐ The thought of it bothers me a bit.

☐ I'm terrified!

2   Here are some expressions you can use to reassure someone. Which do you prefer?

•   There's nothing to worry about. You'll do a wonderful job.

•   You'll be fine. Nothing can go wrong.

•   Things will be OK. We're all supporting you.

•   Try not to worry. It might not be as hard as you think.

Practice

Practise expressing fears and reassuring someone in pairs. One of you should explain what he/she has to do. The other should give reassurance. Then swap over. Base your dialogues on these situations:

* Fear of taking an exam

* Fear of competing in a race or a match

* Fear of giving a talk in front of the school

* Fear of going to the dentist.

3 Pre-listening task

You are going to listen to five people talking about their experiences of challenges. First, match these words with the correct definitions.

a	(finger) nail	1	small insect that sucks blood
b	charity event		
c	shave	2	thin hard covering on the end of a finger
d	trail	3	remove hair with a razor
e	mosquito	4	person you don't know
f	stranger	5	activity to raise money for those who need it
		6	walking path through the countryside

From looking at these words, try to guess what challenges the speakers might talk about.

4 Listening: How people react to challenges

Listen to the five speakers. Which speaker:

a regrets that they couldn't complete their challenge? ☐

b felt sad when their challenge was over? ☐

c thinks the challenge has made them more confident? ☐

d learnt something about themselves that they don't like? ☐

e was surprised by other people's reactions after they completed their challenge? ☐

5 Pre-reading discussion

> **Critical thinking** You are going to read about Monica, a woman who faced a personal difficulty: she didn't learn to read until she was an adult. Discuss the following questions with a partner:

1 What everyday problems do you think not being able to read would present?

2 Why might someone who was unable to read not try to get help to learn?

3 What effect do you think not being able to read might have on them?

6 Vocabulary check

Make sure you know the meaning of these words; they are important for understanding the text. Use a dictionary if necessary.

stomach ache   bully (verb)   illiterate
fool (verb)   volunteer (noun)

When you come to the phrasal verb *let on* (Paragraph 3), use context clues to predict what it means.

7 Reading: Textual organisation

Read the text carefully and match each paragraph (1–7) with one of these headings. If there are words you don't know, try to predict their meaning using context clues.

a Effects on Sally's education

b Hiding the problem

c Unhappy school days

d Qualifying as a parent-educator

e Sally's birth

f Monica's work today

g Learning to read

Facing Fears

1 Monica Chand's childhood memories are of terrible stomach aches each morning before school, of missing lessons through illness and falling so far behind that she understood little but did not dare to ask for help, and of silent misery as children bullied her. She says, 'When I had Sally, 17 years ago, I was determined it would not be the same for her.' She is sitting in her tidy flat, drinking tea. Sally, her teenage daughter, joins us.

2 Monica is describing how it feels to be unable to read and write in a world where just about everything we do, and how we are judged, depends on our literacy skills. Few people, she says, realise what it means to be unable to read a road sign, safety instructions or the contents of a food packet, or how it feels when every form you have to fill in is an impossible task. Few understand what people do to disguise their inability to read and write. Monica explains, 'I would have the names of places I wanted to go to written down, and then I'd show this and ask someone to help, explaining that I'd left my glasses at home or some such story. You get good at fooling other people, but you can't fool yourself.'

3 Her husband, Ravi, who died earlier this year, was unaware of her secret. She says, 'I'd just ask him to do the things I couldn't cope with and he accepted that. But it really came home to me when Sally was born. I felt very insecure as a mother, and as she grew up everyone around me was saying, "You must read to her." I felt so stupid because I couldn't.' Even then she did not tell Ravi, although she smiles now and says, 'I think he must have known in his heart of hearts, but he was such a sweet man he never let on. I made sure he did the reading with Sally – I'd say I had to cook dinner and that it was a good way for them to be close.'

4 Things changed when Sally went to primary school, and Monica became a volunteer in the school, helping children. One morning the headteacher said they wanted to offer her a paid job as a helper. 'I just froze. I knew that would involve reading and writing – the things I'd avoided so far. But the headteacher had recognised my problem. She did reading with me every day so that I could take the job. As I learnt, she put me in with older children, and I realised I could read and write. It was like a miracle.'

5 Then Monica joined a parents' group, and the new headteacher asked them to write a book for parents teaching their children. Monica says, 'My first reaction was, "Ooh, I can't do that," but then I realised I could contribute – to help other parents like me.' By now, she was doing a training course to become a parent-educator. 'The day I got my certificate – the first in my life – Sally and I went out for a really nice meal to celebrate.'

6 These struggles are in the past. Monica works in several schools and has just returned from a conference in Cyprus where she gave a presentation on involving parents in reading. She also has a highly successful blog, which gets thousands of hits from users who post comments about her inspirational ideas.

7 Monica talks about her daughter, Sally. 'Perhaps I pushed her harder than other parents because I knew what failing feels like, and I suppose I was living my life through her. But we were both bursting with pride the day she did really well in her exams. I was in tears in front of everyone at school.' Sally is no less proud. She is sitting on the arm of the sofa near her mother, listening, and her smile is warm. She says, 'I think it was brave of Mum. She's also shown me how important it is to take opportunities when they come.'

8 Comprehension check

Read the text again carefully and answer the questions.

1 How do you think Monica felt at school?

   A   Embarrassed and lonely.

   B   Angry and upset.

   C   Scared and in pain.

2 According to Monica, most people don't really understand:

   A   How many people are illiterate.

   B   What life is like if you are illiterate.

   C   How to help people who are illiterate.

3 Why did Monica say she had left her glasses at home?

   A   To make strangers feel sorry for her.

   B   To avoid admitting that she couldn't read.

   C   As a way of starting a conversation with a stranger.

4 How did Monica's illiteracy affect her when Sally was young?

   A   She was terrified her husband would think she was stupid.

   B   She felt annoyed that people were judging her.

   C   She felt guilty that she couldn't read to Sally.

5 The headteacher of the primary school offered Monica a paid job:

   A   because she didn't realise Monica couldn't read and write.

   B   even though Monica couldn't read and write.

   C   because Monica couldn't read and write.

6 Read the statements about Sally. Which one can we *not* know from reading the text?

   A   Her mother put pressure on her to achieve at school.

   B   Sally is confident about meeting challenges.

   C   As a child, Sally guessed that her mother couldn't read.

9 Text style and features

The text in Section B7 is fairly typical of the kind of interview article that we often find in magazines or in the 'Lifestyle' section of newspapers (whether in print or online). The purpose of such articles is to entertain and inspire the reader, while often also providing some interesting or useful information about an issue.

Which of the following are features of the style and content of this particular article? Underline examples in the text.

a   Much of it is written in the present tense (She says . . . , She explains . . .).

b   The setting of the interview is part of the article: we know where the interview takes place.

c   It has a 'question + answer' format.

d   It includes anecdotes about the interviewee's life (written in the third person).

e   It includes direct quotes from the interviewee.

f   It includes quotes from other members of the interviewee's family or friends.

g   The interviewee is someone famous.

h   The interview has a particular 'angle': it focuses on a particular aspect of the interviewee's life.

i   It includes factual information for the reader about a particular issue and 'helpline'/website links in case they want to know more.

INTERNATIONAL OVERVIEW

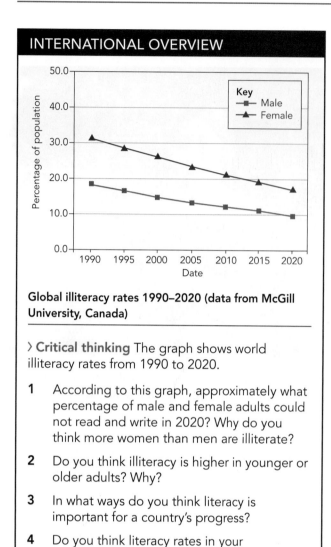

Global illiteracy rates 1990–2020 (data from McGill University, Canada)

> **Critical thinking** The graph shows world illiteracy rates from 1990 to 2020.

1 According to this graph, approximately what percentage of male and female adults could not read and write in 2020? Why do you think more women than men are illiterate?

2 Do you think illiteracy is higher in younger or older adults? Why?

3 In what ways do you think literacy is important for a country's progress?

4 Do you think literacy rates in your own country are higher or lower than the average?

> accurate   appropriate   desperate
>
> separate   delicate   fortunate
>
> considerate   definite

11 Approaches to spelling

1 Select the strategies you use to help you spell.

- [ ] I remember how the word looks on the page (visual recall).
- [ ] I use spelling rules and patterns (like *qu-* or *-ight*).
- [ ] I break words into syllables (e.g. qua/li/fi/ca/tion).
- [ ] I get spelling clues from words in the same word family (e.g. <u>know</u>–<u>know</u>ledge; <u>pleas</u>ed–<u>pleas</u>ure–un<u>pleas</u>ant).
- [ ] I make up silly ways of remembering the word (e.g. *separate*: there's <u>a rat</u> in se<u>par</u>ate; *because*: <u>b</u>ig <u>e</u>lephants <u>c</u>an <u>a</u>lways <u>u</u>nderstand <u>s</u>mall <u>e</u>lephants).

2 As a class, discuss which strategies are most popular. Does anyone use any other strategies?

You can improve your spelling by using a combination of these approaches.

🎧 1.2 10 Pronunciation and spelling

'Monica Chand was illiterate for many years.'

In English, for some words ending in *-ate* the spelling and pronunciation are obvious: words like *date* or *translate*. Other words like *illiterate* and *chocolate* have the weak *schwa* sound shown by the symbol ə (as in the word *the*).

Listen and practise the pronunciation of the adjectives in the box. Watch out for the spelling in the last word. The ending of *definite* sounds like the other adjectives, but note the *-ite* spelling. *Definitely* is one of the most commonly misspelt words in the English language.

12 Why do we misspell words?

Some words are tricky to spell. But it can be easier to remember the spelling if we identify *why* they are tricky. Do this exercise with a partner.

1 Look at these words that students often spell wrong. Make sure you understand the meaning of each one, using a dictionary if necessary. Can you pronounce it properly? Say it aloud to your partner to check.

> cupboard   responsible   beautiful
>
> accommodation   autumn   receipt
>
> exhausted   definitely   wrist   batteries

2 Decide what makes each word extra hard to spell. For example: Is there a silent letter that we don't pronounce? Does the spelling change from singular to plural, or when we form a comparative adjective?

3 Think of some other words that you or your partner find hard to spell. Try to identify why these words are tricky.

13 Look, say, cover, write, check

This is a very useful method for learning spellings, which we will use throughout this course. It can be used with other strategies, such as the ones in Section B11.

Look: Look at the word and identify anything that might be tricky (see Section B12).

Say: Break the word into syllables and say each syllable to yourself (in your head or aloud). You can say each syllable as it looks, even if you know this is not the correct pronunciation, as this will help to 'fix' the letters in your head and make sure you don't miss out any silent letters (e.g. Wed-nes-day). Now take a 'mental photograph' of the whole word.

Cover: Cover the word so you can't see it.

Write: Write it from memory.

Check: Check carefully whether you got it right. If not, repeat all the stages.

Try out this method for the list of words in the exercise in Section B12.

C Personal qualities

1 Vocabulary practice: Describing people's qualities

Look at the adjectives and phrases in the box, which describe people's qualities and personalities. Some of them are used in a positive sense (to describe a quality we admire), while others are more negative.

1 With a partner, check that you understand their meaning. Use a dictionary if you're not sure.

2 Split the words into three categories with the headings: Positive, Negative, Neutral / It depends.

> shy   outgoing   absent-minded
>
> confident   over-confident   sensitive
>
> quiet   ambitious   considerate
>
> obstinate   narrow-minded   open-minded
>
> trustworthy   reliable
>
> has a good sense of humour
>
> keeps himself to himself / herself to herself
>
> untidy   generous   argumentative
>
> laid back   judgemental   cheerful
>
> grumpy   imaginative   calm
>
> friendly   highly strung   practical

2 Vocabulary practice

For each of the following scenarios, choose words from the previous exercise. Then compare your choices with a partner. How far do you agree?

A You are sharing a flat with two friends but you need another person. Choose the three words that best describe your ideal flatmate.

B Now choose three words to describe the worst possible flatmate!

C You are about to go on a working holiday for three months in a foreign country. Describe three qualities of the person you would like to go with.

D Describe three qualities of the person you would like to start a small business with.

3 Negative prefixes

1 Make the character traits below into their opposites by adding one of these prefixes:

dis-   *im-*   *in-*   *ir-*   *un-*

> responsible   secure   efficient
>
> loyal   trustworthy   considerate
>
> mature   reliable   honest

2 Now put the negative words into sentences to show their meanings.

4 What are they like?

We sometimes try to guess people's personalities or feelings from their appearance and their expression.

> She looks quite cheerful.
>
> He looks rather shy.

It's also possible to form compound adjectives with *-looking*:

> A cheerful-looking woman answered the door.
>
> The new pilot was rather shy-looking.

Look at this photo of Alexander, a successful entrepreneur. Make some guesses about his personality using *He looks* or *-looking*.

5 Demonstrating personal qualities through actions

Alexander was 17 when he started his own business selling mobile phones. He became a multi-millionaire at the age of 21. Alexander (known as Alex) has now decided to share his business skills to help others start their own small business. He particularly encourages applications from people who want to start a business in an area of high unemployment.

Read these comments about Alexander made by people who have worked with him. Then answer the question that follows.

> When he's deciding whether to invest in a business idea, he gets negative comments, such as 'It's not worth it, Alex; that project is a waste of money. The applicant is too uneducated to do well.' But he doesn't think like that. He believes everyone deserves a chance to succeed.

He has invested in small businesses with no guarantee of success, but he says that it was worth it because now, all over the world, people are running a business they are proud of.

He thinks there are still huge economic problems and lots of poverty. But he reminds us that if we make the world a fairer place, everyone will benefit.

When he hears about an exciting project, he's filled with enthusiasm. He relies on colleagues saying, 'Wait a minute Alex, you've got to do this or do that to avoid disaster.'

He thinks that encouraging people to believe in their future is vital. Even if others think he is too optimistic, he just has to do what he thinks is right.

Can we draw the following conclusions about Alex? Answer yes or no.

Alex has:

a   the courage to take risks

b   benefited from positive advice

c   bad memories he cannot forget

d   accepted stress as part of his life

e   support from people around him

f   trouble trusting others

g   self-belief

h   a positive outlook

i   determination

j   difficulty adjusting to change.

6 Criticising negative qualities

When we are describing someone's less good qualities, we sometimes use 'tentative' language to avoid being too direct (unless we know the person extremely well or dislike them). Compare these examples:

She's immature. / She's a bit immature at times.

He's unreliable. / He's not always very reliable.

He's inconsiderate. / He can be rather inconsiderate.

1   Imagine you are a colleague of Alex's who admires him but doesn't always agree with what he does. You're discussing him with another colleague. Try to think of any slight criticisms that you might make of him, using the information in the comments in Section C5. Compare your ideas with a partner.

2   Think about your own language and culture. Would you make criticisms in the same tentative way, or would you be more direct? Discuss as a class.

7 Discussion

⟩ **Critical thinking** Discuss the following with a partner:

1   Alex might be successful, but is he happy? What are your views?

2   Is there anything about Alex's approach to life you would choose for yourself? Try to explain why.

3   Do you think Alex is a good example to younger people? Could he be a role model (a person who inspires others to copy them)? Why / Why not?

8 Improving a description

Read the following short description of a person. Does it give you a good mental picture of the person? With a partner, discuss what you think of it and how you could improve it.

> *I've known my friend Shannon for six years. We met when we were both at primary school. We were ten. She had really long red hair. Her hair was wavy. It was tied back with a green ribbon. That's the first thing I noticed about her.*
>
> *Shannon is loyal, quiet, considerate, tidy, imaginative and cheerful. She used to be shy but now she's more confident. She's forgetful, too. There are some things I really admire about her.*
>
> *She loves spiders. She wants to be an architect when she's older.*

9 Comparing style

Compare the style in the following description with that in the previous exercise. Do you get a better picture of the person? Consider what improvements (if any) have been made and discuss your thoughts with a partner.

> I've known Hassan since we met at a summer drama school as seven year olds, many years ago. I remember he was wearing red trousers and a bright-yellow woolly hat, which he never wanted to take off. This was typical of his loud and outgoing personality, and he's still like that now!
>
> Something people admire about Hassan is his ability to cheer people up when things go wrong. Last week he took a group of younger children for a football-themed birthday picnic in the countryside – but we forgot the footballs! So instead, Hassan entertained the kids with funny stories and organised a game of hide-and-seek, which they loved. He's a good listener, too, so when I was upset because my dad was in hospital, he encouraged me to talk about how I was feeling. He's very generous in giving up his time for other people, although he can be a bit unreliable with time-keeping in his own life. He's always turning up late for meetings, cinema trips, even exams, which gets him into trouble sometimes – but then he'll walk in with a lovely smile and everyone will forgive him!

10 Writing your own description

Choose someone that you know to describe. Here are some tips for your description:

*   Don't try to describe everything about the person. Choose just a few key characteristics and give specific examples.

*   If you describe physical features or clothes, try to link them with character traits.

*   Use some adjectives (e.g. from Sections C1 and C3) but don't overdo it.

*   Avoid too many short, simple sentences – link them together.

*   Consider including one negative personality feature – politely!

11 Spelling homophones

In the exercise in Section B11 we considered some common reasons why students misspell words. Another cause of errors is when a word sounds the same as another word but has a different spelling – in other words, it's a homophone.

1   Find and correct the spelling error in each of the following sentences.

   a   You need piece and quiet for your work.

   b   I read the hole book in one evening.

   c   We're not aloud to stay out late.

   d   They built the school on the sight of an old factory.

   e   They forgot to take there shoes off when they entered my house.

   f   If you don't hurry, your going to be late again.

   g   He hasn't decided weather to take the exam this year.

   h   You need to bare in mind that summer evenings can be quite chilly.

   i   The car crashed because its breaks failed.

   j   His injury took a long time to heel.

2   Can you think of any more examples? Discuss them as a class. The two photos give you a clue to another pair of homophones.

D People we look up to

1 Vocabulary practice: Multi-word verbs for relationships and attitudes to people

Read these sentences containing multi-word verbs. Match the meaning of the multi-word verb in italics with one of the definitions below.

   a   Ivan really *looks up to* his stepmother: she's a good influence on him.

   b   Unfortunately, some employers *look down on* applicants who haven't studied at university, even if they are highly skilled.

   c   He's a sociable and open-minded person who *gets on with* everyone.

   d   Li Mei *takes after* her mother: they are both so argumentative!

   e   She didn't want to *let her friends down*, so she came to the wedding with a broken leg.

   f   My sister has *fallen out with* my mum again. They're not talking to each other.

   1   disappoint someone by not doing something

   2   admire and respect someone

   3   have an argument and stop being friendly with someone

   4   think that you are better than someone

   5   be similar (in looks or behaviour) to someone in your family, especially a parent

   6   have a friendly relationship with someone

2 Discussion

Write down the names of three people who you look up to. Why do you think these people should be admired? Compare ideas as a class. Did you choose living people, or did anyone name a historical figure?

3 Pre-listening tasks

1 Study the information in the glossary below; it refers to the dialogue you are about to hear. Use a world map to find the geographical areas.

> ### GLOSSARY
>
> **Dubai:** one of the seven emirates (states) of the United Arab Emirates (UAE)
>
> **Saudi Arabia:** a country in Western Asia
>
> **Zhejiang:** a province in eastern China, next to the East China Sea
>
> **Nobel prize:** one of six international prizes awarded each year (for chemistry, physics, medicine, literature, peace and economics)

2 What do we mean by *people with special needs*?

3 What do we mean if we say someone is named after their mother or father?

4 Listening: Podcast

You are going to listen to a podcast recorded for a student radio station. Choose the best answer for each question.

1 According to Yasmin:

A we can't admire someone if we don't agree with their beliefs.

B over time, we change the way that we judge people's achievements.

C we shouldn't name streets or buildings after people who don't deserve our admiration.

Tu Youyou was awarded the Nobel Prize in Physiology or Medicine in 2015

2 Yasmin understands how hard the walk across the seven United Arab Emirates is because:

A she has done it herself.

B she has personal experience of similar activities.

C she has a good imagination.

3 Yasmin says that Jalal Bin Thaneya wanted to complete his challenges in order to:

A improve the lives of people with special needs.

B support people with special needs, including someone in his family.

C make people realise that disability affects them personally.

4 According to Yasmin, what did Tu Youyou do that showed courage?

A She decided to look for a cure for malaria.

B She worked away from her family.

C She tested the new medicine on herself.

5　According to Yasmin, did Tu Youyou's anti-malaria medicine make her famous?

　　A　Not at first, but people found out about her many years later.

　　B　She was well-known at first, but now she's forgotten.

　　C　It made her more famous than she deserves.

5　Discussion

> **Critical thinking** Discuss the questions in pairs.

1　Do you agree with what Yasmin says about admiring people? To what extent is it possible to admire someone's work (for example, their art or their sports skills) if we dislike the way they lead their life?

2　Why do we put up statues of people? Would it be better not to?

3　Tu Youyou only became well-known when she was in her seventies. Do you know of any other people who became famous only when they were very old, or after their death?

4　If you made an important medical discovery or invented something important, would you want to be famous for it? What might be the advantages of not being well-known?

6　Writing from notes

1　Some people deserve to be more famous than they are. Have you heard of Joseph Lister? Write down any facts you know about him. To give you an idea, look at the photo but imagine we're in the 1840s.

How would this scene be different then? If you were a patient having a surgical operation in those days, what would have been your chances of survival?

2　Now try to write the following description of Joseph Lister in full. You may need to change the form of some words and add others.

I want / describe Joseph Lister. He be / surgeon who / be born / England / 1827. In those days / many patients die / after operations because their wounds / become / badly infect. Lister wonder if / **bacteria** / air / which make / meat **decay** / also make / wounds **septic**.

Lister decide / clean / everything which touch / patient's wounds / carbolic acid. Carbolic acid / destroy / all germs. As a result / these **precautions** / patients recover quickly / operations. The rate / infection / fall dramatically.

Lister develop / safe, antiseptic operations / which be / major medical advance. He receive / many awards / his work / and today / known as 'the father of modern surgery'. I admire him because / he be dedicated / unselfish. He take / great personal risks / make this discovery. Surgery / use to be / highly dangerous. People be / terrify / surgeon's knife. Lister change / all that. Modern surgery be / life-saver.

GLOSSARY

bacteria: organisms that cause disease

decay: go bad, rot

septic: badly infected

precautions: actions taken to avoid danger

7 Looking for a 'local hero'

Imagine that you are browsing on the forum of your local town's community website, where people post information about local issues. You read the following notice.

Think about who you might nominate, and why. If you prefer, you can make someone up. With a partner, discuss what you might say about them.

WANTED

Nominations for the award of
'Local hero of the year'

Do you know someone who volunteers regularly to make a difference in our town? Or perhaps they have worked especially hard helping the public, always with a smile, and have never been thanked? Or maybe they did that one extra special brave or kind thing that deserves recognition?

Tell us about them, and they may win a prize at our 'Local hero of the year' ceremony! Let us know:

- who they are and what they are like
- what they do (or have done) that deserves an award.

Please email your nomination to the forum administrator.

8 Drafting your nomination

Write your nomination, recommending somebody to be 'Local hero of the year'. As you write, consider who will be reading it (the forum administrator and probably a group of other adults). Do you know them well? Think about the *register* (formal or informal?) and the *tone* (amusing, or respectful?).

Use the following structure:

> **Introduction:** Briefly say why you are writing.
>
> **Useful phrases:**
>
> *I am writing to nominate [the person] for . . .*
>
> *I hope that you will consider [the person] . . .*

Hello,

_____
_____
_____

_____
_____
_____

_____
_____

_____

> **Middle section:** Explain who the person is and describe what they do / have done.

> **Ending:** Briefly summarise why the person deserves the award.

9 Giving feedback

Swap your finished draft with a partner. Read your partner's draft and answer the following questions:

- How convincing is the nomination? Would you give this person the award? (If not, what other information is needed to support the nomination?)

- Is the tone of the writing suitable, or is it too informal or too formal?

- Can you spot any spelling mistakes or other errors?

Exchange feedback with your partner, and make any necessary improvements to your own draft.

10 Language study: Using apostrophes

In English, we use an apostrophe (') for two main purposes. Study these examples, and decide why the apostrophe is used in each case.

a   Someone's put a lot of effort into this.

b   I found someone's phone under the sofa.

Practice

1   In this set of sentences, the apostrophe is used to show where one or more letters are omitted. We use these 'contracted forms' in speech and less formal writing. With a partner, write out the full (non-contracted) version of the words in italics.

a   *You're going* to watch a film with friends.

b   He disappeared to Malaysia, where *he's lived* happily ever since.

c   *Don't set* the wrong goals in the first place.

d   *You'll be* fine.

e   When Ravi was alive, *I'd ask* him to do the things I couldn't cope with.

f   I explained that *I'd left* my glasses at home.

g   *He's always* turning up late for meetings.

2   The following examples include an apostrophe used to show possession. Study how the apostrophe is used and write out some rules.

•   These are my husband's keys.

•   My brothers' names are Phil, Matt and Billy.

•   I spoke to the children's favourite teacher.

•   You should listen to other people's opinions.

3   Even native speakers of English make mistakes with apostrophes. Try to spot what is wrong with the following signs.

A Please leave **ALL** trolley's next to the supermarket exit.

B WOMENS TOILETS **CLOSED** FOR CLEANING

C **IMPORTANT CUSTOMER NOTICE**

Please note: our store has changed it's opening hours.

GRAMMAR SPOTLIGHT

Present simple and continuous

One of the uses of the present simple is to describe facts that are usually or always true:

> **I avoid** *the kind of situations that may hurt me.*

> **I** mainly **watch** *videos that people have recommended.*

The present continuous is used to talk about things that are happening at this moment:

> **Monica is describing how** *it feels to be unable to read and write.*

> *She* **is sitting** *in her flat in south London.*

Some verbs do not usually take the continuous form:

> **I don't understand.** *Can you explain that again?*

Verbs like this include: *believe, belong, contain, know, like, love, mean, own, prefer, seem, suppose, understand, want, wish.*

Practice

1   Look at the quiz questions in Section A1 and underline five examples of the present simple.

2   Look at the last paragraph of the text in Section B7 and underline one example of the present continuous.

3   Complete these sentences using the correct present tense of the verb in brackets.

a   That's strange – Josh _____ with his friend Ken. He never normally _____ with anyone. (*argue*)

b   You _____ very quiet this morning. Are you OK? (*seem*)

c   Tanya is very generous. Helping other people _____ her happy. (*make*)

Complete the practice activities in your Workbook.

READING AND WRITING

Reading and writing: open response

Read the article about a phobia (an extreme fear or anxiety), and then answer the questions.

Can you cure a phobia?

Phobia sufferers experience extreme fear of something that's unlikely to harm them. Taking your children to feed the ducks is a normal and pleasurable activity for most parents. But for Kelly Phillips, a young mother of two, it posed a terrifying challenge. Kelly has had a phobia about birds since childhood. Even seeing one on the roof or flying high above her would throw her into a blind panic. The disorder, called ornithophobia, had ruined her life, and meant that she struggled even to do the shopping in case she encountered a bird on the way there.

But what lies behind such fears? People with phobias have a pure, illogical terror of an object or situation, often convincing themselves that something disastrous is about to happen. So people afraid of spiders (arachnophobes) may fear they will be poisoned by a bite, while those with claustrophobia (fear of closed spaces) will avoid using a lift, imagining it will break and they will be left to die. Their fear then provokes physical symptoms such as rapid breathing, sweating and a fast-beating heart. Such reactions are part of the 'fight or flight' response, which can be useful for life and death situations, such as if there is a lion nearby. But for phobias, it's no use telling people they are not thinking sensibly: they already know that.

It wasn't clear what started Kelly's ornithophobia. It might have been a reaction to a bird flying at her as a child, as witnessed by her elder sister, since very upsetting incidents in childhood can generate such fears. (Some claustrophobics recall being trapped in a crowded place for a long period, for instance.) Over-anxious parents giving off signals that certain things are dangerous can also be responsible; this is most probably the case for Kelly, with teasing from classmates adding to her fears. Whatever the cause, sufferers may be left too scared even to go for a walk on their own.

Kelly agreed to take part in a step-by-step treatment programme, with other ornithophobics, beginning with a trip to a park to feed the birds. Even coming into contact with bird food left quite a few participants in tears and threatening to walk off, but one or two in the group managed to help the others through it. The next step was visiting a zoo, where each had to handle a small bird that was used to humans.

The sufferers were taught to deal with their anxiety symptoms by focusing on breathing and relaxation, and distracting themselves from their negative thoughts by focusing on something in the here and now; for example, the wallpaper, or even their own feet.

For the final step, the group had to handle larger, mice-hunting birds. The purpose here was for them to realise for themselves that, despite their appearance, these rather terrifying-looking creatures are harmless. It was an important exercise as phobics tend to generalise, believing all birds – or all spiders, for example – are a threat. Kelly chose a small bird that hopped onto her head, from where she had to pull it onto her hand.

So, did these experiences help? Well, we revisited those who took part in the programme, and all reported having overcome their fears. As for Kelly, she is a changed woman. Despite some minor panic attacks, she has learnt to deal with her anxiety. She even sent us a happy family shot of her with her family feeding the ducks in the park.

CONTINUED

1 When did Kelly's phobia begin?

_____ [1]

2 What is the name for the body's reaction to an emergency such as a dangerous animal?

_____ [1]

3 According to the article, who is most likely to have caused Kelly's phobia?

_____ [1]

4 Why did the treatment programme advise the ornithophobics to stare at their feet?

_____ [1]

5 What important fact were participants supposed to learn in the last part of the programme?

_____ [1]

6 What everyday activities (excluding feeding the birds) are stressful for people who suffer from phobias?

Give **three** examples.

_____ [1]

_____ [1]

_____ [1]

[Total: 8]

Reading and writing: informal

You recently had to do something that made you feel scared.

Write an email to tell a friend about it.

In your email, you should:
- describe what you had to do and how you felt about it
- explain how you overcame your fear
- say what you have learnt from this experience.

Write about 120 to 160 words. [15]

[Total: 15]

Reading and writing: informal

Last week, your school invited a well-known person to give a talk to your class.

Write an email telling your friend about it.

In your email, you should:
- say who the speaker was and why they came
- explain what you admire about them
- describe what they talked about.

Write about 120 to 160 words. [15]

[Total: 15]

CONTINUED

Reading and writing: formal

Your school is planning to make a video to help younger students who will be starting at your school next year feel welcome and less nervous. Your headteacher wants your class's opinions about this, and you have been asked to write a report.

In your report, say why a video is a good idea, <u>and</u> suggest what should be included.

Here are some comments from students in your class:

> A video provides information quickly and easily.

> It would be good to show sports and clubs, not just lessons.

> The new students could watch it again later if they forget something.

> Interviews with some friendly students might make the new students feel more relaxed.

Now write a report for the headteacher.

The comments above may give you some ideas, and you should also use some ideas of your own.

Write about 120 to 160 words. [15]

[Total: 15]

LISTENING

Listening: interview

You will hear Victor, a radio presenter, asking Carlos Gomez, a teenage blogger, some questions about his hobby as part of a radio feature on developing potential in young people. For each question, choose the correct answer, **A**, **B** or **C**, and put a tick (✓) in the appropriate box.

You will hear the interview twice.

Now look at questions 1–8.

1 The main reason Carlos started his blog was because:
   A   teenage blogs are very interesting to read. ☐
   B   he thought he had the skills to write a blog. ☐
   C   other blogs mainly reflected the interests of teenage boys. ☐ [1]

2 When choosing to write about inventors, Carlos concentrates on:
   A   teenage boy inventors. ☐
   B   famous inventors. ☐
   C   little-known inventors. ☐ [1]

3 Carlos's book review section is popular with:
   A   people of all ages. ☐
   B   booksellers. ☐
   C   shopkeepers. ☐ [1]

CONTINUED

4 One of the boys reading his blog changed from:

   A watching action movies to reading. ☐

   B posting comments on social media to reading. ☐

   C playing computer games to reading. ☐ [1]

5 What does Carlos think about the artwork in the series of *Wonderworld* books?

   A He admires it. ☐

   B He finds it weird. ☐

   C He considers it not very good. ☐ [1]

6 We know the Wonderworld series is very popular at his school because:

   A students have bought the original artwork. ☐

   B many students are waiting for a copy. ☐

   C students want to buy sets of the Wonderworld series. ☐ [1]

7 Carlos updates his blog on a regular basis because:

   A he does not want to disappoint his regular readers. ☐

   B he frequently has free time in the evening and at lunchtime. ☐

   C he always has fresh news to share with users. ☐ [1]

8 His advice for those who want to write a blog is to:

   A have an attractive visual presentation. ☐

   B make it enjoyable for readers. ☐

   C have good grammar and spelling. ☐ [1]

[Total: 8]

SPEAKING

Warm-up questions

Warm-up questions help you feel more relaxed before you move on to answering assessed questions.

Take turns asking and answering the questions. Speak for 1–2 minutes.

- Where do you live?
- What is your favourite school subject?
- What did you do during your last holiday?

Interview

Read the questions. In pairs, decide who will play the interviewer and who will play the student. Then role-play the interview. Speak for about 2–3 minutes. Change roles and role-play the interview again.

Your personality and your friends

- Can you tell me about your personality?
- In what ways are your friends like you or different from you?
- What kind of person do you think you would not get on well with, and why?

Short talk

Read the options and compare them. You have one minute to prepare your talk. Now give a short talk to your partner. Speak for about 2 minutes. Change roles and listen to your partner's talk.

Getting to know people

You are starting a new school or university next term, and the school/university has recommended two ways to get to know all the other students before term starts:

- an online chat group
- an informal meeting at the school/university with drinks and snacks.

Discuss the advantages and disadvantages of each option. Say which you would prefer, and why.

Discussion

Read the discussion questions. In pairs, decide who will play the interviewer and who will play the student. Then role-play the discussion. Speak for about 3 minutes. Change roles and role-play the interview again.

- Can you tell things about people from their clothes and physical appearance? What do you think?
- Are people who have no brothers or sisters less sociable than people who do have brothers and sisters? What do you think?
- Is there an aspect of your personality that you would like to lose or develop?
- People's personalities can change when they are online. Do you agree?

SELF-ASSESSMENT CHECKLIST

Reflect on what you have learnt in this unit. For each area listed, decide whether you feel confident or need more practice. If you feel you need more practice, you will find some ideas to help you in Advice for Success. Come back to your self-assessment scores later in your course and see if your confidence has improved.

I can ...	Need more practice	Fairly confident
discuss issues related to goals, achievements and qualities we admire, using appropriate vocabulary		
understand the audience, purpose and features of different text types		
describe people and their qualities		
understand the speaker's ideas and attitudes as I listen		
write a formal email for a specific purpose and audience		

ADVICE FOR SUCCESS

This section is to help you help yourself. Choose the suggestions you like and adapt them if you want to. Make notes about what you do and how it helped you.

Extending your skills

1   Use a search engine to find and read articles about people who interest you (from modern celebrities to long-dead inventors, artists, etc.). Look out for language describing their qualities and achievements.

2   Watch online videos, TV programmes or talks (e.g. TED talks) about people and their lives. How does the presenter feel about the people, and how do they convey that?

3   Read a blog giving advice on a 'lifestyle issue', such as goal setting, similar to the one in this unit (use a search engine). Look at the style and language features.

4   Become more familiar with a range of text types and styles of English (from formal to informal) by reading from a variety of sources: magazines, novels, blogs, instructions, advertisements, and so on. Practise asking yourself who they are aimed at and what their purpose is, and notice how this affects their style and features.

5   Look out for opportunities to write English in the 'real world' (e.g. contacting a website to ask questions about a product or commenting on a suitable online blog or forum).

Showcasing your skills

6   Try to use a range of vocabulary in writing tasks, not just simple words.

7   Read the instructions for writing tasks very carefully and check what you are asked to do. For example, describing a person is unlikely to be the only focus of the task.

8   Check that you know who you are writing to and think about whether you should be writing formally (e.g. to an adult you don't know well) or informally (e.g. to a friend).

9   Check that you know why you are writing, and make sure you take account of that in your content.

10   Check your spelling. Even when spelling is not assessed, a misspelling might change the meaning of a word.

11   In listening tasks, some questions test your ability to use inference (which means 'reading between the lines'). You need to listen for clues: the answers may not be given to you directly.

12   Always do a first draft of your written work and be prepared to redraft it. Show your written work to a friend or English-speaking adult, asking for their advice – not just about language errors but also about your ideas and writing style. If you are describing someone, have you created a good picture? If you are writing to someone you don't know, have you explained your purpose clearly but politely?

13   Get into the habit of using a good dictionary and making use of all the information it provides (see Section A8).

Scores for the quiz in Section A1

Mostly As

You like to play things safe: maybe try taking a few risks? Be less passive, and think about what you really want. Ask yourself whether you would get more from life if you took a bit more responsibility for yourself and your own happiness.

Mostly Bs

Generally, you seem to be a happy, chilled and well-balanced kind of person; you take notice of other people's opinions, but you don't let them tie you down. You live your own life and you know what you want – and you cope well when things don't go your way.

Mostly Cs

You tend to put a lot of pressure on yourself because you are very conscious of what other people think of you. Be a bit kinder to yourself and a bit more relaxed – maybe you're trying too hard to be perfect.

> Unit 2

Fitness and well-being

LEARNING INTENTIONS

In this unit you will:

- Explore the topic of fitness, health, sport and well-being

- Focus on how to take notes effectively

- Read and understand a more formal text, exploring its features

- Extract information from short audio clips without knowing the context in advance

- Explore how sentence stress conveys meaning in speech

02 Watch the video about fitness and well-being in the digital coursebook.

BEFORE YOU START

Look at the photo on this page.

a   Have you ever done the activity in the photo, or would you like to? Why / why not?

b   Do you consider it a sport? Why / why not?

c   What are the health benefits of skateboarding, in your opinion?

d   Name some other fitness activities that you can do outside, without the need to join a club or spend a lot of money.

A What is a healthy lifestyle?

1 Top tips

1 〉 **Critical thinking** People often talk about the need to have a 'healthy lifestyle' – but what is that? Does it mean the same for everybody? With a partner, create your own top tips for a healthy lifestyle, using ideas from the box or your own ideas. Write eight top tips, each beginning with a suitable verb.

Example: *Eat plenty of fresh fruit and vegetables.*

varied diet	processed food
sugary drinks	fruit and vegetables
team sports	vitamin supplements
fresh air	exercise, such as walking
gym	right amount of sleep
stress levels	mental health
water	work–life balance
teeth	time with friends and family
meat	time looking at screens
regular check-ups at the doctor's	

2 Compare your top tips with another pair's. Are they broadly the same, or are there things you disagree about?

2 Keeping the conversation going

You are going to have a conversation with a partner on the topic of health and well-being, but you will focus on keeping the conversation going for as long as possible. Here are some suggestions to help you.

- Avoid 'conversation killers' (one-word answers). Try to give details.

- When your partner says something, ask follow-up questions with *what*, *why*, *when*, *who* or *how (much/long/often)*.

- Check what your partner means if you're not sure (e.g. *So do you mean that . . . ? Are you saying that . . . ?*)

- Change the subject a little if you don't want to answer a personal question (e.g. *I'd rather not answer that, but I can say that . . .*).

- Show interest (e.g. *That's interesting! Could you tell me more about . . . ?*)

Talk about the topics in the box with your partner. You can discuss them in any order.

> People my age don't look after their health enough.

> Exercising and eating healthily are too expensive.

> A healthy lifestyle is more important for older people than young people.

3 Pre-reading

You are going to read Part 1 of a magazine article called 'Now feeling on top of the world'. It's about Shalimar, a digital artist, who changed her lifestyle habits. First, look just at the title and photo, and quickly read the first sentence (in bold). Then answer these questions.

1 Who is the 'audience' for this article?

   A Other digital artists.

   B Doctors or scientists.

   C The general public.

2 What is the purpose of the article?

   A To make people identify with Shalimar and consider changing their own lifestyle.

   B To give advice on running a digital gaming company.

   C To give a scientific explanation of a medical condition.

4 Read and make notes

Now read all of Part 1. Don't worry if there are words you don't recognise – try to predict their meaning from context clues. As you read, make notes under the following headings:

Why Shalimar became unfit :

• . . . .

Examples of Shalimar's unhealthy lifestyle:

• . . . .

• . . . .

• . . . .

• . . . .

• . . . .

Compare your notes with a partner.

Now feeling on top of the world (Part 1)

Digital artist Shalimar was so busy building her own online gaming company she never noticed she was getting unfit – until the day she couldn't run for a bus.

5 Shalimar Lee was late for work one morning and, as her usual number 14 bus came around the corner, 10 she sped up. As she climbed aboard, her heart was beating so fast she could hardly speak to the driver. 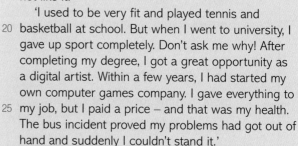 15 She thought she might be going to collapse. This finally made her face the fact that she was seriously unfit, and she did not like it.

'I used to be very fit and played tennis and 20 basketball at school. But when I went to university, I gave up sport completely. Don't ask me why! After completing my degree, I got a great opportunity as a digital artist. Within a few years, I had started my own computer games company. I gave everything to 25 my job, but I paid a price – and that was my health. The bus incident proved my problems had got out of hand and suddenly I couldn't stand it.'

For Shalimar, however, the idea of going on a fitness regime was inconceivable. 'I simply didn't 30 think I had the time. Even when I wasn't at work, I was thinking of new storylines for my games, researching or updating my blog.' Her online games, which are internationally known, centre around a family of penguins, and Shalimar has already 35 achieved the status of a minor celebrity in the blogosphere.

'I got so immersed in work, I never took a meal break and worked ridiculously long hours. I would sip high-energy drinks all day long and nibble biscuits. 40 When I got home, I'd slump in front of the TV, and, rather than cook a proper meal, I snacked on toast and chocolate spread. There was never anything much in the fridge anyway.' Not surprisingly, she didn't sleep well and would wake up feeling as if she 45 needed another eight hours: 'I felt sluggish all the time, but I couldn't imagine how to change things.'

5 Making suggestions

Write some suggestions for how Shalimar could lead a healthier lifestyle without giving up her online design work based on notes you made.

You could use the following language:

If she . . . ., she would . . . .
She could . . .

6 Read and compare

Now read Part 2 of the text. Find and underline information in the text that tells you what Shalimar actually did to improve her lifestyle. Write **S** in the margin where the suggestion is the same as one of yours, or **D** if it's different.

Now feeling on top of the world (Part 2)

No one ever mentioned that Shalimar seemed exhausted. No one, that is, until her mum decided to pluck up the courage. 'I was visiting my family one weekend. Mum waited until I was relaxed after
5 lunch and then plunged in. She had read that a new gym in the neighbourhood was starting up a fitness programme that not only included exercise, but also offered information on developing a healthy lifestyle. Mum persuaded me that we should both give the
10 programme a try.' Shalimar wasn't exactly thrilled but felt she ought to go. After the very first class, she was hooked.

'I got fitter immediately. The exercises were good fun. Gabrielle, our instructor, was so motivational and
15 gave us loads of encouragement. She also told us about easy ways to replace bad habits with healthy ones, such as getting off the bus a stop earlier, and making time to shop for fresh ingredients. I used to leave feeling on top of the world.'
20 Shalimar explains that the programme focuses on making small changes that you can fit into your lifestyle. This, she feels, is the key to its success: 'I'm strict with myself now. However busy I am, I make up my packed lunch every day and leave the office
25 to eat it in a park down the road.' Her office is on the fourth floor, and she now uses the stairs as much as possible instead of the lift. She also avoids fizzy drinks and drinks tea or water instead. 'I didn't need to go crazy to get healthy. Just a few simple, sensible
30 changes have made all the difference.'

It's hard to believe Shalimar was ever so unfit that she couldn't run for a bus. 'I'm still busy but I don't feel exhausted anymore. I'm sure eating properly has also given my brain a boost because I find it so much
35 easier to conjure up new ideas for my games. I've got rid of my old habits for good and they are never coming back!'

Shalimar's business is also going from strength to strength. Her new computer game about a cute baby
40 giraffe is about to be launched onto the market. 'The team and I are so excited. I think this is going to be our most successful product yet.'

7 Post-reading discussion

> **Critical thinking** Discuss the following in small groups:

1   Do you think the small changes that Shalimar has made will be successful? Were any of your own suggestions better?

2   Why do you think some people find it so difficult to change an unhealthy lifestyle?

3   Shalimar's mother had to *pluck up the courage* (Part 2, line 3) to suggest to her daughter that she should get fitter: in other words, she found it difficult to talk about it. If people don't want to get fit, is that their individual choice or should we try to make them change their habits? Why?

4   Shalimar feels that a healthy diet has *given her brain a boost* (Part 2, line 34). Does our physical health really affect our mental health, and vice versa?

8 Words in context

1   Find the following words in the text (Parts 1 and 2). Then, using their context to help you, match them with the correct meaning.

Part 1

a   *sped up* (line 10)

b   *inconceivable* (line 29)

c   *immersed* (line 37)

d   *sip* (line 38)

e   *nibble* (line 39)

f   *slump* (line 40)

Part 2

g   *pluck up the courage* (line 3)

h   *thrilled* (line 10)

i   *boost* (line 34)

j   *go from strength to strength* (line 38–39)

Meanings

1   enjoy something so much you can't stop (informal)

2   become more and more successful

3   very involved in something, concentrating hard

4   force yourself to do something that scares you

5   eat with small bites

6   drink slowly with small mouthfuls

7   sit or fall heavily (lazily or in pain)

8   get faster

9   very excited

10   impossible to imagine

2   Use words from the list above (a–j) in the gaps, in the correct form.

a   The old man was _____ to hear that his grandson's online business was

_____ .

b   The skaters _____ when they reached the last part of the race.

c   The employee _____ his water nervously, trying to _____ to ask his boss for a pay rise.

d   The teacher's encouraging words _____ the student's confidence.

e   I didn't hear the doorbell because I was completely _____ in the essay I was writing.

f   It's _____ that she could win the race, since she's done no training at all.

INTERNATIONAL OVERVIEW

Global population by age group

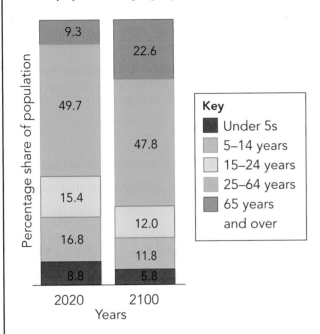

Distribution of global population by age group, 2020 and 2100 (projected)

> **Critical thinking** Study the chart, which shows the projected percentage of people throughout the world for five age groups in two different years (one in the recent past, one in the future). Answer the questions.

1 a What proportion of the population were 65 and over in 2020?

   b What proportion are expected to be 65 and over by 2100?

2 a Which age group will have declined in size the most by 2100?

   b Which is the only age group that will have increased in size by 2100?

3 What do you think are the causes of these big changes?

4 How will this change in the proportion of old and young people affect our lives? Make a list. What could be problematic? How could we try to prepare for it?

9 Sentence stress

John and Ella are watching an international football match on TV. Poland are playing against Finland.

1 Listen to the dialogue while you read, and notice which words or syllables the speakers emphasise (they are underlined). Why are these words or syllables emphasised?

Ella: Is Poland playing in the blue and green?

John: No, Poland's playing in the <u>yell</u>ow and green.

Ella: Did you say <u>Fin</u>land was in the yellow and green?

John: No, I said <u>Po</u>land was in the yellow and green.

Ella: Is Poland playing <u>France</u> this season?

John: Poland plays France <u>every</u> season.

Ella: Did Poland win a few of their matches last season?

John: They won <u>all</u> their matches last season!

2 Now practise reading the dialogue in pairs, pronouncing the main stress as shown.

Why is a different word stressed in each answer?

10 Practising sentence stress to convey meaning

Read the two-line dialogues about football. For each dialogue, decide with a partner where the main stress should fall in B's reply. (There may be more than one.) Underline the word or syllable. Then practise each dialogue together.

a A: Is anybody from your family going to see the game tomorrow?

   B: Everybody's going to see the game tomorrow.

b A: Were you surprised about Kelly's behaviour on the pitch last night?

   B: I'm never surprised about Kelly's behaviour!

c A: Do you think the match will be as exciting as the last one?

   B: I don't think any match could be as exciting.

d A: Did you think the referee acted fairly?

   B: No one thought the referee acted fairly.

e A: Didn't the women's team win the Crown Cup two years ago?

   B: Actually, it was the Union Cup, and they won it last year!

f A: Do you think Lucas pushed the goalkeeper?

   B: I don't think he did, I know he did because I saw him do it!

11 Spelling: Adding suffixes to words ending in –e

A suffix is a group of letters added to the end of a word – for example, the suffix *-ful* can be added to *use* to make the adjective *useful*.

1 Look at these two groups of words from the texts in Sections A4 and A6. They are words that are formed from base words ending in *-e* by adding the suffixes *-ing*, *-ible*, *-ly* and *-ment*.

A	B
gaming (gam<u>e</u>)	completely (complet<u>e</u>)
updating (updat<u>e</u>)	immediately (immediat<u>e</u>)
sensible (sens<u>e</u>)	encouragement (encourag<u>e</u>)

What happens to the *-e* from the end of the base word in groups A and B? Try to suggest a reason for the difference.

2 Look at these two sets of suffixes.

Beginning with a vowel	Beginning with a consonant
-ing	-ful
-ive	-less
-able	-ment

Make one to three new words by adding suffixes from the table to each of the following base words. If the suffix begins with a vowel, take off the *-e*. When it begins with a consonant, keep the *-e*.

a excite   e expense

b care   f achieve

c advise   g hope

d create

3 There are some exceptions to the rule that *-e* disappears when the suffix begins with a vowel. Look at the following examples.

changeable	courageous
noticeable	replaceable

After *c* or *g*, the *-e* is kept – for a specific reason. Try to read these words spelt wrongly without the *-e*. How might you pronounce them?

- changable ✗
- replacable ✗

The consonants *c* and *g* have two different pronunciations in English (for example, c in *ice* or *doctor*) or g in *page* or *leg*.

4   Unfortunately, there are two other common exceptions with the *-able* suffix, which don't follow a rule and have to be memorised: *likeable* and *sizeable*. Use a dictionary to check the meaning of these words and find examples of when they might be used.

12 Spelling practice

Read this newspaper report about teaching traditional dance in schools. Applying the rules for adding suffixes to words with a final *-e*, add the correct suffixes to the words in brackets.

Choose from the following suffixes:

-ative	-ing	-ion	-ish	-ment
	-able	-tion	-ity	-ivity

An **(a)** _____ (*increase*) number of schools are **(b)** _____ (*replace*) some of their more traditional sports lessons with dance. It is a brilliant way of **(c)** _____ (*have*) fun and an **(d)** _____ (*excite*) way to keep fit. Dance provides students with a chance to express their **(e)** _____ (*create*). Even the younger ones can learn simple ways of **(f)** _____ (*move*) to music, and after just a few weeks, their **(g)** _____ (*improve*) is very **(h)** _____ (*notice*). Older pupils who lack **(i)** _____ (*motivate*) when it comes to competitive sport find **(j)** _____ (*dance*) very **(k)** _____ (*stimulate*). Secondary school teachers say **(l)** _____ (*participate*) in such an enjoyable activity needs no **(m)** _____ (*encourage*).

A **(n)** _____ (*size*) number of schools have been **(o)** _____ (*participate*) in the annual Schools Festival of Dance since it started ten years ago. The Festival is a wonderful **(p)** _____ (*celebrate*) of both modern and traditional dance. Last year, the **(q)** _____ (*style*) costumes, great **(r)** _____ (*diverse*) of dances and **(s)** _____ (*imagine*) approaches made the evening particularly **(t)** _____ (*memory*).

13 Word families

By adding prefixes or suffixes, English creates 'families' of words with a common base word. Understanding word families can help you predict the meaning of unfamiliar words and expand your vocabulary. However, it's important to use a dictionary to check that you are forming words correctly.

Examples of word families:

responsible – responsibility, irresponsible, irresponsibility

belief – believed, believer, disbelief, believable, unbelievable, unbelievably

Practice

Create your own word families starting with each of these base words:

a	hope	d	patient
b	change	e	compete
c	achieve	f	decide

B Note-taking and sports

1 Discussion

Discuss the following as a class.

1   What do we do when we make notes? Why is note-taking useful?

2   Do you usually make notes by hand or on a laptop or tablet? What's the difference, and which do you prefer?

3   Is there a difference between notes you would make for yourself and notes that somebody else might need to read?

4   Think back to the note-taking task that you carried out in Section A4. What aspects of the task were most challenging? Try to be precise.

2 How to make notes

Do the following exercise with a partner. Start by reading the short text below about a musician who took up yoga. Your task is to write notes about three ways in which yoga helped him.

1   Start by finding and underlining or highlighting the three points within the text. Number them 1, 2 and 3. Check that you and your partner agree.

Twenty-five-year-old classical guitarist Jonas Hornik took up yoga five years ago during a stressful period of his life when he was building his career playing four concerts a week while also dealing with the death of his only brother. Not only did the yoga classes teach him to relax and, in his words, 'say goodbye to all the stress', but there was another unexpected benefit too. The other members of his morning yoga group, none of them musicians, soon became very close and supportive friends. As a result, the whole experience provided him with a much-needed new focus in life outside of music.

2 A student correctly identified the first of the three points and made the notes below. She knew that it is fine to use the same words as in the original text, but there are some other problems with what she wrote. Discuss with your partner.

> **How yoga helped Jonas Hornik**
>
> • The first point is that the yoga classes teach him to relax and, in his words, 'say goodbye to all the stress'

3 Cross out the words in the student's notes that you don't need. Also make one essential grammar change.

3 Note-taking practice

1 Now try writing notes based on another short text, using the method you have learnt in Section B2. Write your notes as two bullet points, under the heading 'Why oranges are better than apples'.

Everybody knows that fruit is good for your health, and in many parts of the world the most commonly eaten fruits are apples and oranges. But, if you had to choose, which of the two should you go for? Well, both fruits contain good levels of nutrients, but an average orange will provide you with about 20 times more vitamin C than an apple, so you should keep this in mind when you're trying to boost your immunity against winter colds. What's more, we can also get the folic acid we need for producing healthy red blood cells from eating oranges, whereas you'll get hardly any at all from an apple. So I'd say the orange wins!

2 Compare what you have written with a partner. You may have used different words to say the same thing, but decide whether you have included extra words you didn't need.

4 Sports vocabulary

1 Most sports and other physical activities have a specific set of words associated with that activity. Look at the table, which has been completed with vocabulary for two activities (badminton and running).

	Sport or activity	
	Badminton	Running
Verb(s)	play badminton	go running, go for a run
Where you do it	badminton court	athletics track or any suitable outdoor area
Special equipment	badminton rackets, shuttlecock, net	heart rate monitor (optional)
Clothing or footwear	clothes that allow you to move around easily (e.g. shorts and T-shirt) + shoes with a thin sole that grips well	breathable clothing, running shoes or trainers

Copy the table and add three more columns for three more sports or physical activities. If possible, choose ones that you enjoy playing, doing or watching, or ones that are popular in your country.

The following words may help you, but you may also need to use a dictionary.

Verb (-*ing*): play, do, go

Where you do it: court, pitch, track, gym, rink, pool, studio, anywhere

Equipment: racket, bat, stick, club, weights, mat, goggles, shin guards, saddle

Clothing/footwear: shoes with studs, helmet, cap, hiking boots, skates

2 Work with a partner, ideally someone who has chosen different sports or activities from you. Tell them about your activities as if they know nothing about them using words you've written in the table.

5 Is sport always fun?

> Critical thinking Many people love taking part in sport; others have more mixed feelings about it. Read the opinions below about school sport, and tick whether you agree, partly agree or disagree. Then compare your thoughts with your partner. Discuss your reasons.

	I agree	I partly agree	I don't agree
'It's too competitive. The same few kids always get picked for the team.'	☐	☐	☐
'It's embarrassing and humiliating for the ones who are no good at it.'	☐	☐	☐
'It's not fair for the kids that are unfit.'	☐	☐	☐
'The sports on offer are too traditional. We should have a wider choice of activities.'	☐	☐	☐
'It's a waste of time. I would rather be studying.'	☐	☐	☐

6 Pre-reading

1 You will be reading a newspaper article about sports day – a primary school event in which 4–11-year-old children take part while their parents watch. Do schools in your country have similar events? Do you think it is a good idea? Discuss as a class.

2 In the article, the writer criticises the sports day at her son's school. Choose the points that you expect the writer to criticise:

☐ the value of the prizes

☐ the competitive aspect of the day

☐ the bad effects of sports day on some children

☐ the skills of the teachers

☐ her own child's poor performance

☐ the fact that sports day takes time away from academic subjects

☐ possible alternatives to traditional sports day.

7 Reading for gist

Read the article fairly quickly, focusing on the main ideas rather than the detail. Try to work out the meaning of any words you don't know from their context, without using a dictionary for now. Did you correctly predict the points in Section B6?

1   One afternoon in the last week of term, I saw three children from my son's school in tears being comforted by teachers. That morning, my 11-year-old had stomach pains and, on talking to other mothers, I heard about other children with stomach ache or difficulty sleeping the night before.

2   What caused so much distress? Sports day – not at a highly competitive independent school, but at a large village primary. For the children who can fly like the wind, it causes no problem. For those who are poorly coordinated, overweight or just not good at sport, it is a nightmare. Even for those who enjoy running, but who fall halfway down the track in front of the entire school and their parents, it can prove a disaster.

3   Why do we put our children through this annual torment? Some may say competition is character-building; or it's taking part that's important, not winning; or that it's a tradition of school life. I just felt immense pity for those children in tears or in pain.

4   Team games at the end of the 'sports' produced some close races, enormous enthusiasm, lots of shouting – and were fun to watch. More importantly, the children who were not so fast, nimble on their feet or skilful with the ball were hidden a little from everyone's gaze. Some of them also had the thrill of being on the winning side.

5   I wish that sports day could be abandoned and replaced with some other summer event. Perhaps an afternoon of team games, with a few races for those who want them, would be less stressful for the children and a lot more fun to watch.

8 Comprehension check

1 Match paragraphs 1–5 with the following summaries of their content:

a How team games produced a positive atmosphere on sports day.

b The reasons why sports days are still a part of school life.

c An alternative to the traditional sports day.

d The explanation for the children's illnesses and fears.

e The physical symptoms that fear of sports day produces.

2 The text has no title. Write a suitable one that summarises what the whole text is about. Then compare your heading with other students. Agree on the best one.

9 Note-taking practice

You are going to write a set of notes based on the article, using the following headings:

• Reasons for having a sports day

• The negative effects of sports day

• Sports day: possible improvements

1 Re-read the article and underline the parts that are relevant to the headings.

2 Write your notes.

3 With a partner, check each other's notes for the following factors:

Content: Have you included all the relevant points? Have you included anything that is not relevant or under the wrong heading?

Language: Are the notes clear and concise?

10 Language study: Compound adjectives with numbers

The writer refers to 'my 11-year-old', meaning 'my 11-year-old child'. Notice that when we put a measurement before the noun it refers to, we:

• add a hyphen (or hyphens)

• use the singular form of the unit of measurement.

Examples:

a 20-metre swimming pool   *a two-part question*

a 40-mile drive   *a fifty-thousand-dollar contract*

Practice

Rewrite each of these sentences using a number + noun form.

a The coach made a fitness video lasting 50 minutes.

b To get into my online account, I need a code consisting of six numbers.

c The racehorse owner bought a mansion worth 10 million dollars.

d They ordered a meal that consisted of five courses.

e I need a coin worth one euro for the changing room locker.

f I'd like a bag of sugar weighing 2 kilograms.

g The doctor worked a shift that lasted for 12 hours.

h The hotel has three stars.

2.2 11 Listening for specific information

You are going to hear two short conversations and one recorded message without knowing in advance what they are about. Your task is to find out specific information, but you will also hear a lot of other information that is *not* what you need.

Before you listen, read the questions carefully and underline or highlight any key words. Then listen to the extracts and answer the questions.

Extract 1

1   What new sport has the girl taken up?

☐ **a** Hockey ☐ **b** Golf ☐ **c** Tennis

2   How many paid lessons has the girl had?

☐ **a** None ☐ **b** Two ☐ **c** Ten

Extract 2

3   According to Hailey, people new to wild swimming should:

☐ **a** check the temperature before swimming.

☐ **b** start swimming in summer.

☐ **c** stay in the water only briefly.

4   What is the most important thing <u>not</u> to do when you are wild swimming, according to Hailey?

☐ **a** Jump into the water

☐ **b** Swim without a wetsuit

☐ **c** Swim alone

Extract 3

5   Is it possible to do the following?

a Visit the leisure centre at 10 a.m. on Sundays. Yes/No

b Play badminton with your own equipment. Yes/No

c Hire a swimming towel for $1. Yes/No

d Attend the keep fit class without a reservation. Yes/No

12 Expressing warnings

Look at these examples of warnings. They are from the interview with Hailey about the possible dangers involved in wild swimming.

- Be careful to allow your body to get used to the temperature.

- Watch out for rocks or strong currents.

- If you jump in, you'll risk getting cold-water shock.

- Make sure there's a safe and easy place to exit the water.

- Never swim alone.

Here are some ways that the person receiving the warning might respond:

- Thanks, I'll do that / I'll remember that.

- That's a good point – I will/won't.

- Thanks for the tip/warning – I wouldn't have thought of that.

1   Write a reply giving a warning in each of the following situations.

Example: *My dad's going to let me try driving his car tomorrow.*

Make sure you practise in a quiet street!

a   My brother's only three, but he wants to learn to swim.

b   My friends have invited me to go sailing with them.

c   I want to go and see that really popular film at the cinema at the weekend.

d   We're going to the beach tomorrow. It's supposed to be really hot!

2   Create mini-conversations with a partner around the situations below, using the following pattern:

Student A: Talk about plans.

Student B: Give a warning.

Student A: Show you've understood the warning.

a   start jogging / need proper running shoes

b   swimming in the sea on holiday / jellyfish

c   hill walking alone / tell someone where you are going

d   mountain biking in a new area / lots of rain recently, ground muddy and slippery

e   lift weights at the gym for first time / proper supervision from instructor

C Fitness and technology

1 Discussion

Most forms of physical activity can be done with very little equipment. But there are many forms of technology that can improve your experience.

What do you know about the following? Have you used any of them? Discuss in a group.

- Fitness videos
- Fitness trackers
- Goal-line technology
- Hawk-eye technology

It's used/useful for . . . -ing

You can use it to . . .

---

2 Pre-reading vocabulary

You are going to read about some different kinds of fitness trackers. Before you do, work with a partner to check that you understand the meaning of the following words.

---

wrist   calories   device   the latter

potentially   a workout   mode   function

smartphone   data   download

---

3 Reading for gist

Start by reading the text quickly to get the general idea. Answer the following questions.

1   What is the purpose of the text?

2   Where might you find this type of text?

3   What sort of person do you think it is aimed at?

GoZone 24/7

Designed to be on your wrist the whole time, as the name suggests, the GoZone 24/7 tracks and measures every aspect of your waking life with pinpoint accuracy, from the steps you take to the calories
5   you burn and the minutes you sleep. The wealth of features includes a stress calculator with links to a menu of deep-breathing exercises to help you reduce that stress, and a punch-strength measuring device for use with activities such as cardio boxing. Although
10 you might question the value of the latter, depending on your personal training habits, one feature that is surely more universally important is the heart-rhythm monitor, which can spot any changes that could indicate heart disease: potentially a life-saver.

15 On the whole, the device is straightforward to set up and, once you have done so correctly, the display of recorded information is clear at a glance. The cleverly designed screen layout positions your achievements immediately above your targets, which motivates
20 you to put in that little extra effort at the end of a tough workout.

Vivace Pro

This rather pricey option would undoubtedly be the winner if we were to judge trackers purely by their ability to look good on your wrist. Most people would happily wear the Vivace Pro as
5   a fashion accessory, if it had nothing further to offer. Fortunately, it has: it can track just about any form of exercise (or non-exercise) on the planet, offering such a confusingly vast menu of options that it might put you off if you're new to
10 fitness tracking. On the other hand, one great feature for all levels of experience is automatic, personalised goal adjustment – so if you miss (or exceed) your daily target of stairs to climb, for example, it will be lowered or increased
15 accordingly.

One small but annoying thing to be aware of is that, while the battery life of the Vivace Pro is great (if you used the active mode continuously, it would last a week), there is, unbelievably,
20 no low battery warning. Leaving this practical detail aside, this new entrant to the fitness tracker market looks likely to be a big hit.

Kilston Sportwatch

With its accompanying smartphone app, the Kilston Sportwatch is the one to choose if you want to make your fitness tracking a sociable experience. Provided your friends have similar devices, it
5   enables you to participate in a range of challenges, which might just get you out in the rain on a cold day instead of choosing to slump on the sofa. What is particularly appealing in these challenges is that your activity levels are measured against your
10 current fitness levels – in other words, it's your effort that is the focus, not whether you achieved a world-beating speed.

Switching between one mode of use and another is simple with this device. One thing in particular
15 worth noting if you are forgetful by nature is that it can automatically detect when you have started a new activity, without waiting for you to set it manually, and it will start tracking your run, walk or swim (it is water-resistant to a depth of 50 metres)
20 all by itself. Overall, this relatively low-budget fitness tracker is the one for a first-timer – although with its sharp-cornered square face, you wouldn't choose it for its looks.

FitterGogo 5

Unlike the other devices in this review, FitterGogo lacks the function to count steps or measure your sleep, for instance. What it does do – and really well, too – is guide you
5   through a unique range of exciting workouts, including dance moves, via instructions you listen to on your headphones, accompanied by your choice of music. Activity completed, you'll get all the usual data about your heart
10 rate, calories burnt, time spent exercising, and so on, but you'll have to reach for your smartphone to view this (via the app that you'll have downloaded). FitterGogo's many fans don't find this an issue, and are happy to
15 exchange lack of instant access to their data for the many advantages this tracker provides. Among these advantages is a system of progression from one level to a slightly harder one each time you achieve a certain score.

20 This gives you a real sense of achievement, motivating you by demonstrating your improving fitness.

Whether it's worth upgrading to the FitterGogo 5 if you already possess an earlier

25 model is down to personal opinion. Unless you value the slightly improved battery life and definitely more comfortable wrist strap, there's little to recommend the switch.

4 Scanning to match information

Now that you have a general idea of the purpose and content, you are going to search the text for specific details. Your task is to match one of the four descriptions in the text to questions a–j below.

The following tips may help you:

- In each question, underline important words that tell you what you have to find.

- Run your eye over the whole text, looking for part of the text that mentions what you are trying to find. Be aware that the answer may be written in different words from the words in the question.

- When you think you have found the right place, read very carefully to check.

Which device:

a   has a feature that will help you relax?

b   reduces your training goals if they are too challenging for you?

c   is less expensive than the others?

d   already has a large number of users?

e   is ugly but easy to use?

f   gives you spoken instructions as you do a fitness exercise?

g   can give you early information about a serious illness?

h   has a disadvantage that the reviewer finds surprising?

i   might be too complicated for a beginner?

j   may be an unnecessary purchase?

5 The writer's opinion

The article is a review. The writer tries to be fair, but she gives you her opinion. Find the words in the text that she uses to do this.

Which words tell you that the writer:

GoZone 24/7

a   . . . thinks the punch-strength measuring device might not be very useful?

b   . . . thinks the heart-rhythm monitor is extremely useful for everybody?

c   . . . admires the screen layout?

Kilston Sportwatch

d   . . . likes the fact that your activity levels are measured against your fitness levels?

FitterGogo 5

e   . . . finds the provided activities unusual and enjoyable?

f   . . . thinks people don't mind having to read data on their phone?

Vivace Pro

g   . . . considers it attractive?

h   . . . thinks it will be very successful?

6 Post-reading discussion

> Critical thinking

1   Would you like to have one of these fitness trackers? (Or maybe you already have one?)

2   What features would you use, or not use? Why?

3 Which of the following comments from teenagers do you agree with? Give reasons.

A 'A lot of people my age give up sport because they think it's boring. This is a way to make it fun again.'

B 'I think they are expensive so, if you've paid a lot of money, you're more likely to keep using it!'

C 'If my parents gave me one, I would be hurt. I would think they were criticising me for being too lazy.'

D 'Could this be dangerous for some people? It might make them do too much exercise.'

E 'If your fitness tracker compares you to other people, it's motivating for the ones who are doing well, but the others will be discouraged and give up.'

7 Pre-listening prediction

You are going to listen to an interview on a radio programme. Two worried parents contacted the show to talk about their 14-year-old children's use of computers and mobile phones at home. The radio programme has invited an expert to reply to the parents.

1 Write down at least two things the parents might be worried about. Write down two things the expert might say to the parents.

2 Check you know the meaning of the following words before listening:

- hormones
- teens
- cyberbullying.

🎧 8 Listening to check predictions

Listen to the conversation. Were your predictions correct?

🎧 9 Listening for detail and attitude

Listen to the audio recording again and answer the questions.

1 According to Jeremy the interviewer, the parents he talked to in the morning felt _____ about their children's use of screens.

A angry

B a little worried

C very worried

2 Manal says that spending very long hours looking at screens _____ harmful for teenagers.

A is

B isn't

C may or may not be

3 According to Manal, if teenagers become moody and unconfident, it may be because:

A they aren't socialising enough with their friends.

B they aren't sleeping long enough.

C they have been looking at harmful material online.

4 It's best not to look at phone or computer screens at bedtime because:

A the hormones in our body will keep us awake.

B our brain will be too active to sleep.

C our body won't produce the hormone we need to sleep.

5 Manal thinks late-night phone use is:

A something that should be punished.

B a common problem, not only for teenagers.

C less of a problem as teenagers become more mature.

6 What does Manal advise the parents to do, since they are worried about dangerous activities online?

   A Make sure their children tell them everything they're doing online.

   B Talk to their children about cyberbullying and unsuitable online content.

   C Communicate well with their children and treat them respectfully.

10 Post-listening discussion

> **Critical thinking** Do you agree with the advice given by Manal? If you were a parent of teenagers who never stopped using their phones or tablets, how would you deal with the situation? Give reasons.

D Different approaches to well-being

1 Sayings

Many languages have well-known, traditional sayings that give advice to people about how to live their lives.

Discuss the following sayings with a partner. What do you think they mean? Do you agree with them? Do you have similar sayings in your own language?

a An apple a day keeps the doctor away.

b An ounce of prevention is better than a pound of cure.

c Early to bed and early to rise makes a man healthy, wealthy and wise.

d Eat to live, not live to eat.

e You are what you eat.

f Laughter is the best medicine.

2 Pre-reading: Predicting audience and purpose

You are going to read a text on a topic related to well-being. Before you read the whole text in Section D4, quickly read the title and just the first paragraph. Answer the questions.

1 What is the writer's main purpose?

   A To entertain you.

   B To give you information.

2 Who is the intended audience?

   A Educated readers with a basic knowledge of biology.

   B Experienced doctors.

   C Children or people with no knowledge of biology.

3 What do you expect to find in the rest of the text?

   A A personal story about the writer's own experience with laughter.

   B More facts and details about how laughing may improve our health.

   C Information about how to sign up for laughter health treatment.

   D The writer encouraging you to laugh more so you will live longer.

3 Reading strategy: Using word families to predict meaning

In Section A12, you practised adding different prefixes or suffixes to a base word to create a family of words with related meanings. It is sometimes possible to predict the meaning of unfamiliar words in a text by relating them to other words in the same word family. For example, if you know the verb *miss*, can you predict the meaning of *unmissable*?

Check that you understand the following words. Then, as you read the text in Section D4, find a word that links to each of these words and predict its meaning.

to measure	energy	to row (a boat)
comfort	different	to vary, various
infection	cooperate (with someone)	
horror	tense (adjective)	to prove

4 Reading

Read the text and answer the questions.

Laughter – benefits and causes

Laughter brings many measurable **physiological** benefits. When we laugh energetically, it increases our body's oxygen levels by raising our heart rate and exercises muscles in our diaphragm, stomach, lungs and face. In fact, 20 seconds of
5 laughter could be considered approximately equivalent to a 3-minute workout on a gym rowing machine. Laughing can also boost the **immune system** by stimulating the body's production of **antibodies** and **T-cells**, thus improving our ability to fight disease.

10   Additionally, our body releases endorphins into our bloodstream during laughter. Endorphins, commonly known as 'happy hormones', help us to relax, but they may also increase our tolerance of pain. In one experiment to test the theory that laughter reduces pain,
15 carried out at Oxford University (UK) in 2011, participants were divided into two groups. One group watched a comedy film while the other viewed a recording of a golf match. Then both groups were monitored to check the length of time they could stand the discomfort of having
20 ice packs strapped to their arms. The comedy-watching group lasted ten percent longer.

    Apart from the physiological benefits, laughter has many social and psychological advantages too. Even though cultures and nationalities can differ greatly in
25 what amuses them, what we have in common is that we all laugh, and it is invariably a bonding experience. Laughter brings us closer together, makes us like each other more, improves communication between us and makes us cooperate more effectively. And this very
30 bonding is itself something that makes us feel calmer and happier. Furthermore, laughter is highly infectious: it has been shown that people laugh aloud much more readily when other people are also laughing. We can assume that this is why, during the **Covid-19 lockdown**, certain
35 radio comedy programmes that normally relied on a live studio audience found that their humour simply no longer worked: without the sound of others laughing, the audience at home failed to find the jokes funny.

    Interestingly, though, research suggests that 80
40 percent of laughter is not really associated with humour at all. Investigations into what makes people laugh when they are with others suggests that we laugh more as a way of connecting with people, of showing that we accept or like them, than because they have said something hilarious. In
45 fact, according to **anthropologist**s, learning to laugh may have contributed to the survival of early humans millions of years ago – not due to the physiological benefits of laughter but because it **facilitated** the formation of cooperative social structures.

50   As well as helping us connect with other people, sharing laughter with them can also be a coping strategy. Take, for example, the 'black humour' enjoyed by those whose jobs take them into life-and-death situations, such as emergency doctors. Or consider reports of people
55 surviving horrendous circumstances (such as being held **hostage**) by exchanging jokes with fellow victims. In cases like these, laughter works by helping to release tension and to maintain some necessary emotional distance from the reality of what is happening.

60   In recent years, attempts have been made to **harness** the benefits of laughter specifically to improve people's well-being. Some hospitals have employed comedians or clowns to entertain patients on wards, and telephone 'laughter lines' have been set up to enable
65 people with health issues to laugh together via group calls. Laughter yoga groups have started up around the world, based on the concept that the fake laughter carried out in a series of exercises with an instructor will bring participants the same benefits as **spontaneous**
70 laughter from watching a hilarious sketch. Do these forms of 'laughter therapy' actually work? Is there any physical evidence that they reduce the symptoms of serious illnesses? Much more research is needed. While most participants report very positively about their experiences
75 with laughter therapy, claims about specific medical benefits have yet to be proved or disproved.

GLOSSARY

physiological: relating to the way the body works

immune system: the body's system for protecting itself against illness

antibody: a substance in the blood that attacks harmful bacteria and viruses

T-cell: a type of white blood cell that helps protect the body against disease

Covid-19 lockdown: the period when people were not allowed to mix with others to avoid spreading the Covid-19 virus

anthropologist: person who studies humans and their habits

facilitate: make something happen more easily

hostage: someone kept as a prisoner in order to force another group of people to do something

harness: control something so that you can use its power

spontaneous: happening suddenly, without planning

1   An experiment was carried out by Oxford University in 2011 to find out:

   A   whether one group would laugh more than the other.

   B   whether endorphins help us tolerate cold better.

   C   whether we notice pain less during laughter.

2   Some radio comedies were unsuccessful during the Covid-19 lockdown because:

   A   people are less amused by jokes when they don't hear others laughing.

   B   the audience in the studio didn't laugh as much as in normal times.

   C   the people listening at home didn't bond with the people telling the jokes.

3   How (according to the writer) did laughter help early man survive?

   A   It made people cooperate with each other better.

   B   It had physiological benefits that made people healthier.

   C   It helped people socialise with a greater number of other people.

4   Why does the writer provide the example of the 'black humour' of members of the emergency services?

   A   Because their kind of humour is particularly extreme.

   B   Because their humour is used for a particular purpose.

   C   Because it is an example of humour that is not meant to be funny.

5   What is the writer's personal opinion about laughter therapy?

   A   It can benefit people's health.

   B   Many people believe in it, but it doesn't work.

   C   We are not told.

5 Vocabulary practice

Find a word or phrase in the text that matches each definition.

a   improve or increase (paragraph 1)

b   checked, tested (paragraph 2)

c   connected with (paragraph 4)

d   someone in the same situation (adjective) (paragraph 5)

e   stop holding something, let something go free (paragraph 5)

f   rooms for patients in a hospital (paragraph 6)

g   made to look real (paragraph 6)

6 Making notes

Imagine that you have to give a talk to another class on 'How laughter helps us', based on information you learnt in the text in Section D4.

1 Make a list of brief notes that you would use to help you remember the key points during your talk. Make sure you:

- use bullet points
- keep your notes short
- leave out anything irrelevant.

2 When you have finished, work with a partner to compare notes. Together, agree on a final set of notes.

7 Style and features

1 Read the following short extract from the beginning of another article on the same topic as the text in Section D4.

Laugh more, live longer!

A good giggle can make you feel better – but it can also do wonders for your body. People who laugh are fitter and can fight off many illnesses.

Gerda Fischer, 19, takes part in laughter yoga sessions three times a week. She says: 'It's the most amazing feeling and I would recommend it to anybody. The exercises are the same as working out at the gym – only much more fun! If everyone did this, doctors would be out of work!'

a Do you think the writer's purpose and intended audience is the same or different compared to 'Laughter – benefits and causes'?

b How are the tone and language different?

2 The following sentence is from 'Laughter – benefits and causes'.

20 seconds of laughter could be considered approximately equivalent to a 3-minute workout on a gym rowing machine.

Find the sentence in the extract 'Laugh more, live longer' above that has the same meaning as this sentence. Carefully compare the words used in the two sentences. Try to explain the reasons for the differences.

3 Look back to the text 'Laughter – benefits and causes'. Tick the statements that are true.

The writer:

a ☐ is mainly interested in facts.

b ☐ tends to use exciting words and exclamation marks to make the text sound more appealing.

c ☐ uses words like *may* and *Research suggests that* to show us show that experts cannot be 100 percent certain.

d ☐ uses quite formal language.

e ☐ avoids giving their personal opinion.

f ☐ tends to use long, complex sentence structures.

g ☐ uses exaggeration.

h ☐ provides dates, numbers and specialised terms.

8 Describing and recommending an activity

Your school online magazine wants to encourage students to take up new sports or hobbies that will boost their physical or mental health (or both). It has a feature called 'I recommend', which consists of an article written by a different student each week. The article describes a sport or hobby, and says why it is enjoyable and good for you.

One student, Mel, wrote the article below, but first he wrote some notes to guide him. Read the notes in his plan, then read the article.

1   As he was writing the article, Mel decided to make one change from the order in his notes. What is it, and why might he have made it?

WRITING PLAN

My activity Go

Introduction Why hobbies are good

1   Description   2 people   How you play   Equipment

2   How I started   10 years ago   Grandpa   Explain why

3   Why I recommend it   Simple to learn   Challenges brain

Helps forget stress   Sociable

Ending   Try – you will enjoy

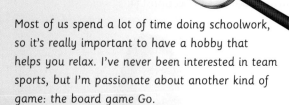

I recommend...

Most of us spend a lot of time doing schoolwork, so it's really important to have a hobby that helps you relax. I've never been interested in team sports, but I'm passionate about another kind of
5   game: the board game Go.

In case you haven't heard of it, Go is a game for two people, which was invented in China over two thousand years ago (but it's much more fun than it sounds!). It's a game of strategy, where each
10   player tries to win more territory on the board than the other. Go can be played on a computer too, but I prefer using a real board and pieces, called 'stones'. This is partly because I already spend a lot of time on my computer so a change of
15   focus suits me, but also because I own a beautiful old wooden board with stones made of black pebbles and white shells, which used to belong to my grandfather.

I recommend Go because the rules are simple to
20   learn, but if you want to play skilfully, it challenges your brain to focus and come up with ways to defeat your opponent. It improves your ability to solve problems, as well as making you forget about anything else that is causing you stress. It can even
25   be quite a sociable game if you join a club or get to know people at tournaments.

I started playing about ten years ago when I was taught by my Japanese grandfather, who has sadly passed away now. As I was a lively, hyperactive
30   six-year-old, he realised that I needed something to help me concentrate and calm down.

Why don't you give Go a try? I'm sure you'll love it!

Mel Ogawa

2   Is there anything you particularly like or dislike about Mel's description? Discuss with a partner.

9 Writing style: Sentence structure

After a previous piece of writing, Mel's teacher criticised him for using too many short, simple sentences. So Mel worked very hard in this article to use more interesting sentence structures, joining up his ideas with suitable words. For example:

'Most of us spend a lot of time doing school work, so it's really important . . .'

'It's a game of strategy, where each player tries to win more territory . . .'

Look back at the article and find some more examples. Underline the words Mel used to link his ideas.

10 Planning and drafting your own article

You are going to write your own article for the 'I recommend . . .' section on your school website.

1   First, think of a sport or other hobby to write about. It should be one that you know a little about and enjoy.

2   Make notes to plan your article. You can use a similar plan to Mel's in Section D8 if you like.

3   Write a first draft of your article. Try to:

*   make it interesting, so other people might want to try your activity

*   explain why your sport/hobby is good for your well-being

*   avoid too many short sentences. Instead, connect them, using linking words.

11 Feedback and redrafting

1   Swap your finished draft with a partner. Read your partner's draft and give them some feedback on the following points:

*   Would the description make people want to try the activity?

*   Has your partner used some longer, more interesting sentence structures with suitable linking words?

*   Can you suggest any improvements?

2   Make any changes to your own writing, following your partner's feedback. Finally, check your work carefully for errors of spelling, punctuation, grammar, and so on.

12 Look, say, cover, write, check

1   Learn these commonly misspelt words using the 'look, say, cover, write, check' method (see Unit 1, Section B12 if you need a reminder).

immediately	exciting	courageous
unforgivable	surprising	imaginative
competition	laughter	enthusiasm
encouragement	physical	skilful

2   Ask a partner to test you when you are confident you have learnt them correctly.

3   Choose six of the words and put each one into a sentence to show its meaning.

GRAMMAR SPOTLIGHT

Zero conditional form with *if*

Look at these examples from the unit:

> It [the game Go] **can** even be quite a sociable game if you **join** a club or get to know people at tournaments.

> If you **swim** regularly, discount rates **are** available at our reception desk.

Here is another example:

> Plants **die** if they **get** no water.

The verbs in the *if* clause and in the main clause are both in the present tense.

Tick the correct explanation. The zero conditional is used:

☐ to talk about facts or rules that are always or generally true

☐ to talk about things that might happen in the future.

First conditional form with *if*

Look at these examples from the unit:

> If you **jump** in, you**'ll risk** getting cold-water shock.

> If you **follow** my safety tips, you**'ll have** a wonderful experience!

The verb in the *if* clause is in the present tense, while the verb in the main clause expresses the future.

Tick the correct explanation. The first conditional is used:

☐ to imagine situations that probably won't happen

☐ to talk about future situations we believe to be real or likely.

Second conditional form with *if*

Look at these examples from the unit:

> The exercises are the same as working out at the gym – only much more fun! If everyone **did** this, doctors **would be** out of work!

> If you **were** a parent of teenagers who never **stopped** using their phones or tablets, how **would you deal** with the situation?

The verb in the *if* clause is past simple tense, while the verb in the main clause is *would* + infinitive form (without *to*).

Tick the correct explanation. The second conditional is used:

☐ to imagine situations that are unlikely or not real

☐ to talk about how something could have been different in the past.

Practice

1 Find further examples of the conditionals described above in the unit, as follows:

   a zero conditional: find an example in Section D8, 'I recommend . . .' paragraph 3.

   b first conditional: find an example in Section C3, 'Vivace Pro'.

   c second conditional: find two examples in Section C3, 'Vivace Pro'.

2 Decide whether the sentences below should be zero, first or second conditional. Then put the verbs in the correct tense.

   a I live 100 miles from the sea but if I (live) closer, I (swim) every day.

   b People come and swim in this pond all winter. If they (be not) regular swimmers, we generally (advise) them to hire a wetsuit.

   c Hurry up and join us in the water! If you (stand) there much longer in your swimming costume, you (get) cold!

Complete the practice activities in your Workbook.

READING AND WRITING

Reading and writing: note-taking

Read the article about why walking is good for you, and then complete the notes.

A life-saving stroll: the many health benefits of a daily walk

'Walking is a man's best medicine', said Hippocrates over 2000 years ago – and a growing body of scientific evidence suggests he wasn't wrong. Yet a recent study has found that four in ten middle-aged adults are failing to manage even one 10-minute walk a month, increasing their risk of developing potentially fatal illnesses.

The latest evidence on the power of walking comes from Canada, where researchers discovered a link between brain function and low-level aerobic exercise. A group of adults who suffer from a medical condition causing memory loss were monitored for six months. Those who walked regularly displayed improved levels of mental functioning.

Two recent studies suggest that walking can be an effective weapon in the battle against cancer, too. The first study showed that women who walk for 180 minutes a week after being diagnosed with breast cancer were roughly half as likely to die from the disease as those who didn't, over an eight-year period. The second study uncovered similar findings, this time for people with bowel cancer.

Most of the benefits scientists have discovered relate to the simple fact that walking gets the blood pumping around the body without putting too much strain on the body. As a result, it reduces the risk of heart attacks or strokes very considerably. This compares very favourably with running, which stresses the muscles and joints, often causing injury. Runners often find that their 'free' form of exercise leads to expensive treatment for damaged knees and hips.

Reducing physical illness is only a part of the picture. A series of psychological experiments suggests that walking naturally boosts our mood, too – even for routine journeys or if we are walking towards something we don't want to do. In one experiment, participants were asked to either tour a university campus on foot or by video link while sitting in front of a screen. Some were also told that they would have to write an essay about the experience at the end – a task that the organisers of the experiment thought the participants would not want to do. They were asked to report their happiness levels at various moments in the experiment. The mood of the video link group dropped during and after the screening. In the group who toured the buildings on foot, even those who knew an essay awaited at the end of the tour reported high happiness levels.

We should not overlook another indirect benefit. By building a regular stroll into your daily routine, you basically ensure that you get outside, rather than staying under different roofs all day long. Once outdoors, you're exposed to the sun's rays, which is how your body absorbs vitamin D – which it uses to keep your bones, teeth and muscles healthy.

And finally, while walking is not necessarily a way to lose weight quickly (unlike running), it will certainly lower your stress levels, and getting off the bus a stop earlier may mean arriving at the office more relaxed. And (unlike your running colleagues) you won't arrive sweating and in need of a shower.

CONTINUED

Imagine you are going to give a talk about walking to your classmates. Use words from the article to help you write some notes.

Make short notes under each heading.

1 Health and wellbeing benefits of walking:

- Improves mental functioning _____

- _____

- _____

- _____ [4]

2 How running is less good than walking, according to the writer:

- _____

- _____

- _____ [3]

[Total: 7]

Reading and writing: informal

You recently went to watch a match or another other live sports event for the first time.

Write an email to tell a friend about it.

In your email, you should:

- describe what you went to see and what happened
- say why you went and who you went with
- explain how you feel about the experience.

Write about 120 to 160 words. [15]

[Total: 15]

Reading and writing: formal

Your class has been discussing how teenagers can use social media in a fun but safe way. The organiser of your school online magazine has asked you to write an article about it.

In your article, say how social media can be useful and enjoyable for teenagers, and suggest how to use it sensibly.

Here are some comments from students in your class:

You can keep in touch with friends far away.

It's great for chatting with people who share a particular interest or problem.

People waste too much time on it.

It's dangerous to give personal information to strangers.

CONTINUED

Now write an article for your school online magazine.

The comments above may give you some ideas, and you should also use some ideas of your own.

Write about 120 to 160 words. [15]

[Total: 15]

Reading and writing: formal

Last week you and your family had lunch at a brand new café called The Healthy Eater's Dream.
The owner would like customers' honest opinions about the café, and you have been asked to write a review.

In your review, say what was enjoyable about the food and the venue, and suggest how it could be improved.

Here are some comments from other members of your family:

> There were some unusual and extremely tasty dishes.

> The portions were rather small.

> The service was a bit slow.

> The walls were beautifully decorated.

Now write a review for the café owner.

The comments above may give you some ideas, and you should also use some ideas of your own.

Write about 120 to 160 words.

LISTENING

Listening: multiple matching

You will hear six people talking about sport.

For questions **1–6**, choose from the list (**A–H**) which idea each speaker expresses. For each speaker, write the correct letter (**A–H**) on the answer line. Use each letter only once. There are two extra letters, which you do not need to use.

You will hear the recordings twice.

CONTINUED

Now look at the information **A–H**.

Information

A   Sport can prepare you for adult life.

B   Young people's experience of sport should be light-hearted.

C   The essence of sport is competition.

D   To be successful in sport, you need to start young.

E   Competitive sport should be introduced by the age of ten.

F   Sport needn't take up a lot of your time.

G   Sport should be a bigger part of the school curriculum.

H   Sportspeople make good role models.

1	Speaker 1	_____	[1]
2	Speaker 2	_____	[1]
3	Speaker 3	_____	[1]
4	Speaker 4	_____	[1]
5	Speaker 5	_____	[1]
6	Speaker 6	_____	[1]

[Total: 6]

SPEAKING

Warm-up questions

Warm-up questions help you feel more relaxed before you move on to answering assessed questions.

Take turns asking and answering the questions. Speak for 1–2 minutes.

- What kind of music do you like?
- Tell me about a place you like visiting.
- What did you do yesterday evening?

Interview

Read the questions. In pairs, decide who will play the interviewer and who will play the student. Then role-play the interview. Speak for about 2–3 minutes. Change roles and role-play the interview again.

Free time

- Can you tell me about the most popular leisure activities in your country?
- How do you and your friends feel about these activities?
- If you had more free time, what activities would you like to do, and why?

Short talk

Read the options and compare them. You have one minute to prepare your talk. Now give a short talk to your partner. Speak for about 2 minutes. Change roles and listen to your partner's talk.

Healthier lifestyle

You have decided you want to get fitter and you are thinking about doing the following:

- going to an exercise class at a gym or sports centre once a week
- going for a run or walk on your own twice a week.

Discuss how easy or difficult these options would be for you. Say which option you would prefer, and why.

CONTINUED

Discussion

Read the discussion questions. In pairs, decide who will play the interviewer and who will play the student. Then role-play the discussion. Speak for about 3 minutes. Change roles and role-play the interview again.

- Do you think people eat more or less healthily than in the past?
- What could your school do to encourage students to have a healthier lifestyle?
- Do you need to be rich to lead a healthy life?
- Should medical treatment be free for everyone?

For even more speaking practice, watch the videos about healthy lifestyles in the digital coursebook

SELF-ASSESSMENT CHECKLIST

Reflect on what you have learnt in this unit. For each area listed, decide whether you feel confident or need more practice. If you feel you need more practice, you will find some ideas to help you in Advice for Success. Come back to your self-assessment scores later in your course and see if your confidence has improved.

I can ...	Need more practice	Fairly confident
discuss issues related to fitness, health, sport and well-being, using appropriate vocabulary		
take notes effectively		
read and understand a more formal text		
understand specific information in short audio clips		
use sentence stress to convey meaning when I speak		

ADVICE FOR SUCCESS

This section is to help you help yourself. Choose the suggestions you like and adapt them if you want to. Make notes about what you do and how it helped you.

Extending your skills

1 Widen your English vocabulary and your knowledge of the topic by finding articles to read online in English on whatever aspect of the topic interests you. You could, for example, use a search engine to look for 'top tips for well-being', 'ways to lead a healthier life', or look at lifestyle blogs on healthier eating, fitness, and so on.

2 Find and follow vloggers who post short videos about issues to do with health and well-being.

CONTINUED

3   If you do a particular sport, consider joining a suitable forum or social media group to swap ideas or get information about it in English. You probably already know a lot of vocabulary connected with your favourite sport, but you could search out information about other less familiar sports to broaden your vocabulary. Video-sharing platforms often have short videos that explain and demonstrate how to do sports or other activities at a beginner level – use these for English practice.

4   Practise reading more formal texts by using a search engine to find information related to topics you are studying at school (such as Science, Geography, etc.). Skim the title and first paragraphs using your awareness of audience and purpose to identify which ones are suitable. Then practise making notes relevant to whatever you are studying.

5   Improve your ability to hear and understand sentence stress by listening to recordings of dialogue (e.g. in audio books) while following short sections of the printed script. Try to identify and underline the stressed words as you listen. Alternatively, identify the words you think will be stressed *before* you listen, then listen to see if you were right.

Showcasing your skills

6   Discussions with a partner in class can be a good opportunity to practise using sentence stress yourself. For example, you could use it in questions to clarify what your partner says (e.g. 'Did you mean/say [*this*] or [*that*]?') It can also be useful to record yourself reading a short passage that includes stressed words, and listening back to see how it sounds.

7   Don't expect to be able to understand every word in a listening task. Listening for stressed words may help you pick out the key points.

8   Always read the listening questions very carefully and underline any key words to help you remember what to listen out for. Notice particularly words such as *not*, *the most (important, etc.)*, *before*/after, first/last, and so on. If you got any answers wrong, read the audioscript afterwards to work out how you got it wrong.

9   More formal texts often include subheadings, diagrams, charts and illustrations. Skim these before you read the whole article to help you get an idea of whether the content is relevant for you.

Unit 3
Where we live

LEARNING INTENTIONS

In this unit you will:

- Explore the topic of home, neighbourhood and places to live

- Continue exploring a range of text types and their features

- Learn skills for writing an email to someone your age

- Listen for gist and then detail in a conversation and a formal talk

- Use stress and intonation appropriately to persuade others or to express a reaction

04 ◄ Watch the video about where we live
in the digital coursebook.

BEFORE YOU START

Look at the photo on this page.

a   Look carefully and describe the kind of neighbourhood in the photo.

b   What practical difficulties might the people living there experience?

c   What might be good about living in such a place?

d   Why do you think the houses have been painted bright colours?

A Our neighbourhood

1 Discussion

1 With a partner, answer the questions about the area where you live.

a How long have you lived there?

b Describe what you would see if you were standing looking out from your front door or the main entrance to your apartment block. Then describe what you would hear.

c To what extent are the following statements true about where you live? Give each statement a number from 5 (I totally agree) to 1 (I don't agree at all). Explain your reasons and give examples.

☐ There is a range of good shops nearby.

☐ There are good transport links and you can travel around easily.

☐ It's a quiet and peaceful place to live.

☐ When you walk around the local area, you often bump into someone you know.

☐ There is a strong community spirit, and people look out for each other.

☐ You can easily access medical facilities if you need them.

☐ There are plenty of sport and leisure facilities to suit all tastes.

☐ It's a great place for people my age.

2 What else is good (or not so good) about living in your local area? (If you and your partner live in the same area, do you agree with each other?)

3 Make a list of public facilities / amenities that you think are important in a town.

2 Homesickness

You are going to read some comments on an online forum called 'The Away Page'. The forum was set up so that young people living away from home for the first time (perhaps as students or doing a first job) could access useful practical information or share thoughts and feelings.

The topic of the comments you will read is homesickness and things that young people miss about home. Before you read, make a list of at least five things you think people in this situation might miss.

3 Reading comments on a forum

1 Now read the comments. Tick any that match your predictions.

2 What did the comments mention that you hadn't thought of?

The Away Page

What do you miss about home?

Anil861
I love my course and student life is great, but sometimes if I'm on my own, I do get a bit of homesickness and I miss things – sometimes quite trivial things. So I wondered . . . what do you guys miss about home?

Splash Turtle
I don't really get homesick, but I do miss having my laundry done for me and not having to think about grocery shopping. And my Dad's cooking (sorry, Mum – I miss yours too!)

Elly5
Bumping into people I know in the street, stopping to chat. Sitting out on the veranda watching the world go by. And my pillow! The ones here in my accommodation are rubbish.

OrangesAndLemons
Sounds really crazy, but I actually miss the silly squabbles with my brothers, fighting over the last roast potato, that kind of stuff. And also gossiping with my sister and sharing secrets at night when everyone's asleep.

BeenWiggly
There's this massive old tree growing out in our back yard at home with chairs under it. It's my gran's favourite place to sit, and we often have a catch-up there over a cup of tea. She never stops talking!

WhyOnEarth
I miss hanging out with my mates from school. I've got new friends here, but it's not the same. And you'll think I'm kidding, but I kind of miss all the nagging from my parents – hang your clothes up, get out of bed . . . When I'm at home, I can't stand being told what to do, but it's weird going out at night without my mum telling me what time to come home!

MissTR
Cinemas, restaurants, decent shops . . . There's nothing like that where I am now, and to get to a supermarket, I have to drive 40 minutes! Living in beautiful surroundings is fab, but sometimes I'd just love to go and grab a burger, or be part of the hustle and bustle in the streets.

SuperCat
Nothing whatsoever! I couldn't wait to get away, and I love having control over my own life and being able to do my own thing. I don't mind doing without some of the home comforts – it's worth it for the freedom.

TedTheMedic
You know, I think what I miss most of all about home is that everyone accepts you for what you are and that's fine. They'll support you even when you screw up. Outside, people are so judgemental.

4 Colloquial language

1   When people comment on a forum, they tend to write very informally as though they were speaking. For example:

- They may not use full sentences.

- They may use short forms of words (e.g. *info* for *information*).

- They may use particular colloquial words and expressions.

Find examples of the first two features in the posts. Then match the colloquial language below with its more formal equivalent.

a	rubbish	1	do whatever you want
b	stuff	2	deal with a situation badly
c	do your own thing	3	thing(s)
d	hang out	4	say something untrue as a joke
e	kid	5	in a way
f	kind of	6	very bad
g	grab	7	spend time with
h	screw up	8	have or do something quickly

2   When do you think it would be acceptable to use this kind of language? When should you avoid using it?

3   a   〉 Critical thinking Why do we change the way we speak depending on who we are speaking to? What would happen if we used the wrong register? Think of examples.

b   Most people are very understanding of mistakes in register from people who are not speaking their first language. But what about people who don't have the skills to use a more formal register in their own language (perhaps because of their background or a lack of educational opportunity)? How might this be a problem for them?

5 Language study: Using the gerund

1   We use a gerund (-*ing* form):

a   after certain verbs (e.g. miss, finish, like, hate, love, enjoy, risk, suggest, deny).

Example: *He suggested going out for a meal.*

b   after certain expressions and phrasal verbs (e.g. spend time, look forward to, give up, get used to, put off).

Example: *We look forward to seeing you next week.*

c   after prepositions.

Example: *I felt really tired after walking all the way home.*

d   as the subject of a sentence.

Example: *Living away from home can be difficult at first.*

Find at least one example corresponding to each of a–d in the forum posts.

2   A few verbs can be followed by either the gerund or infinitive form, depending on their meaning (e.g. remember, try, stop, go on).

Find an example of both forms (gerund and infinitive) following one of these verbs in the forum posts. Discuss the difference in meaning with a partner.

Think of examples of both forms for the other three verbs listed, and discuss the difference in meaning. Use a dictionary to help you if necessary.

3   Imagine that you are living away from home, perhaps for study or work. With a partner, discuss what you might *enjoy* about the experience and what you would *miss* about home.

6 Pre-listening task

You are going to listen to a discussion between two officials, John and Pamela, about creating a new facility for local teenagers. Money is available to convert a disused warehouse and local young people were asked to give their views about how it should be used. Pamela starts by identifying the two main ideas they received from teenagers.

Before you listen, look over the definitions of these words and phrases. Tick the ones that you already know.

- [ ] maintenance: keeping something in good condition
- [ ] to unwind: to relax
- [ ] a drain on resources: a constant, large waste of money
- [ ] wear and tear = slight damage from repeated use
- [ ] budget: spending plan, money for something specific
- [ ] rowdy: noisy and causing trouble
- [ ] residential: where people live (adjective)
- [ ] supervisor: person who has responsibility for something or for some people
- [ ] to give something the go-ahead: to give permission for something to happen

 ## 7 Listening for gist

Listen to the conversation for general meaning first, and find answers to the three questions.

a   What facility does Pamela want?

b   What facility does John want?

c   What does Pamela say that shows she is changing her mind?

8 Detailed listening

Now listen for detail and choose the correct answers.

1   Pamela feels a study centre would be:

   A   inexpensive to operate.

   B   cheap to run but unpopular.

   C   used only at weekends.

2   John thinks the public library is:

   A   very popular with students.

   B   very busy but well-staffed.

   C   a very good, convenient facility.

3   Pamela believes leaving school with good qualifications is:

   A   more important for teenagers than good social facilities.

   B   a guarantee of entry to a good job or further study.

   C   less relevant for modern teenagers than it was in the past.

4   John thinks a youth club would be:

   A   a place where all students could make friends.

   B   fair to both academic and less academic students.

   C   a way to help teenagers prepare well for the future.

5 John says that the parents' opinion is:

A against a youth club.

B in favour of a study centre.

C unknown.

6 With regard to teenagers' behaviour, Pamela:

A agrees with John.

B disagrees with John.

C feels very angry.

7 John thinks it would be possible to pay a supervisor a salary for:

A more than one year.

B six or seven months.

C up to one year.

8 Pamela agrees to the youth club because:

A so many local people want one.

B a capable supervisor will be in charge.

C there have been so many teenage tragedies.

9 Post-listening discussion

Discuss the following as a class:

1 In general, whose views do you sympathise with – John's or Pamela's? Why?

2 We are told that Pamela and John are 'officials'. Using inference skills, say which statement you think best expresses their working relationship.

A John is Pamela's boss.

B Pamela is John's boss.

C They are both on equal terms.

Try to explain your choice.

10 Persuading: Stress and intonation

In their discussion, John and Pamela use the following polite phrases to persuade each other to listen to their point of view. Listen to the phrases, noticing the intonation (the way the voice rises or falls) and how the words in **bold** letters are stressed.

- Do you **really** think it's a good idea to . . . ?
- (That) sounds all right in **theory**, but in **practice** . . .
- I take your **point, but** . . .
- (That)'s all very well, **but** . . .
- That's true, **but** . . .
- Look at it **this** way: . . .

Practise saying each phrase aloud to each other. How could you complete each one?

11 Arguing for a new facility for your community

> Critical thinking Work as a group of three. Each of you will be arguing in favour of a particular new facility for the area where you live.

1 Start by agreeing on three possible facilities that you think would benefit some or all members of your community. Decide who will argue for which facility.

2 Note down some points that you can make in favour of your facility, and some further reasons why the other two facilities are not a good idea.

3 Hold your discussion. At the end, decide whose argument was most convincing.

67

INTERNATIONAL OVERVIEW

> Critical thinking **Moving out of home**

1   A 'multi-generational home' is one where several generations of a family live together under the same roof (for example, children living with their parents as well as grandparents or even great-grandparents). In your country, is this common or unusual? Do you know of any other countries which are different from your country in this respect? What are the advantages of a multi-generational home?

2   Look at the table and map, which show the average age at which adult children leave their parents' home permanently in a number of European countries. Answer the questions below.

Average age of leaving home (2019)

Country	Age
Italy	30.1
Spain	29.5
Greece	28.9
Turkey	27.5
UK	24.6
Germany	23.7
France	23.6
Finland	21.8
Sweden	17.8

Average age of leaving home in 2019 in various European countries

a   In which country do children stay in their parents' home the longest? In which do they leave at the youngest age?

b   For what reasons do you think children move out of their parents' home? Why might they stay longer in some countries (or areas) than others?

B Living in different locations

1 Discussion

> **Critical thinking** With a partner, discuss what it might be like to live in an area similar to those shown in the photos. What would be the advantages and disadvantages? Which would you prefer, if you had to live in one or the other, and why?

A small, isolated village in a cold climate

A very popular tourist destination

2 Jigsaw reading

You are going to read a text about two rather unusual places to live. You and a partner will read different sections of the text – about Derinkuyu and Coober Pedy. Then you will come together and share what you have learnt.

1   Read the introduction (lines 1–8), then read only your part of the text quickly to answer the following questions about your section. Make brief notes as a reminder to yourself.

    a   Where is this place?

    b   Why was it built?

    c   How old is it?

    d   Who lives/lived there?

    e   How is it used today?

2   Compare your answers with your partner's answers. What is similar and what is different in the two places?

Living underground

Since prehistoric times, humans have used and lived in caves. For example, there is evidence that the Zhoukoudian caves in what is now Beijing, China, were inhabited 750000 years ago. Let's
5 look at two rather more recent examples of human settlement underground, considering both the factors involved in choosing this type of **dwelling** and some of its features.

Derinkuyu, Turkey

10 The underground city of Derinkuyu is in Cappadocia, an area consisting mainly of high **volcanic plateaus** in modern-day Turkey. It is believed that Derinkuyu is one of several hundred underground cities in the area, of
15 which only a few have been **excavated**.

The city is built on 18 separate levels, linked by sloping tunnels and stairs, which extend 85 metres down into the ground. There would have been rooms for individual families, as well
20 as communal spaces for people to meet, eat, worship and study. It is thought that as many as 20000 people may have lived in the underground city, which provided all the basic essentials for living: **ventilation** shafts to allow fresh air to
25 circulate; wells to provide fresh water; storage space for food; even stables and an area for the livestock, to provide the population with fresh milk and meat. Lighting would have been by flaming torches, and black soot stains on the
30 roof of the tunnels can still be seen today.

This vast underground network came about because of the unusual **geology** of the area. The soft underlying rock, created over millions of years from volcanic ash, was **eroded** into caves
35 and columns by the action of wind and water. Ancient peoples would have been easily able to expand these to create their own man-made tunnels and chambers.

Caves in Derinkuyu

Archaeologists are unable to give an accurate
40 age for the city, since the oldest underground structures may have formed naturally; however, most suspect the Anatolian Hittite people may be responsible for the construction, some 3500 years ago. Others, though, believe it is
45 more likely to have been the Phrygians, with their known architectural skills. Whichever is true, it seems probable that the city was built principally as a means for the local people to defend themselves from attack by their
50 enemies. In the centuries that followed, later inhabitants would have used the city for a similar purpose, expanding and adapting the accommodation to create a safe haven to suit their own requirements. A number of features
55 confirm this theory, including the huge circular stone doors, which could only be opened from the inside. Thus each separate level of the city could be closed off from invaders.

A secondary purpose may have been to provide
60 cool storage for food supplies, protecting them from climate extremes on the surface.

Today, half of the site of Derinkuyu is inaccessible, but the remainder can be visited through popular guided tours.

65 Coober Pedy, Australia

Located in an area of stony, treeless desert, the town of Coober Pedy is in the state of South Australia. Although the area in general has been inhabited by Aboriginal people for 70 thousands of years, it was only in 1915 that a sizeable town was established here. This happened as a result of a chance discovery of opals by the son of a gold **prospector**. Opals are precious stones, often multi-coloured, 75 with varying amounts of white, blue and green, and 70 percent of the world's production is now linked to Coober Pedy.

Following the discovery, mining for opals began, and people were drawn to the area in 80 the hope of making their fortune. However, the climate in this part of Australia is **harsh**, with an average summer temperature of 37°C and very cold nights. So the earliest inhabitants adapted to this hostile environment by seeking 85 shelter in the holes that they dug to find the opals. (It has been suggested that some of the prospectors, having recently served in the **trenches** during the First World War, made the most of their wartime experience of 90 digging tunnels.)

Understanding how this was possible requires a basic knowledge of the area's geology. The rocks on which Coober Pedy lies were formed 97–100 million years ago when the 95 area was covered by a warm, shallow sea, which gradually retreated, depositing layers of **sediment**. Over time, this formed a soft sedimentary rock, which is relatively easy to excavate. Thus the miners were easily able to 100 create a living space for themselves under the ground, which allowed them to live in a cool, sheltered space with a constant and much more comfortable temperature.

Opal mining continues, but an important 105 secondary source of income for the town today is tourism. Coober Pedy has successfully marketed itself as an interesting and unusual destination for visitors, and has expanded the existing underground town by 110 building **subterranean** facilities for tourists such as hotels, bars, shops and a church. But it is still the case that at least 50 percent of the town's year-round population live entirely or partly underground, some in large and 105 complex networks of self-built rooms.

GLOSSARY

dwelling: home

volcanic: from volcanoes (mountains with holes that can release hot liquid rocks and gases)

plateau: large, raised, flat area of land

excavate: remove earth to find what is below

ventilation: movement of fresh air in and out

livestock: farm animals

geology: the study of rocks

erode: remove the surface of rocks (by water or wind)

archaeologist: person who studies objects found in the ground to learn about history

prospector: person who searches for gold, oil or other minerals

harsh: cruel, too strong

trench: long, deep hole in the ground to allow soldiers to be protected from the enemy

sediment: sand, mud, etc. at the bottom of a sea or river

subterranean: under the ground

3 Comprehension and note-taking

Re-read the text more carefully and answer the following questions. (The questions are grouped into two sections, so you can answer questions about one or both sections.)

Derinkuyu

1   Make short notes about what the people of Derinkuyu ate and drank while sheltering underground. Write three bullet points.

2   What evidence have archaeologists found to prove that the following are true?

   a   It was possible to see where you were going in the underground corridors.

   b   The city was used as a place of safety.

3   Explain why the geology:

   a   made it possible to build the city under the ground.

   b   makes it difficult to know how old the underground city is.

Coober Pedy

1   Make short notes about the following:

   a   How the town of Coober Pedy came to exist (write three bullet points).

   b   How the inhabitants of Coober Pedy make a living today (write two bullet points).

2   The writer does not know for certain whether the reason why earliest inhabitants built underground tunnels is that they were soldiers with experience of digging trenches in the war. Which words does the writer use to show uncertainty?

4 Style

Here are some sentences from the text. Try rewriting them in a less formal style (as if you were a tour guide talking to a group of visitors).

Example: *Archaeologists are unable to give an accurate age for the city* → Nobody really knows how old the city is.

a   Understanding how this was possible requires a basic knowledge of the area's geology.

b   Opal mining continues, but an important secondary source of income for the town today is tourism.

c   It seems probable that the city was built principally as a means for the local people to defend themselves.

5 Prefixes

In the text, the opals are described as *multi-coloured*, the tourist facilities are *subterranean* and the local people's underground houses are *self-built*.

1   What is the meaning of the following prefixes:

   a   *multi-?*

   b   *sub-?*

   c   *self-?*

2   In pairs, discuss the meaning of the following:

   a   a *multi-purpose* tool

   b   a piece of *sub-standard* work

   c   a *self-catering* holiday

3   Think of another example for each prefix.

6 Promoting a tourist attraction

Imagine you are a tour operator, promoting tours of Derinkuyu or Coober Pedy (choose one or the other) to tourists. Write a brief description of the place (maximum four or five sentences) summarising what is special about the place and persuading people to come on your tour. Use information from the text.

Come and enjoy . . .

You'll have an opportunity to see / hear about / experience . . .

fascinating   unique

one of the world's most . . .

---

7 Spelling: Doubling consonants when adding suffixes

Adding a suffix can change a verb tense, make an adjective comparative or superlative, or change nouns into adjectives. It can also affect the spelling of the word that it is added to.

Look at these examples of verbs where the infinitive form ends in a consonant.

One-syllable infinitive form

sit – sitting	nag – nagging
stop – stopping	shout – shouted
seek – seeking	start – started
kid – kidding	dig – digging

Multi-syllable infinitive form

inhabit – inhabited	visit – visiting
retreat – retreated	correct – corrected
begin – beginning	regret – regretted
deposit – depositing	occur – occurring

Practice

1   In the verbs above, circle all the double consonants to occur before -ed or -ing.

2   With a partner, try to work out when the consonant doubles and when it does not.
    Tick the correct rules.

    a   One-syllable words ending in a consonant.

       A   The consonant always doubles when it follows a vowel.

       B   The consonant doubles when the word ends in a single consonant following a single vowel.

    b   Multi-syllable words ending in a consonant

       A   The rules are the same as for one-syllable words in all cases.

       B   The rules are the same, except that a word ending in -t never doubles.

       C   The rules are the same, but only when the stress is on the last syllable of the infinitive form.

3   What is the rule for words ending in -w, -x- or -y? Do they double? Think about the verbs show, fix and display.

Note that the rules in tasks 1–3 above apply for adjectives and adverbs as well as verbs.

8 Spelling practice

1   Complete the words in the following sentences, doubling the final consonant where necessary.

    a   That music is loud___ than I can bear!

    b   Yesterday was the hot___ day of the year.

    c   Ibrahim has stop___ eating meat.

    d   Late for work, she grab___ her bag and ran out of the house.

    e   It's sad to see homeless people beg___ in the streets.

    f   Finland has a much cool___ climate than my country.

g   Lighting fires is ban___ here during the summer months.

h   The hotel manager greet___ the new guests as they arrived.

i   They went to watch a box___ match.

2   Repeat the same task with the multi-syllable words below.

a   People love visit___ the old castle.

b   He was sent to prison for commit___ several serious crimes.

c   Last year, the government prohibit___ the sale of rare birds.

d   Please stop gossip___ about other people's problems.

e   I would have prefer___ to have a room on a higher floor.

f   Grandma keeps forget___ to feed the goldfish.

9 Look, say, cover, write, check

1   Learn these commonly misspelt words using the 'look, say, cover, write, check' method (see Unit 1, Section B12 if you need a reminder).

beginning	preferred	shopping
occurrence	happened	traveller
dropped	development	permitted
multimillionaire	gradually	successful

2   Ask a partner to test you when you are confident you have learnt them correctly.

3   Choose six of the words and put each one into a sentence to show its meaning.

10 House or home?

What is the difference in meaning between a house and a home?

Decide whether the word *house* or *home* should be used in each of the following words or phrases, and match the word or phrase with its meaning.

a   a green_____

b   Make yourself at _____!

c   a _____ match

d   _____made

e   to get on like a _____ on fire

f   to feel at _____

g   to move _____

h   on the _____

i   to work from _____

j   _____sick

1   free, without payment (e.g. a meal in a restaurant)

2   unhappy because of being away from home

3   to form a great friendship with someone (used informally)

4   to feel comfortable and relaxed in a new place

5   a game of football played in the team's own area

6   to do a job at home which you would normally do in an office

7   a glass building for growing fruit and vegetables

8   an expression you might say to a guest to welcome them

9   made in someone's house, not in a factory (e.g. a cake)

10 to change the place where you live

C Describing places and belongings

1 Order of adjectives

When adjectives are used before a noun, they follow a particular order:

Opinion → size → age → shape → colour → origin → material → purpose → (noun)

Look at this phrase from the text in Section B2:

. . . huge circular stone doors, which could only be opened from the inside.

Size goes before shape, and shape goes before material.

Put the following adjectives into the correct order. Use the information above to help you.

a   I've lost a bag. (*sports, canvas, red*)

b   We stayed in a house. (*three-bedroomed, Swedish, beautiful*)

c   The archaeologist dug up a coin. (*copper, eight-sided, unusual*)

d   The new boss is a woman. (*friendly, Egyptian, middle-aged*)

e   I want to buy a jacket. (*leather, good-quality, black*)

f   I've bought a coat. (*warm, winter, woollen*)

g   Thieves stole a teapot. (*Moroccan, silver, priceless*)

2 Developing your writing style

Using more than three adjectives before a noun sounds odd and can be confusing. You can 'break up' a long description by adding a clause instead.

Examples:

- Adjectives + noun + with (extra details):

  *He decided to wear a cool white cotton shirt **with short sleeves**.*

- Adjectives + noun + made of (material):

  *Her great-grandmother owned an amazing, long, purple cloak **made of velvet and silk**.*

  Note that commas are sometimes used between adjectives in longer sequences.

- Adjective + noun + which (a variety of information):

  *She was wearing an Italian gold watch, **which looked very expensive**.*

  *He has a reliable old scooter, **which he doesn't mind lending to people**.*

Practice

Combine each group of sentences into one longer sentence. Use the correct adjective order and a clause where appropriate. When you've finished, compare your answers with a partner's.

a   He gave her a box. The box was made of wood. It had a picture of a famous story on the lid. It was Russian. It was an unusual box.

b   He keeps his granddaughter's photo in a photo frame. It's in the shape of a diamond. It's small. It used to belong to his mother.

c   She bought herself a set of headphones. They are noise-cancelling. Their quality is high. They work really well. They were expensive.

d   It's a frying pan. It's copper. It's heavy. It's French. It has a lid.

e   Someone's taken my mug. It has my name on it. It's blue. It's a ceramic mug. It's used for coffee.

f   Rosanna decided to wear a long dress. It was green and white. It was made of silk. She had bought it in America.

3 Describing a personal object

Read the description.

Next to the computer where I work, I have a pretty, heart-shaped, white stone, which shines a little when I hold it up to the light. When I first picked it up, it felt like a gift from the sea, and now it brings back memories of that day on the beach when I made a life-changing decision.

Think of an object that is important to you for some reason. It might hold particular memories, but it might simply be something that's extremely useful to you, or perhaps it was a present. Write two sentences to describe your object. Then share your description with a partner.

4 Using all the senses in describing a place

Readers of a student website were asked to write about their favourite places. Read one student's description.

When I've got some free time, I love visiting our local market. It's a large, outdoor market by the seafront, which is always busy. Even if I'm not going to buy anything, I really like the atmosphere, people of all ages and the cheerful sounds of stallholders calling to each other.

I'm usually tempted by the brightly coloured fruit, displayed so carefully, and am impressed by the gorgeous cloth on sale. As the market is so close to the sea, you can't escape the strong, fishy odours that mix with the smells of herbs, plants and vegetables. There's a second-hand stall I browse through, too, unable to resist the chance of finding something valuable. I once bought a wonderful old Chinese candlestick for just 50 cents! When I'm at the market, I forget all about my everyday problems. I just relax, unwind and enjoy the sights and sounds around me.

Read the text again and underline the descriptive phrases. Then group them according to:

- Size and location
- Colours
- Atmosphere
- Emotions
- Smells
- Opinions
- Sounds

5 Writing about a favourite place

1 Now imagine yourself in a favourite place of your own. Are you alone, or with family or friends? What are you doing? Take in all the sights, colours, sounds and smells of the place, and think about the way you feel when you go there.

2 Write a description, trying to include references to sights, sounds, smells and atmosphere, and so on, as in the example in Section C4. Use a dictionary to help. Remember to explain *why* this is a place you like.

Some of the following descriptive words and phrases may help.

Smells
sweet   fresh   smoky

Sounds
cheerful sound of talk and laughter   peaceful noisy sound of birds calling

Colours
bright   shining   rich   gorgeous   soft

Atmosphere
calm safe   warm and friendly   lively   cosy comfortable   appealing   relaxing   brightly lit mysterious

Where is it?
off the beaten track   right in the centre of town only five minutes away   isolated hard to get to but worth the effort

Expressing feelings

When I'm there I . . .

. . . feel close to my family or friends / like the solitude / enjoy my own company.

. . . relax and unwind / forget my everyday problems.

. . . feel excited / happy / secure.

. . . experience the beauty of nature / enjoy the wonderful things people have created.

6 Pre-listening tasks

You are going to listen to a podcast about the painting below, which is entitled *The Hunters in the Snow* and was painted by Pieter Bruegel the Elder.

1 First check that you know or can work out the meaning of these words and phrases, which you will hear in the audio recording:

Dutch	to commission	spear
mill	pioneer	contemporaries

2 Now look carefully at the picture and, with a partner, describe what you can see. What is the mood of the painting? What do you like or dislike about it?

Hunters in the Snow, **painted by Pieter Bruegel in the 16th century**

7 Listening for gist

Listen to the podcast for the first time to get a general idea. Read the following questions and try to answer them, but try to look at the painting as you listen.

1   Who do you think the podcast is intended for, and why do you think so?

   A   Art experts.

   B   Adults with a general interest in art.

   C   Younger schoolchildren.

   D   Anyone who wants something fun to listen to for a few minutes of relaxation.

2   Which of the following are discussed in the podcast?

   A   Why the painting was created.

   B   The mood of the painting, according to the speaker.

   C   Why the speaker likes the painting.

   D   Details in the painting.

   E   Where you can go to see the painting.

8 Listening comprehension

Read the questions carefully, underlining any important words. Then listen again and choose the best answers.

1   _____ of Bruegel's paintings of the seasons exist(s) today.

   A   One

   B   Five

   C   Six

2   Bruegel painted the hunters facing away from us so that:

   A   we look where they are looking.

   B   we look at the scene, not at the hunters.

   C   we see the scene like a map.

3   We know from looking at the hunters that they:

   A   didn't catch anything.

   B   are very experienced.

   C   didn't achieve what they wanted to.

4 The scene illustrated in *The Hunters in the Snow*:

A is based on the artist's home village.

B comes entirely from the artist's imagination.

C represents more than one real place.

5 The term *genre painting* (painting pictures of ordinary people) was:

A created by Bruegel.

B created at the time Bruegel was painting.

C created after the time Bruegel was painting.

6 According to the speaker, Bruegel included the frozen waterwheel in the painting to:

A increase the sense of cold.

B match the colours in the pond and sky.

C demonstrate that they were experiencing a Little Ice Age.

9 Post-listening discussion

› Critical thinking Discuss the questions in pairs, then as a class.

1 How far do you agree or disagree with what the speaker said about the scene in the painting?

2 In the podcast, *The Hunters in the Snow* was described as 'one of the most famous images in the art of western Europe'. Had you seen the picture before? Do you learn about art and famous artworks at school? Do you think learning about art is important? Why / why not?

3 Can you name any famous artists (living or dead) from your own country? Describe what kind of works they have created.

10 Reading: Scanning for details

You are going to read about some people living in an unusual and challenging situation. They are, or have been, wildlife wardens, living in basic accommodation on islands off the coast of England and Wales.

Read some of the comments their friends might have made before they went off to their islands. Then scan the text below to see whether each comment is true, false or partly true. Write the number of the paragraph that gives you the answer.

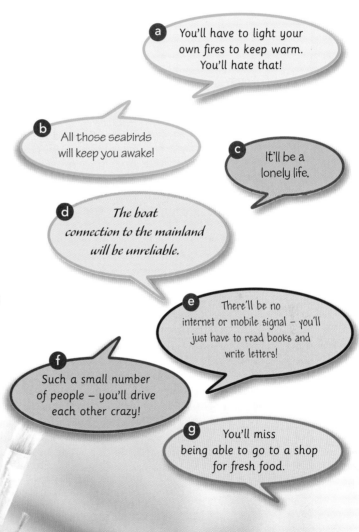

a You'll have to light your own fires to keep warm. You'll hate that!

b All those seabirds will keep you awake!

c It'll be a lonely life.

d *The boat connection to the mainland will be unreliable.*

e There'll be no internet or mobile signal – you'll just have to read books and write letters!

f Such a small number of people – you'll drive each other crazy!

g You'll miss being able to go to a shop for fresh food.

Extreme conditions, loud birds and fresh food by boat – could you live on a remote island?

The wardens of Britain's small islands talk about daily life with little more than thousands of puffins for company

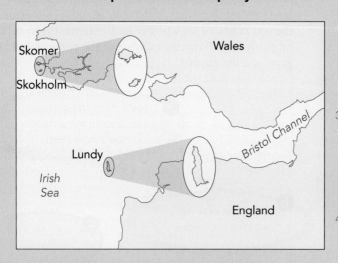

1. 'Living on the island was absolutely amazing,' says Stubbings. Alongside his partner, Bee Bueche, he has completed six years working on Skomer, 720 acres of seabird-populated rocks off the Pembrokeshire coast.

2. The appeal of a small island, Bueche says, is not just being closer to nature – it is being self-sufficient. 'Everything that breaks, you have to fix yourself,' she says. 'It's

Skomer Island, with Midland Isle in the foreground

challenging and exciting – you have to look after yourself, use your brain, **initiative** and imagination. Even not being cosy is great – you wake up and feel the cold and chop wood and put the woodburner on. It makes me feel really alive.'

3. Like most people overseeing the wildlife of small islands, Stubbings and Bueche were drawn to this work through their love of birds: thousands of them, including the noisy nocturnal shearwaters. Many people would struggle to sleep in this cacophony; Stubbings and Bueche found it calming.

4. People who escape to islands where humans are a tiny minority might be assumed to enjoy solitude, if not **misanthropy**. Plenty of people apply for jobs on Skomer seeking to be alone, Stubbings says, but they would be disappointed. 'You have to tell them that's really not what you're going to find.' It is 'a hustly bustly' workplace, he says. 'You never get five minutes to yourself. People come and knock on your door asking questions at 8 p.m., 9 p.m., 10 p.m.'

5. Their working day as Skomer wardens began with a call to the boatman to see if the weather would permit boats to run. Skomer receives 250 day-trippers during the peak bird-breeding months of May and June and accommodates 16 overnight guests. As well as birds and seals to count, there are beds to make, staff and volunteers to organise, and **VIPs** from international ecologists to film-makers to support. 'People probably want to hear we're wild and remote and cut off from the world,' Stubbings says. 'The **brutal** truth is, these days, you're not. Everyone has got internet and mobile phones in their pockets.'

6. Stubbings and Bueche's neighbours on nearby Skokholm, Brown and Eagle, live in a lighthouse, surrounded by puffins, but appear more practical than dreamy. 'We're a bit like **tour reps**,' Brown says, as if **striving** to make his job seem particularly

having a drink in the sunshine or going snorkelling together. There's always **tiffs** between people, but they tend to work themselves out most of the time.'

11 'It's not for everyone,' Bueche says of small-island life. 'If you wanted a family, you'd really struggle, but we decided this life is for us.' She finds her appreciation of the mainland deepened by her small-island **exile**. 'A hot shower! Central heating! A comfy bed! If you fancy a cucumber, you can go to the shop and get it. When you live on the mainland, you don't get any **elation** from going and buying a cucumber. After being on an island, you start to really value these things again.'

unappealing. 'When people first think about island residents, they think of an isolated existence. But I imagine we meet more people during the year than most people on the mainland.'

7 They receive a fresh food delivery by boat once a month. 'There's no reason not to eat well on an island. We have a lot of root vegetables,' Brown says. 'We've got loads of tinned and dried stuff if our delivery doesn't happen,' Eagle laughs.

8 It sounds austere, but Brown says it is much more luxurious than when he began. 'When I started out on the island, it was still gas lights and no hot water unless you boiled it. These days, we've got solar power and solar hot water and a 4G signal. It has got much easier.'

9 The weather is the force that most shapes the life of Dean Woodfin Jones, the warden of Lundy, across the Bristol Channel from Brown and Eagle on Skokholm. 'Mother nature is truly in charge here,' he says. Lundy – 1100 acres of **granite**, sitting high above the waves – feels like a huge ship and is likened to one by Woodfin Jones, who sees Lundy's 29 residents as a kind of crew. I asked one islander how she got on with her fellow residents. 'Carefully,' she replied. Small-island communities can be **claustrophobic**. As Stubbings puts it: 'If you can't cope with the **insularity**, you're going to explode, because you're on a small island with a small group of people.'

10 Small talk is crucial on small islands. Social bonds must be renewed each day and misunderstandings **nipped in the bud** before they **blossom** into **feuds**. 'You get some brilliant characters here. We've got a really good group at the moment. We're quite social and like

GLOSSARY

initiative: ability to make decisions without being told what to do

nocturnal: active at night

misanthropy: dislike of other people

VIP: very important person

brutal: cruel

tour rep: person responsible for looking after holiday-makers (rep = representative)

strive: try very hard

granite: type of (very hard) rock

claustrophobia: fear of being in a small space

insularity: lack of contact with people outside your own small community

nip something in the bud: stop a problem when it's small, before it grows

blossom: grow (like a flower on a fruit tree)

feud: argument lasting a long period of time

tiff: small disagreement

exile: separation from your home country or town (e.g. for political reasons)

elation: extreme happiness

11 Comprehension check

Read the text again carefully and answer these questions.

1   Why did Stubbings and Bueche want to be wardens in the first place? Which words tell you this?

2   Which word suggests that the writer of the article doesn't enjoy the sound of birds.

3   Explain in your own words the difference between people's expectations of life on Skomer and what it is really like. Look at paragraph 4.

4   Why do you think some people are disappointed to learn that the islanders have mobile phones and the internet?

5   Why do you think Brown was 'striving to make his job seem particularly unappealing'?

6   Explain Dean Woodfin Jones's attitude towards the weather.

7   Explain in your own words how, according to the writer, you should behave towards other people on the island in order to maintain good relationships.

8   How does Bueche feel about visiting the mainland now?

12 Post-reading discussion

Discuss the following with a partner.

1   Based on information in the text, describe the qualities you would need to be a successful warden on these islands.

2   Do you think you would be able to do this job? Why / why not?

🎧 [3.4] 13 Showing reactions with stress and intonation

1   Listen to the following descriptions of places. Notice how the most important words, which show strong, definite feelings, are stressed.

   a   What an **amazing** place! It would make a **great** change from life in the city.

   b   What a **lovely** place! I'm sure I'd appreciate the special **atmosphere**.

   c   What **fun**! It would be a **superb** place to relax on holiday.

   d   How **fascinating**! My friends and I **love** wildlife. We **must** go there.

   e   How **interesting**! Now I'll see it through **new eyes**!

2   Practise saying the sentences to your partner. Make sure you sound enthusiastic. Stress the important words that show your attitude.

3   Notice the language structure:

   What (+ *a*) + noun / noun phrase

   How + adjective

   Make up a suitable response to each piece of news that a friend tells you, using *How . . . !* or *What . . . !*

   a   I'm going to live in Canada for a year with my family.

   b   We found a gold ring behind an old cupboard in our kitchen.

   c   Our new neighbours are really noisy. They woke me up last night.

   d   I've been offered the opportunity to work as a wildlife warden on an island.

   e   My aunt gave me a new mobile phone as a present.

   f   I thought I heard somebody come into our house in the middle of the night.

D Welcoming an exchange visitor

1 Reassuring your guest

Many young people take part in exchange visits with students of their own age, to learn more about another culture and improve their language skills. They take turns going abroad to stay with each other's family.

Imagine that your family is going to take part in an exchange visit. Your guest, who is about your age but you have not met before, is coming from overseas to stay with you for three weeks.

Your guest may be a bit nervous, not knowing what to expect, so think about what you could say in an email to put them at ease. Make your home and your local area sound inviting. Write some notes under the following headings:

- Positive things about my home and family

- Exciting places to visit in my area

- Other enjoyable things to do together

What aspects of your home life or area would you *not* want to draw attention to (if any)? Why?

2 Email beginnings and endings

Below are some common phrases used to begin and end an informal email. Complete them using the words from the box. There is one word you don't need.

all	to	to	from	forget	for	for

Beginnings

1 It was great _____ get your last email.

2 Thanks _____ your email.

3 Just a quick email _____ let you know . . .

Endings

1 That's _____ for now.

2 Looking forward to hearing _____ you.

3 Don't _____ to email soon.

3 Example email

Now read this example email. Underline the phrases used to welcome the visitor. Then answer the questions below.

To... Zoltan
Cc...
Subject: Your visit

Hi Zoltan,

I'm really pleased you're coming to stay with us soon. My family consists of my mum, dad and my younger sister Astrid. We're an easy-going, ordinary family and my parents are very approachable. They let us do more or less what we like as long as we tell them about it first. I think you will enjoy sharing family dinners with us all.

One thing I should mention is that we are vegetarian, but my parents always cook delicious meals, so I don't think you will mind not having meat.

We live in a modern three-bedroomed house with a small front and back garden. It's about ten minutes' walk from the town centre, which has plenty of shops, three cinemas, cafés and a weekly market. We also have a brand new leisure centre with a pool, so bring your swimming things! If you enjoy history, I'll show you our town museum, which has some fascinating information about local history.

I've made a list of the most interesting things to see in the area. I heard you are keen on watching football so I've booked two tickets to see a big match while you're here. I got my driving licence last month, and Mum has promised to let me use the car. We can explore the nearby hills and perhaps even camp for a night or two. The wildlife and countryside won't be as spectacular as where you live, but it's very peaceful and we might even see some wild ponies.

I can't wait to meet you, Zoltan! Have a safe journey here.

Best wishes,

Matt

1 What information does Matt provide about:

  a his family?

  b his home?

  c what he has planned for Zoltan's visit?

2 How does Matt show that he has considered the feelings of his guest? Give examples.

3 How does Matt begin the email, after the greeting? Why is this a good way to start the email?

4 The email is divided into paragraphs. Why is this helpful? What is each paragraph about?

5 Would you say that the email is too formal, too informal or about right?

4 Finding a suitable tone

In pairs, read the following sentences taken from students' emails. Tick the sentences that would make you feel at ease if you received the email. Put a cross next to the ones that would worry you.

a It'll be lovely to see you. ☐

b We're all looking forward to meeting you. ☐

c The food here will be rather unpleasant for you. ☐

d When you are in the house, try to behave with respect to my parents. ☐

e My friend, you can come and enjoy yourself but my family is very strict. ☐

f You'll soon feel at home. ☐

g The place is safe. You do not need to be afraid when walking – there aren't many thieves. ☐

h I would like to tell you that my parents are very good and they don't like people who drink too much. ☐

i We can promise you the best time of your life. ☐

j We will visit our countryside every day because here that is the only place worth visiting. ☐

k My family are selfish and want someone to do things for them but I know this will not be a problem. ☐

l We're going to have a wonderful time together. ☐

m We can go cycling through our beautiful countryside and have great parties on the beach. ☐

n As I have already told you, this is a very small place, so don't think about shopping malls, theatres, cinemas, and so on. ☐

Choose three of the sentences above that don't sound right, and rewrite them to make them sound more appropriate and friendly.

5 Correcting mistakes

The following email is from Zoltan, who is writing to thank Matt for his holiday. It contains some mistakes.

1 Underline any sentences or words that are too formal.

2 Find and correct the mistakes, which are to do with:

  • prepositions   • punctuation

  • missing words • spelling

  • word order   • agreement of subject and verb (singular/plural).

  • verb tense

3 Show where the email should be divided into paragraphs.

4 Finally, rewrite the whole email correctly.

Hi Matt,

I'm back! I am writing to you to offer you my most sincere thanks. I've had a great time to stay with you and you're family last week. You were all really kindness for me. I've got so much good memories of the trip. Everyone were so friendly – your family, the nieghbours, all the students at the college. Tell you're mum she is the best cooker in the world! Can she came and live with us hear? I really liked your town, by the way. I think you are lucky to live there. I had such a good time – we done so many interesting thing! I send you some photos of our camping trip in my forthcoming email? You must come and stay with us soon! Do you remember I told you that our house is near a big lovely lake? Well, Dad's just fixed the boat which means we can go out on the lake on it, if you like! The beaches here are great and now the summer is in the way we'll able go swimming all the days. I know how much you love. Whenever the weathers is not so good, we can go to some of shops by the town centre – tourists love all the shops! I look forward to receive an email from you as soon as it is convenient for you to send one.

Best wishes,

Zoltan

6 Presenting information positively

In Matt's email to Zoltan, he told Zoltan about his family's vegetarian diet as follows:

One thing I should mention is that we are vegetarian, but my parents always cook delicious meals, so I don't think you will mind not having meat.

Matt wanted to explain the situation but without making it sound like a negative thing, in case Zoltan is a meat eater.

Try to complete these sentences by balancing any negative ideas with more positive ones.

a   Even though he is a nuisance at times, my little brother . . .

b   Despite being too dangerous for swimming, our local river . . .

c   Although we're a long way from the bright lights of the city, . . .

d   My parents can be rather strict, yet . . .

e   You may find our way of life a bit strange at first, but . . .

f   We don't have a perfect house, but . . .

7 Further practice with tone and register

Work with a partner.

1   You recently arranged a surprise party for your parents' wedding anniversary. You went to a lot of trouble to make the party a success. Unfortunately, your cousin was ill and unable to attend.

Which of the following would you say to your cousin? Why?

a   Where were you? Everyone expected you to come.

b   Why didn't you arrive? You should have been there.

c   It is such a pity you couldn't make it.

d   You disappointed us very much.

2   Discuss what you might say in each situation. Use an appropriate tone.

a   Your elderly aunt sent you a parcel containing a ceramic jug as a present, but she hadn't wrapped it very well and it was cracked when you received it.

b   The student you will be doing an exchange with has arranged to take you swimming with a group of friends, but you can't swim.

8 Reordering an email

The following email describes a surprise party. It is written to a cousin who missed the celebration. Put the sentences in the correct order. Divide the sentences into paragraphs. What overall impression do you think the email will make on the recipient?

Dear Ella,

a   As you know, Mum and Dad didn't know anything about the party in advance.

b   Just before the end, Uncle Dan let off lots of fireworks in the garden.

c   She had decorated the house beautifully.

d   Perhaps the DVD I'm sending you of the occasion will be a little compensation.

e   However, everyone understood that you were still feeling weak after the operation.

f   So you can imagine their surprise when, instead of going to the Blue Fountain, we arrived at Auntie Mei's house.

g   Hope you feel better soon.

h   No one looked tired or seemed inclined to go early.

i   It was a great pity you couldn't come.

j   Although many of the guests must have been over 60, the party went on until the early hours.

k   Despite the fact that we all missed you, we had a lovely day.

l   This was a wonderful way to round off the occasion.

m   Once again, I know how disappointed you were not to be there.

n   Just a short email to let you know about Mum and Dad's anniversary party.

o   They assumed I was taking them to a restaurant to celebrate.

Lots of love,

Krystyna

9 Writing an email to a family member

Your cousin went to live abroad with her family when she was only two or three years old. Her parents have arranged with your family that she will come and stay with you all for a holiday. You have never actually met before. Write an email to your cousin in which you:

- introduce yourself
- describe your family and where you live
- tell her about enjoyable things to do together and places to visit.

10 Reviewing your email

When you have drafted your email, read it through carefully using the following checklist.

☐ Check that you have remembered to mention your cousin's visit.

☐ Check the content. Have you covered points listed in Section D9?

☐ Check the tone and register. Is it neither too formal nor very informal? Is it friendly and welcoming?

☐ Check that you've written in paragraphs.

☐ Check for mistakes. (Look back at Section D5 for a list of things to check for.)

Make any necessary improvements. Then swap emails with a partner so you can check each other's work.

GRAMMAR SPOTLIGHT

Passives

Passive forms are made up of the verb *be* plus a past participle:

> The window frames **are / are being / were / have been / will be** (etc.) painted light blue.

Look at this example from the reading text in Section B2:

> The area **has been inhabited** by Aboriginal people for thousands of years.

The passive form is used here because the main focus of the sentence is *the area* (the subject of the sentence), so that is placed at the beginning of the sentence. If we were more interested in the *people*, we would use the *active* form:

> Aboriginal people **have inhabited** this area for thousands of years.

We also use the passive form when the person/ thing responsible for the action is not known or is unimportant, or when we don't know or prefer not to say who carried out an action.

> The leisure centre **was built** five years ago.

> A mobile phone **was stolen** from this office yesterday afternoon.

Passive forms are more common in more formal writing and in texts which explain how things work (for example, scientific processes).

In more formal written texts, the following forms are often used: *It is said that . . . It is known that . . .* , and so on. For example:

> It is believed that Derinkuyu is one of several hundred underground cities in the area.

This creates an impersonal tone and focuses on the information being presented rather than the people who discovered the information.

Particular uses

Passives are formed in the same way with multi-word verbs. Study these pairs of examples, where the active form becomes passive:

The construction firm carried out the work over six weeks.

→ *The work was carried out over six weeks.*

When nobody claimed the bike after a month, the person who found it gave it away.

→ *After a month, the bike was given away.*

As a child, my great-aunt looked after me.

→ *As a child, I was looked after by my great-aunt.*

An indirect object can become the subject of a passive verb. Study these examples:

Sydney University offered a place to Marianne.

→ *Marianne was offered a place at Sydney University.*

Someone lent a valuable old camera to my friend for her photography course.

→ *My friend was lent a valuable old camera for her photography course.*

This construction is common with verbs like *give, offer, lend* and *send*.

Practice

1 With a partner, discuss the difference between the following two sentences and in what context they might be used:

   You can collect parcels any time you like.

   Parcels can be collected between 9 a.m. and 3 p.m.

2 Look at the text 'Living underground' in Section B2 and underline further examples of passive forms.

3 Rewrite the following sentences using a passive form. In each case, consider whether 'by (someone)' is necessary.

   a The artist painted the scene in the open air.

   b A kind neighbour of mine lent me the tools to fix our broken tap.

   c Geologists believe that these rocks are 200 million years old.

   d Ivan's boss sacked Ivan for being late every day.

Complete the practice activities in your Workbook.

READING AND WRITING

Reading and writing: multiple matching

Read the article where four people (**A–D**) talk about a place which is special to them. Then answer questions **(a)–(i)**.

A special place

A Anh

When I turn the key in the door of my shoe shop, I am in my favourite place. I stand in the middle of the shop floor for a few seconds, gazing over the rows of stylish shoes in gorgeous colours. I used to sell my shoes in the market and I enjoyed the cheerful community atmosphere, but when I began to make a decent profit, I moved to this modern mall out of town. The mall is so good for my business. It makes up for the amount of time I spend getting there. I think some of the customers are put off by the price of the shoes, but I tell them that, although the shoes might be expensive, they cost nothing to try on! That bit of encouragement works very well and business is good! When the last customer leaves, it's time for me to go home too, but I must admit I like to wait for a while, enjoying the peace in the empty shop.

B Roberto

My sister, Elsie, and I love going to our uncle's farm in the school holidays. Living in a small city flat makes you really appreciate the space and freedom in the countryside. When we are there, we relax, unwind and forget all about schoolwork and busy timetables. I enjoy waking up to the sound of the cows and sheep on the farm and feeling the whole day is ahead of me. I used to think getting up early was not for me, but when I'm at the farm, I find myself wanting to get out of bed and get going, which I never expected. Even though the farm is isolated and there isn't any internet access, we find so many brilliant things to do, like riding on the quad bikes, swimming in the river or having a picnic. Sometimes we help my uncle with the farm work. Elsie loves looking after the cows and I help with the sheep. We have delicious food too. My aunt fills the fridge with snacks and fresh juices, and we help ourselves whenever we're hungry.

C Hayley

My favourite place is a cosy café with a roof-top terrace – not everyone knows about it. I go there at weekends and sit outside, surrounded by plants, watching the bees collecting honey from the flowers, which is a wonderful way to calm yourself if you are anxious. At the café, I feel part of a simpler, more natural world. The owner is an artist and helps other local artists make a living by letting them display their paintings. The pictures are of the most unspoilt places in our community, like the beaches and woods. They remind me of happy times spent collecting shells or splashing in the sea, but the pictures are too expensive for me to buy. There are some artistic cards on sale, though, and I can afford one of them from time to time. I know my friends would like the café too, but I usually go alone and enjoy my own company for a change. I do sometimes feel it is maybe a little selfish of me not to share such an appealing place with them.

CONTINUED

> **D Xing**
>
> I got my job in the Science Research Institute only a few months ago, just after leaving college, and I love it. People think a laboratory is a dull, sterile environment. but to me it is a magical place, full of possibilities. As soon as I arrive, I put on my lab coat and feel very purposeful. I spend a lot of time doing experiments to develop a new kind of treatment for sick children. We have made some discoveries that I really didn't expect, and the outcome is hopeful. If we actually developed a complete cure, it would be a dream come true. The working atmosphere in the team is warm and friendly. Some team members are much more experienced than me, but they never mind answering my questions or considering my suggestions for different ways to do things. We're not serious or working hard all the time, of course. We often stop to laugh, especially when my colleague Tim tells one of his jokes!

For each statement, write the correct letter A, B, C or D on the line.

Which person gives the following information?

a	The fact that they occasionally buy things	_____	[1]
b	A description of happy times without technology	_____	[1]
c	An explanation of how they persuade people	_____	[1]
d	A wish for the future	_____	[1]
e	Their opinion that the workplace has pros and cons	_____	[1]
f	A recommendation for reducing stress levels	_____	[1]
g	Something surprising the writer learnt about themselves	_____	[1]
h	A confession about feeling guilty sometimes	_____	[1]
i	A description of how others treat them	_____	[1]

[Total: 9]

Reading and writing: informal

You recently took part in a project to clean up your neighbourhood and improve your local park.

Write an email to tell a friend about it.

In your email, you should:

- describe what you did and why
- explain how the improvements will benefit local people
- encourage your friend to get involved in something similar.

Write about 120 to 160 words.

Reading and writing: formal

Your school recently held a community event where students taught elderly people how to use email and make video phone calls. Your school wants students' opinions about the event, and you have been asked to write a report.

CONTINUED

In your report, say how elderly people benefited from the event and suggest how it could be improved.

Here are some comments from students in your class:

> We helped the elderly people communicate with their families.

> There weren't enough computers.

> It made us feel proud and more confident.

> We needed more time to chat afterwards.

Write a report for the organisers of the event.

The comments above may give you some ideas, and you should also use some ideas of your own.

Write about 120 to 160 words.

[15]

[Total: 15]

LISTENING

Listening: dialogue

In Listening exams, exercises like this may have more recordings and questions than given below. Your teacher will be able to give you more examples.

You will hear three short recordings. For each question, choose the correct answer, **A**, **B**, **C** or **D**, and put a tick (✓) in the appropriate box.

You will hear each recording twice.

1   Which flat does the man think his daughter Ariane should choose?

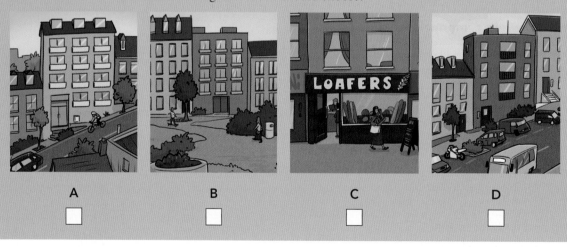

A	B	C	D
☐	☐	☐	☐

[1]

CONTINUED

2　What present has the boy got from his grandmother?

A	B	C	D
☐	☐	☐	☐	[1]

3　Where should Ireshi meet the girl and her father?

A	B	C	D
☐	☐	☐	☐	[1]

[Total: 3]

SPEAKING

Warm-up questions

Warm-up questions help you feel more relaxed before you move on to answering assessed questions.

Take turns asking and answering the questions. Speak for 1–2 minutes.

- Tell me about your favourite foods.
- How do you usually travel to school?
- What would you like to do when you finish school?

Interview

**Read the questions. In pairs, decide who will play the interviewer and who will play the student.
Then role-play the interview. Speak for about 2–3 minutes. Change roles and role-play the interview again.**

Living arrangements

- Can you tell me who you live with? Do you get on well?
- Would you like to live alone or would you prefer to share your home with lots of people?
- When you are very old, would you like to live with your children if you have any?

CONTINUED

Short talk

Read the options and compare them. You have one minute to prepare your talk. Now give a short talk to your partner. Speak for about 2 minutes. Change roles and listen to your partner's talk.

Visit to a foreign country

Your teacher is considering a visit to an English-speaking country to help students improve their language skills. There are two options:

- the whole class staying in a hotel with daily lessons in a language school
- each student staying with a different family.

Discuss the advantages and disadvantages of each option. Say which option you would prefer, and why.

Discussion

Read the discussion questions. In pairs, decide who will play the interviewer and who will play the student. Then role-play the discussion. Speak for about 3 minutes. Change roles and role-play the interview again.

- Is it easy to find somewhere to live in your town or city, or is there a shortage of homes?
- Are there enough parks and open spaces in your city?
- If you could make one change to your town or city, what would it be?
- If you came back one hundred years in the future, how might your home town or city have changed?

Interview

Read the questions. In pairs, decide who will play the interviewer and who will play the student. Then role-play the interview. Speak for about 2–3 minutes. Change roles and role-play the interview again.

Your home

- Can you tell me about your favourite place in your home?
- What thing in your home would you replace if you could?
- Do you think most private homes are more comfortable now than 50 years ago?

Short talk

Read the options and compare them. You have one minute to prepare your talk. Now give a short talk to your partner. Speak for about 2 minutes. Change roles and listen to your partner's talk.

A lost possession

You have just lost something that's very precious to you, but not valuable. You must have dropped it while visiting another town. You are considering two ways of finding it:

- travel back to the town and look for it everywhere you went
- advertise on that town's online community page.

Compare the two options and say which one would be better, and why.

CONTINUED

Discussion

Read the discussion questions. In pairs, decide who will play the interviewer and who will play the student. Then role-play the discussion. Speak for about 3 minutes. Change roles and role-play the interview again.

• If you found something in the street, would you have the right to keep it?

• Most people have too many possessions. What do you think?

• The objects that make us most happy are not the most valuable. Do you agree?

• Is it better to spend money on possessions or experiences?

SELF-ASSESSMENT CHECKLIST

Reflect on what you have learnt in this unit. For each area listed, decide whether you feel confident or need more practice. If you feel you need more practice, you will find some ideas to help you in Advice for Success. Come back to your self-assessment scores later in your course and see if your confidence has improved.

I can ...	Need more practice	Fairly confident
discuss issues related to home, neighbourhood and places to live, using appropriate vocabulary		
recognise the features of some different text types		
write an email to someone my age		
understand gist and then detail in a longer audio		
use stress and intonation appropriately to persuade others or to express a reaction		

ADVICE FOR SUCCESS

This section is to help you help yourself. Choose the suggestions you like and adapt them if you want to. Make notes about what you do and how it helped you.

Extending your skills

1 Listen to spoken English, focusing on the intonation patterns that people use in different contexts or to express different emotions. Radio plays are particularly useful for this.

2 Improve your understanding of register by listening to spoken English in a variety of contexts (from formal news programmes to chat shows or dramas that you can find online). Continue reading a range of text types to learn more about the features of written English in different genres, too.

3 Use a search engine to find descriptions of unusual places where people live, either on travel or tourist websites, or in a more academic context (e.g. history or geography).

4 Look at reviews of places to visit on websites such as TripAdvisor (where members of the public can post their opinions) to see the more informal language used.

5 Look at descriptions of places in more literary contexts to see examples of how adjectives are used to describe places.

6 Use a search engine to read about an artist you like. To find descriptions of particular artworks (written or spoken), try looking at the websites of famous art galleries.

7 Practise writing emails to English speakers of your own age or even swap emails in English with a friend who speaks the same first language as you.

Showcasing your skills

8 Always proofread your writing, looking out for the points listed in Sections D5 and D10.

9 When you look up words in a dictionary, use the examples provided to check the context(s) in which the word is used. Also check whether the dictionary says that the word is informal.

Our impact on the planet

LEARNING INTENTIONS

In this unit you will:

- Explore the topic of our environment

- Scan for information in a magazine article

- Listen for detailed information in a formal talk

- Use linking devices to organise and present a point of view

- Write a report giving both sides of an argument

05 ◄ Watch the video about our impact on the planet in the digital coursebook.

BEFORE YOU START

Look at the photo on this page.

a Describe what you can see in the photograph.

b Are there examples of either of these near where you live?

c What do you think the photographer was trying to achieve through this image?

d What impact do these two ways of generating power have on our planet?

A Global warming and industry

1 Global warming vocabulary

Complete the gaps in the paragraph below with the following expressions. There is one more expression than you need. Do not use any expression more than once.

climate change	greenhouse gases
carbon emissions	global warming
carbon footprint	fossil fuels
environmental pollution	

_____(a) means a continuing rise in the Earth's average temperature. Many scientists think that this is the result of our production of _____(b), such as carbon dioxide, which are released when we burn _____(c) (coal, oil and natural gas). These greenhouse gases become trapped and warm the Earth's atmosphere.

A _____(d) measures the total greenhouse gas emissions caused by the activities of a person, group or country. Richer countries have a bigger carbon footprint per person.

There are fears that global warming is causing _____(e) and so many governments are aiming to reduce their _____(f).

2 Discussion

1   Read the following statements about climate change. One of them is incorrect. Discuss the ideas with a partner and cross out the incorrect statement.

a   Trees absorb and store carbon dioxide, so deforestation leads to an increase in greenhouse gases in our atmosphere.

b   Wind, waves and sunlight are all renewable sources of energy. These can help reduce climate change.

c   Nuclear energy is radioactive and produces greenhouse gases, which cause climate change.

d   Climate change has caused unpredictable global weather patterns, including floods, severe winters, drought and desertification.

2   〉 Critical thinking How might the way of life in your country change if the climate became much warmer and drier, or much wetter and colder? Discuss the possible benefits and disadvantages.

3 **> Critical thinking** Look at one student's ideas about how to reduce her and her family's carbon footprint. Make your own list with two or three more ideas of your own. Discuss with a partner which ideas are best and explain why.

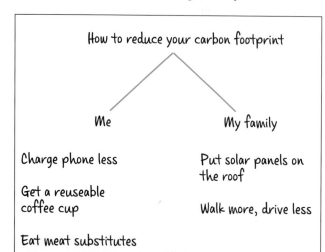

How to reduce your carbon footprint

Me

Charge phone less

Get a reuseable coffee cup

Eat meat substitutes

My family

Put solar panels on the roof

Walk more, drive less

3 Pre-listening tasks

1 You are going to listen to an environmentalist who is giving a talk to a group of students. He explains the connection between the fast fashion industry and global warming. As a class, discuss what you understand by 'fast fashion'.

2 Before you listen, make sure you know the meaning of these words.

| garments | petroleum |
| landfill | mattresses |

4 Listening for detail

1 You are going to complete some notes about the talk. Read through the notes below first and predict what kind of word you will need in each gap: a number? A noun? A verb?

2 Listen to the talk, then complete the notes below. Write one or two words for each gap.

Size of the industry

a Worldwide, we buy about _____ new items of clothing per year.

b The average number of new clothing items per year for someone in the USA is _____.

c It is predicted that in 2050, the total amount of new clothes purchased globally will rise to _____ tonnes.

Impact on the environment

d Eight percent of all _____ emissions are caused by the fashion industry.

e The industry uses vast amounts of non-renewable _____ such as petroleum.

f Pesticides cause pollution in the surrounding area and health risks for _____.

g In countries such as Vietnam, the industry uses up precious local resources such as _____.

Recycling

h   The majority of clothing we no longer want is either _____ or sent to _____.

i   One percent of clothes sent for recycling are used to make _____.

5 Post-listening discussion

> Critical thinking Discuss as a class:

• Did anything surprise you in the talk that you have just listened to?

• Do you think that the major clothing brands are doing enough to try to improve their sustainability?

6 Reading: Scanning practice

You are going to read a magazine article about possible alternatives to fast fashion. Scan the article to find the answer to the following questions.

Which of the five alternatives:

a   is still at the experimental stage?

b   is ideal for people on a low income?

c   uses materials that would otherwise kill living creatures?

d   was inspired by experiences from the creator's own childhood?

e   uses something farmers had previously thrown away?

SLOWING DOWN THE FAST FASHION TREND

Evidence of climate change is all around us, and sustainability is the word on everyone's lips. As a result, many of us have been thinking a little harder about our
5 shopping habits. Do we really need that orange silk jumpsuit, the one that fashion vlogger promoted?

Here, we take a look at five alternatives to fast fashion.

10 Clothes swapping
Swapology was the brainchild of New Zealander Alice Wills-Johnson. While clothes swap parties already existed, during the Covid pandemic lockdown Alice was desperate to
15 find a way to carry on swapping clothes safely and without the need for face-to-face contact. So she created an online platform that enables members (for a modest subscription) to swap clothing from their own wardrobes
20 for items on the site, using a system of points. It allows those on a budget who want to live more sustainably to do so without giving up the pleasure of having a regular selection of new (to them) clothes.

25 Fabric from fruit
Piñatex®, a leather substitute made from pineapple leaf fibre, is one of a number of new clothing textiles made using byproducts from food crop production – including banana
30 peel, coconut husks and coffee grounds. The pineapple leaf fibre, which used to be sent to landfill or burnt, now provides a valuable source of extra income to the pineapple farmers in the Philippines, and Piñatex® is
35 used to make high-quality shoes, jackets and bags. Carmen Hijosa, from Spain, developed the product because she became concerned about the use of chemicals in traditional leather production, which results in serious
40 environmental damage.

Recycling marine rubbish

Spanish fashion company EcoAlf specialises in upmarket clothing using a range of recycled materials. When company founder Javier
45 Goyeneche became aware of the quantities of **trash** brought to the surface during fishing in the Mediterranean, he set up a campaign called Upcycling the Oceans, hoping to make a difference. Through collaboration with the
50 local fishing industry, his company has been able to collect and recycle tonnes of marine debris, including plastic bottles and discarded nylon fishing nets. This debris would take 600 years to decompose, trapping and destroying
55 marine life in the meantime.

Upcycling

One person's trash is another person's treasure, according to Kriti Tula, founder of Delhi-based fashion brand Doodlage. For Tula,
60 fast fashion is a new concept in India and one that she hopes to reverse. She says she grew up in a no-waste culture: if something broke, it was repaired or reused in some other way. Doodlage purchases waste fabric from big
65 fashion manufacturers (mainly cutting-room scraps or unwanted surplus stock) and uses the creativity of its design team to turn these odd scraps into unique clothing items, which they sell online and through stores across India.

70 ## Growing your own clothes

Could we do away with raw materials and grow our own clothes in a lab? That's the idea behind BioCouture, a system being developed by American Suzanne Lee. She uses
75 microorganisms in a fermentation method that grows bacterial cellulose in large tubs, which spreads out to form sheets of thin leather-like material. The cellulose can grow around a mould, leading to the exciting possibility that
80 it could form itself into a shoe or body shape. What is more, since the material is completely non-toxic and organic, when you no longer need it, you can add it to your garden **compost** heap!

GLOSSARY

trash: rubbish (US term)

compost: decayed plant material used as medium for growing plants

7 Vocabulary practice

Match the words from the article with their definitions.

a   brainchild
b   substitute
c   byproduct
d   upmarket
e   debris
f   mould

1   high quality and expensive
2   container that makes its contents take a particular shape
3   scattered pieces of rubbish
4   replacement
5   original idea or invention
6   something that is produced as a result of another process

8 Post-reading discussion

Discuss in pairs:

- Do any of the alternatives to fast fashion mentioned in the magazine article appeal to you?

- Which (if any) are likely to be most successful at persuading us to give up our fast-fashion buying habits?

- 〉 Critical thinking What other possible ways can you think of to make the fashion industry more sustainable?

- Whose responsibility is it to solve the problem: ours, or the big fashion brands?

9 Language study: Using connectives to guide the reader

It is easier to find your way around an unfamiliar town if you use signposts to guide you from street to street. Similarly, in a text, a good writer leads you through their argument by showing you where they are going.

Expressing reasons and consequences

Look at these sentences. Do we know the connection between them?

His parents bought him some new running shoes. He went on a run every day.

1   Now try connecting the sentences into one sentence, first using *so* and then using *because*.

What is the difference in meaning between the two new sentences you have created?

A writer can express the **reason** for something:

*They cancelled the open-air concert **because** / **since** it was raining / **because of** / **due to** the rain.*

Or a writer can express the **consequence** of something:

*The weather has been dreadful this year, **so** they have cancelled many events.*

*The weather has been dreadful this year. **Therefore** / **That's why** they have cancelled . . .*

***As a result of** the dreadful weather, they have cancelled many events.*

2   With a partner, try connecting the following sentences in as many different ways as you can.

> *The recycling centre was successful.*
>
> *They opened a bigger one nearby.*

Adding extra information

A writer may also 'signpost' that they are about to add extra information:

*Her climate change talk was sold out so she's repeating it tomorrow. **In addition,** / **Furthermore,** / **What's more,** she's going to post the video on her website. / She's going to post the video on her website **as well.***

3   With a partner, think of possible extra information to add to the following sentence.

> *A reusable cup is really cheap to buy.*

4   Look back to the article 'Slowing down the fast fashion trend'. Find at least four examples of the writer expressing reason or consequence, or adding extra information.

10 Completing a text

Read this extract from a leaflet advertising a new beginners' sewing course. With a partner, try to fill the gaps with words expressing reason or consequence, or adding extra information.

Sewing for beginners

Many people don't repair slight damage to their clothes (like moth holes or lost buttons) ....(a) they lack basic sewing skills. ....(b), they throw away clothes that could last for years. .... (c), they feel bad about wasting a lovely garment that's now going to end up in landfill. If that sounds like you, why not enrol in our new beginners' sewing course? Places are limited, ... (d) be quick!

INTERNATIONAL OVERVIEW

The pie chart shows where most of the world's greenhouse gas emissions come from by sector. Study the chart and answer the questions below with a partner.

1   Which sector is responsible for the most greenhouse gases?

2   You buy a bar of chocolate. Name all the sectors in the pie chart that will have emitted greenhouse gases to give you that bar of chocolate.

3   You drive to a local restaurant and buy hot takeaway food, which you then eat at home while looking at your mobile. Again, which sectors in the pie chart were involved in making this possible?

4   Choose three of the sectors. Think of something that your country (or another country familiar to you) is doing to *reduce* their greenhouse gas emissions for that sector.

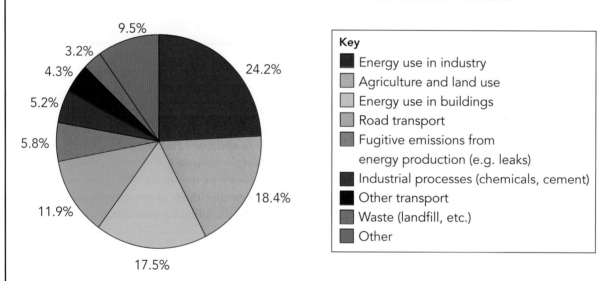

9.5%
3.2%
4.3%
5.2%
5.8%
11.9%
17.5%
24.2%
18.4%

Key
- ■ Energy use in industry
- ■ Agriculture and land use
- ■ Energy use in buildings
- ■ Road transport
- ■ Fugitive emissions from energy production (e.g. leaks)
- ■ Industrial processes (chemicals, cement)
- ■ Other transport
- ■ Waste (landfill, etc.)
- ■ Other

Global greenhouse gas emissions by sector, 2016 (data from Climate Watch, the World Resources Institute, 2020)

Notes

Total greenhouse gas emissions in 2016 were 49.4 billion tonnes.

Agriculture and land use includes livestock production, rice cultivation, deforestation, etc.

Energy use in buildings includes heating, lighting and appliances in both homes and commercial buildings.

In Waste, the greenhouse gas is mainly methane from decomposing organic material.

B Transport

1 Discussion

Discuss with a partner what form of transport, if any, you use to:

- get to school or college
- go shopping
- visit friends
- go to places of entertainment.

How satisfied do you feel with the forms of transport you use? Is there any form of transport you would prefer? Try to explain your views.

2 Pre-listening task

Before you listen, make sure you know the meaning of these words and expressions.

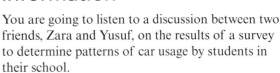

get a lift from someone

exhaust fumes

EVs

3 Listening to check information

You are going to listen to a discussion between two friends, Zara and Yusuf, on the results of a survey to determine patterns of car usage by students in their school.

1   Read the notes that Zara made while she was talking to Yusuf. Some of her notes are wrong. Listen to find the mistakes and correct them.

a   Average weekly number of car journeys: 11–20

b   9 percent make 50+ car journeys weekly.

c   80 students admitted using a car when it was not necessary.

d   14 percent walk to school regularly; 33 percent always come by car.

e   Reasons for not coming to school by public transport:
  - expensive
  - crowded.

f   Parents' opinions of roads for walking or cycling: too much pollution.

g   Two-thirds don't want to get a car as adults.

h   Additional comments: Would prefer to drive an EV.

4 Post-listening discussion

> Critical thinking How do the results of the survey compare with your personal usage of the car?

Read the following statements about car usage. For each statement, underline the words that best represent your view. Then compare your answers with a partner. Try to justify your answers if you and your partner disagree.

a Five years from now, there *will / may / probably will not* be more EVs (electric vehicles) than petrol cars in my country.

b EVs *will / might / will not* play an important part in slowing down global warming.

c A car share scheme *would / would not* solve the problem of too many cars on our roads.

d Improving public transport is *a waste of time / a great idea*. Most people *will never leave the comfort of their own private car / would gladly use public transport if it were efficient and comfortable / would willingly use public transport* to save the environment.

e By the time I'm middle-aged, *it's very likely / possible / unlikely* we will have driverless cars.

Discuss your answers with a partner.

5 Euphemisms

Yusuf says students are 'just too lazy to walk anywhere'. This is a very direct statement. If he was telling the school the results of the survey, he would probably avoid this remark because he could cause offence. He might prefer to use a euphemism (a polite way of expressing something rude or very strong) like 'students are reluctant to give up the comfort of a car ride'.

Practice

Match the common euphemisms in italics with their meanings.

a Her coat *had seen better days.*

b I need the *bathroom.*

c Discounts for *senior citizens.*

d She's *between jobs.*

e He's *careful with his money.*

f The house is *in need of some modernisation.*

g She's *being economical with the truth.*

h Our neighbour has *passed away.*

1 in a poor state and needs repairs

2 toilet

3 died

4 being dishonest, telling lies

5 old people

6 unemployed

7 mean, not generous

8 was shabby, perhaps had holes in it

6 Asking for a favour

Study this dialogue:

Joe: Dad, could you do me a favour? Would you mind giving me a lift to the sports hall? I've got a basketball game.

Dad: When do you want to go?

Joe: In about half an hour.

Dad: Oh, all right.

Joe: Thanks, Dad. Are you sure it's not too much trouble?

Dad: No, I need to go out anyway.

Joe: Well, thanks a lot. That's nice of you.

Asking for a favour

Could you do me a favour?

Can I ask you something?

Would you mind giving me a lift?

Could you please . . . ?

Checking

Are you sure it's not too much trouble?

Are you sure it's all right with you?

Are you sure it's not too inconvenient?

Are you certain it's not too much bother?

I hope it doesn't put you out.

Are you sure it's OK? I don't want to be a nuisance.

Expressing thanks

Thanks, that's nice of you.

Thanks a lot. That really helps me out.

Thanks very much. I really appreciate it.

Practice

Take turns asking for a favour in the following situations. Work in pairs.

- You need a lift to the cinema.

- You need to be picked up from a party.

- You need someone to take a parcel to the post office for you.

- You've filled in an online form (in English) and you need someone to check you've done it correctly.

- You need to borrow a tennis racket.

- You need someone to help you carry some heavy boxes to your bedroom / the car.

7 Spelling and pronunciation: The letter g

The letter *g* is a hard sound in words like *organic, grow* and *garment*. The phonetic symbol is /g/.

The letters *gu* in words like guilty and guest are also pronounced /g/. (In a few words, like *extinguish* and *language*, *gu* is pronounced /gw/.)

Notice how *g* is pronounced in *Egypt*, *gist* and *damage*. This is sometimes called 'soft g' and the phonetic symbol is /dʒ/. What other words do you know that have this sound?

Practice

1   Listen to the words on the audio recording. Mark them **G** for a hard **g**, pronounced /g/.

Mark them **g** for a soft **g**, pronounced /dʒ/.

a	budget	☐	g	oxygen	☐
b	rigorously	☐	h	apology	☐
c	challenge	☐	i	vegan	☐
d	vlogger	☐	j	registered	☐
e	shortage	☐	k	figure	☐
f	guarantee	☐	l	average	☐

2   The sounds /g/ and /dʒ/ are voiced sounds. If you place your fingers on the spot where your vocal cords are and say the sounds, you will feel your vocal cords vibrate. Practise saying the words in the list clearly to your partner. Do they think you are pronouncing the words correctly?

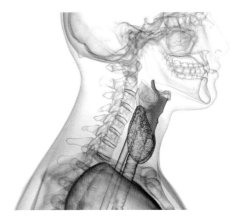

8 Spelling patterns

Did you notice how all the /dʒ/ sounds in the previous exercise were followed by the letters *e, i* or *y*? Look back at the word list and circle this spelling pattern for each soft-g word.

Note that there are some exceptions to this rule. Hard /g/ sounds are also sometimes followed by *e* or *i*, as in the words *get*, *tiger* and *girl*.

9 Vocabulary check

Choose a word from the list in Section B7 to match each of the following sentences:

a   She should offer one for breaking your vase.

b   We breathe in this gas.

c   Someone who doesn't eat any animal products.

d   A person who creates a video blog.

e   It's worthwhile but sometimes difficult too.

f   To promise that something will happen.

g   A limited amount of money available.

h   Another word for 'number'.

i   The aircraft should be checked in this way if a fault is suspected.

10 Odd word out

Circle the odd word out in each list below. Say why it is different.

a
hygienic	general	vegetable	agility
	surgeon	privilege	changeable
	regard	manager	encourage

b
grateful	vague	magazine	guard
Portuguese	pigeon	dialogue	angry
	catalogue	guidance	arrogant

11 Look, say, cover, write, check

1   Learn these commonly misspelt words using the 'look, say, cover, write, check' method (see Unit 1, Section B12 if you need a reminder).

changeable	luggage	rigorously
environment	vegetables	catalogue
Portuguese	guarantee	Egyptian
privilege	drought	guard

2   Ask a partner to test you when you are confident you have learnt them correctly.

3   Choose six of the words and put each one into a sentence to show its meaning.

C Looking for solutions

1 Pre-reading discussion

> **Critical thinking** Do you own a bicycle or an e-bike? How often do you cycle and where do you usually go to? If you do not own a bicycle, would you like one?

In pairs, work out the advantages and disadvantages of cycling as a form of transport. When you have finished, compare your ideas with those of other pairs and add any new points to your list.

Advantages
It doesn't pollute the environment.

Disadvantages
You get wet when it's raining.

2 Reading for gist

You are going to read an article about a Mexican woman who cycles in Mexico City.

Skim-read the article quickly to get a general idea of the content. Which summary below is the most appropriate?

A   Despite many continuing problems in the city, it's now possible to improve your mental health by going for a cycle ride.

B   Because people of all ages are using bicycles more, the city is safer and pollution levels have dropped.

C   Thanks to improved facilities in the city, people of all ages and experience levels can enjoy cycling there.

Meet the cyclist changing the streets of Mexico City into a bike lane for all

In Mexico City, young families, senior citizens and all genders are reclaiming their health, their streets and their transportation network by taking to the streets on bicycles.

1 When Gaby Hernández Castillo was told she'd have to wait three months for approval for a car loan, she grabbed her bicycle and hit the streets of Mexico City. By doing so, she cut her two-hour metro commute down by half. Gaby also came to realize how Mexico City offers thousands of miles of protected bike lanes, secure warehouses around the city for overnight bike storage, multiple bike-sharing platforms, dozens of group rides each week, and a strong network of cycling advocates. When the car dealership called a few months later to offer her the loan, she declined; by now, she had become a cycling enthusiast.

2 Gaby began her **advocacy** with Mujeres en Bici (Women on Bicycles), a women's bicycle advocacy organization that started the first free bike school in Mexico City. Here participants learn to ride a bike as well as strategies for riding safely in the street and how to make basic repairs. They set up shop on Reforma Avenue during the city's weekly **Ciclovía**, when the city shuts down major thoroughfares to cars for cyclist and pedestrian use only. The group now operates three other schools in different parts of the city, some locations offering daily classes and events.

3 Cycling is increasing in popularity for riders of all ages in Mexico City. Gaby says that many women in their sixties, who weren't allowed to ride bikes as children because 'that's not what girls did' at the time, are excited to learn to ride. These cycling seniors feel like rebels and get a sense of empowerment on two wheels. While some just ride in their **neighborhoods** and during the Sunday Ciclovía, others have become members of cycling organizations and are joining longer rides out of the city.

4 While much of the cycling infrastructure in Mexico City is geared towards locals, visitors can take advantage of the city's efforts and explore the metropolis from a saddle. Main streets with bike lanes such as Reforma, or car-free areas like Chapultapec Park, are the safest areas, especially for those without much experience. The Sunday Ciclovía is fun for riders of all skill levels and is the perfect place for tourists, who can ride on car-free streets that are normally packed with vehicles.

5 What's next for Mexico City's cycling advocates? According to Gaby, getting bureaucrats to require Mexican drivers to undergo competence and safety testing before receiving their license. 'There's so much more to be done,' she says, 'but we've made so much progress.'

GLOSSARY

advocacy: public support for a particular idea

Ciclovía: Spanish word for a route that is only for cyclists

neighborhood: US spelling of *neighbourhood*, the area where you live

3 Comprehension check

Answer the questions.

1 What made Gaby start cycling?

2 Which word in paragraph 1 tells us she used her bicycle to get to work?

3 What happened when the car dealership finally agreed to lend her money for a car?

4 How does Mujeres in Bici encourage women into cycling? Give two details.

5 According to the article, what are the benefits of cycling for older female cyclists?

6 In paragraph 4, what do you think is meant by the city's *efforts*?

7 For inexperienced cyclists, what is the advantage of cycling on a Sunday?

8 What would Gaby like the city authorities to do in order to make motorists drive more safely?

4 Vocabulary in context

Find words in each paragraph of the article that match the definitions given below.

			Word
1	a	People who support a particular action or belief	
	b	A business that buys and sells something	
	c	Said no to something	
2	d	Public road or street	
3	e	A person who doesn't obey rules or who fights against something	
4	f	The systems and services (e.g. roads/buildings) that make something possible	
	g	Intended for, aimed at	
	h	Large city	
5	i	People working in an office, especially in a government department	
	j	Skill	

5 Reordering an article

The following text, taken from an article on a school website, puts forward the pros and cons of cycling.

Try to reorder it so that it is in a logical sequence. The first and final sentences are provided. Finally, decide where the new paragraphs should start.

The pros and cons of cycling
Cycling is an enjoyable, efficient and liberating mode of transport which has many benefits.

a Cycling at night can be particularly dangerous, especially along dark country roads.

b In addition, owning a bike frees you from dependence on your parents to take you to places.

c However, some of these problems can be eliminated if you take sensible precautions, such as using lights at night and wearing reflector strips.

d Cycling can be dangerous on busy streets and you can be seriously hurt if you are knocked off your bike by a motorist.

e In the first place, cycling is cheap because second-hand bikes are not expensive.

f Attending a cycling training scheme also enables you to cycle more safely and may help you identify the less polluted routes.

g Although cycling has many advantages, there are some drawbacks too.

h Moreover, many roads are polluted by traffic fumes, which makes cycling unpleasant and unhealthy.

i You can also save money by carrying out simple repairs yourself.

j It also removes the frustrations of waiting around for a bus to turn up.

In conclusion, although there are some drawbacks, I feel that the personal enjoyment and freedom you get from cycling outweigh the disadvantages.

6 What makes a good argument?

1 When you have reordered the article correctly, read it through or write it out in full to get a feeling of how the text flows.

2 The rearranged text could be described as 'balanced'. Why, do you think?

3 The last paragraph shows the writer's point of view. Is this a good way of concluding an argument? Why / Why not?

4 A convincing article should help the reader understand the issues. Do you think the article 'The pros and cons of cycling' achieves this? Try to explain how you feel to your group.

7 Presenting contrasting ideas in the same paragraph

'The pros and cons of cycling' devotes separate paragraphs to the advantages and disadvantages of cycling. It then sums up at the end. An alternative to this approach is to consider contrasting ideas in the same paragraph.

The following extract comes from an article about whether cycle helmets should be made compulsory.

1 Circle the word that contrasts one idea with its opposite.

I recognise that a feeling of freedom is part of the pleasure of cycling. Nevertheless, in my opinion, it is essential that cyclists are made aware of the dangers of not wearing a helmet.

2 Now rewrite the extract using a different linking word or phrase. Choose from: *although, however, but, yet, in spite of, despite*. Make changes to the extract if you think it is necessary.

8 Presenting more contrasting ideas

Study the incomplete sentences below. Notice the use of a contrast word in each one. Then try to complete each sentence in an appropriate way.

a Car accidents continue to increase *despite . . .*

b Electric vehicles are still more expensive than petrol cars. *Nevertheless, . . .*

c A new airport is planned for our area *in spite of . . .*

d I have always been a keen supporter of the private car. *However, . . .*

e It seems unfair to stop cars going into the town centre, *yet . . .*

f A good train service would help to reduce our carbon footprint. *On the other hand, . . .*

g I would always travel by sea rather than by air even *though . . .*

9 Language study: Further connectives

In this unit, we have looked at ways of making your argument easier to follow using suitable connectives to express reason, consequence, contrast or to add extra examples. Look at the following connectives, which are used for three purposes: to list points in order, to sum up the main points of an argument, or to add emphasis (to show that something is particularly important). With a partner, write the words under the correct heading.

> Secondly   Above all   Lastly   To sum up
>
> Next   Undoubtedly   Firstly
>
> Taking everything into account   Finally
>
> There is no doubt that   In particular
>
> In conclusion

Listing points	Summing up	Adding emphasis

10 Group brainstorm

> **Critical thinking** Brainstorming is a group activity to help you come up with ideas on a topic. It's important because you can't write a convincing argument unless you have strong ideas to work with.

In your group, discuss this scenario:

Imagine that the local council is considering creating a new car park near a shopping centre for the convenience of shoppers. It would involve cutting down City View Wood, a small public woodland area. Brainstorm points for and against the idea.

Should City View Wood be cut down to provide a car park for shoppers?

11 Text completion

A local student, Roland Chang, heard about the proposal to cut down the wood. He felt very strongly about it so he wrote to his local newspaper. Study his email carefully with a partner. Then try to complete each gap with appropriate linking words from the choices given.

a   However / On the other hand / Although / Because

b   In addition / In the first place / Nevertheless / But

c   to sum up / also / in my view / nevertheless

d   On the other hand / At the beginning / Furthermore / Finally

e   secondly / not at all / because / such as

f   for example / yet / thirdly / so

g   In addition / Therefore / Consequently / However

h   also / but / thirdly / last but not least

i   In the end / In my opinion / On the contrary / For instance

j   For example / After all / In fact / On the other hand

Dear Editor,

I was disappointed when I heard of the proposals to cut down City View Wood to make a car park for shoppers.

(**a**) _____ I agree that the town is short of car parks, this solution would be insensitive and wrong. (**b**) _____, the wood is an area of natural beauty. There are many ancient trees of an unusual kind. I often go there for a picnic or just to relax at weekends. The wood is (**c**) _____ a vital habitat for birds, animals and insects. If the trees were cut down, many species would be lost.

(**d**) _____, the wood is right in the centre of a heavily polluted part of town. The trees help to make the air cleaner (**e**) _____ they trap dust, smoke and fume particles in their branches and leaves. The council says it is worried about global warming, (**f**) _____ trees help reduce the build-up of gases that contribute to global warming because they feed on carbon dioxide emissions. (**g**) _____, that area (**h**) _____ suffers from high noise levels from passing lorries and the railway line. The trees help reduce the noise levels and have a beneficial effect on the whole environment. (**i**) _____, cutting down the wood would be stupid, greedy and pointless. A car park may well attract shoppers to the town and increase the shopkeepers' trade. (**j**) _____, a unique and beautiful place would be destroyed. I would be very interested in hearing what your other readers think.

Yours faithfully,

Roland Chang

12 Discussion

Discuss the following questions with a partner, then as a class.

- Do you think the email is too formal, too informal or about right? Try to explain why.

- How does Roland show an awareness of his audience in the letter?

- Obviously, Roland is opposed to the council's plans. How convincing do you think his argument is? Try to mention particular examples to justify your opinion.

13 Words often confused

The pairs of words below, some of which are taken from Roland's letter, are often confused. Complete each sentence with the correct alternative.

1 council/counsel

   a   The _____ meets once a month.

   b   The doctor may also _____ you about your personal problems.

2 affect/effect

   a   The medicine didn't have any _____ on my cold.

   b   The new rules _____ all aircraft over 30 years old.

3 there/they're/their

   a   _____ are plenty of pegs for the children's coats and lockers for _____ shoes.

   b   They said if _____ going to be late, they will let us know.

4 loose/lose

   a   You must be careful not to _____ your passport.

   b   Since I lost weight, my trousers have been too _____.

5 alternate/alternative

   a   I have to work on _____ weekends.

   b   The last bus had gone so walking home was the only _____.

6 lightning/lightening

   a   The house was struck by _____.

   b   The sun came up, gradually _____ the sky.

7 practice/practise

   a   He tries to _____ the guitar once a day.

   b   We have music _____ on Tuesdays.

8   passed/past

    a   Have you seen Henry in the _____ few days? Yes, I _____ him in the street on Saturday.

    b   Luckily, we all _____ our maths test.

D The community's views

1 Pre-reading discussion

> **Critical thinking** Study the photograph and try to describe it. How do you think the people in the cars are feeling? Motorways (sometimes called highways) are the main roads that link towns or cities. What causes traffic jams to build up on motorways? Is there any way of preventing them?

Brainstorming

Divide into two groups. Group A should try to list all the advantages of motorways. Group B should aim to list all the disadvantages.

When you have finished, compare your ideas. Can you add any new ideas between you?

2 Reading an email expressing a point of view

> **Critical thinking** Rosville's council is supporting government plans to build a new motorway. This will link Rosville to the capital city and some other large cities.

1   Do you think this will be a good development for Rosville? Who is likely to benefit? Who might be against the idea? Try to think of reasons for your opinions.

2   The email below was sent to the Editor of Rosville's online newspaper. Scan the email quickly to see whether it includes the points you thought of in your discussion in the previous exercise.

Dear Editor,

We are delighted that a new motorway is being planned for Rosville because it will bring so many benefits to the town.

In the first place, Rosville has suffered from the recession – many young people are unemployed after leaving school. The motorway will bring a much-needed boost to business, as travel and transport will be faster, cheaper and more efficient. Consequently, businesses will find life easier, new companies will be attracted to Rosville, and there will be more jobs for everyone.

Furthermore, the new motorway will not only reduce commuting time for the large number of people who travel to the city daily but it will also provide them with a safer and more relaxing journey to work.

Many readers might be worried about pollution from increased traffic. On the contrary, pollution is likely to decrease as so many new trees, especially chosen for their ability to absorb car fumes, will be planted.

Finally, the new motorway will also serve as a bypass for the large lorries that now go through Rosville town centre.

There is no doubt that the motorway will really put Rosville on the map. If we want a bright future for ourselves and our children, we should all support it.

Yours faithfully,

The Rosville Business Group

3 Comprehension check

Re-read the email more carefully.

1   Where will the email in in Section D2 appear?

2   What are the writer's main points in favour of a new motorway?

3   How does the writer make their argument convincing?

4   Here are some definitions of words in the email. Try to find the words and underline them.

   a   a bad period in the country's economy

   b   something that helps and encourages

   c   routes linking one place to another

   d   to travel between home and work every day

   e   a main road built to avoid a town

4 Analysing the email

Work in pairs to answer the following questions on the email in Section D2. They will help you to analyse the way the model argument is structured.

1   Underline the word in the opening paragraph that expresses emotion. Which word introduces a reason for the feeling? Underline it. An opening paragraph should grab the reader's attention. Does this paragraph do that?

2   Which words are used in paragraph 3 for emphasis?

3   Paragraph 4 considers an opposing point of view. What is it? Which phrase is used to introduce a contrasting opinion?

4   *Finally* is used at the start of paragraph 5. Why?

5   The last paragraph of an email of this type should not leave the reader in any doubt as to what the writer thinks. It should have a confident tone. What do you think of the final paragraph of this email?

5 Putting forward an opposing viewpoint

The Rosville Nature Society held a meeting to discuss the email from the Rosville Business Group that appeared in the local newspaper. They decided to write an email in reply. Read the notes they made about points they wanted to include, then think of one more point of your own. (Think back to the advantages/disadvantages of motorways that you listed earlier.)

- Building motorway would destroy the environment
- It is not true that it would reduce commuters' travel time
- The idea that pollution would decrease is absurd!
- The motorway would split Rosville in two
- _____

6 Writing an email expressing your views

Below is an outline for the email that the Rosville Nature Society want to write. They want to make five points. With a partner, decide how to complete each space in the email and note down your ideas. Try to add structure to your argument by using linking words.

Dear Editor,

We were _____ to hear _____

_____ .

[1] we believe _____

_____

[2] _____

_____

[3] _____

_____

[4] _____

_____

[5] _____

_____

Please, people of Rosville, [*say what you want them to

do*] _____

Yours faithfully,

The Rosville Nature Society

7 Relating to your target audience

Your email or article should reflect the interest of those who are going to read it. These people are called your 'target audience'.

Study the extracts A–E below. Decide with a partner whether each extract comes from:

- a school magazine
- a letter to a local newspaper
- an e-newsletter for elderly people
- a music- and video-sharing website
- a formal report.

Decide whether the target audience in each case is:

- school pupils
- elderly people
- the general public
- the headteacher
- internet users.

A   I don't agree with the last post. I absolutely love the words to this song. It really captures the idea of fighting to save a troubled world. The images that go with the music really work for me as well.

B   Most of us already have problems getting to school on time. The proposed cuts to the bus service will make things even worse. I suggest we have an urgent meeting to discuss a plan of action in the Common Room next Wednesday lunchtime.

C   I am writing to express my concern about your suggestion printed in yesterday's *Evening News* that the greenhouse effect has no scientific basis. Like many of the readers of this newspaper, I have no doubt that the greenhouse effect is a reality that is becoming steadily worse.

D   Like most people of my age, I welcome the news that Redline buses are offering senior citizens free bus passes at weekends. Go to www. redlineseniorpass.com for further information.

E   To sum up, our visit to the environmental centre to see bicycles being made from recycled metal and rubber was so worthwhile. If we could have permission for another visit later this term, our class would love to go again.

8 Understanding a balanced report task

Look back briefly at the three emails sent to a newspaper (Sections C11, D2 and D5). In all three of them, the writer expresses a strong point of view and wants to persuade their readers to agree with it.

A report, on the other hand, presents facts in a clear, formal and objective way. It may offer conclusions and recommendations, but avoiding emotional or personal language.

Look at the following example of a report-writing task:

> Students at your school have recently been given an outdoor, covered seating area where they can sit at breaktimes. The covered area is at the far side of the school grounds, away from the main school buildings. Your headteacher wants to find out what students think of their new facility and whether it would be a good idea to construct a similar covered area for the younger students (8–12 years). Write a report for the headteacher giving your views.

Your report should start with an introduction. Which of the following introductions do you think would be more appropriate, and why?

A The new seating area is absolutely amazing, and we would like to thank Mr Matuga, our headteacher, for arranging it. I spend all my breaktimes there with my mates!

B This is a report for our headteacher Mr Matuga about the senior school seating area, which we have been using for two months now. We have interviewed all the students to find out what they think of this new facility.

9 Writing a balanced report using a framework

Now write your report, using the following framework as a guide. In the final paragraph, you can say clearly whether you think the new facility is a success. You should also say whether a similar facility would be good for the younger children.

Introduction

(See example in Section D8 – or write your own.)

Main paragraphs

Positive points about the facility:
- protection from hot sun / some students concerned about sun damage
- very useful in recent stormy weather / heavy rain / thankful we can go under cover
- small tables are useful for packed lunches / writing
- new friendships made as students from wider range of classes and different ages mix
- peaceful in this part of the school grounds / can hear the birdsong / enjoy nature / relax properly
- return to school refreshed / right mood to study.

Negative points about the facility:
- some distance from main buildings / quite a long walk (but students now getting more used to it)
- fixed seats – inconvenient for friendship groups / chatting
- not enough recycling bins – litter / insects / smells.

Conclusion
- Successful facility. Popularity gradually increasing. Consider adding seats not fixed to ground.
- Should younger children have similar facility – yes! Possibly situate it near the water fountain / they get thirsty running around.

10 Preparing points for your own report

> **Critical thinking** Study the following writing task, based on a stimulus in the form of comments.

The comments from local people are ideas to help you write your report. However, your report will be better if you:

- add your own ideas

- use your own words – try not to copy word for word from the comments.

Do the following exercise in pairs.

1 Decide whether each comment is *for* or *against* the proposal.

2 Choose one comment *for* and one *against*. Try to express the idea using different words and new ideas. For example:

The new marina would allow people from the city to get to know our region, and they would also spend money in our local shops and restaurants.

There are proposals to develop a river near your home. A marina would be built, and tourists would be encouraged to come and use the river for boating and fishing. The council has asked you to write a report saying *what you think of this idea.*

Here are some comments from local people. You can use these for ideas, or use ideas of your own.

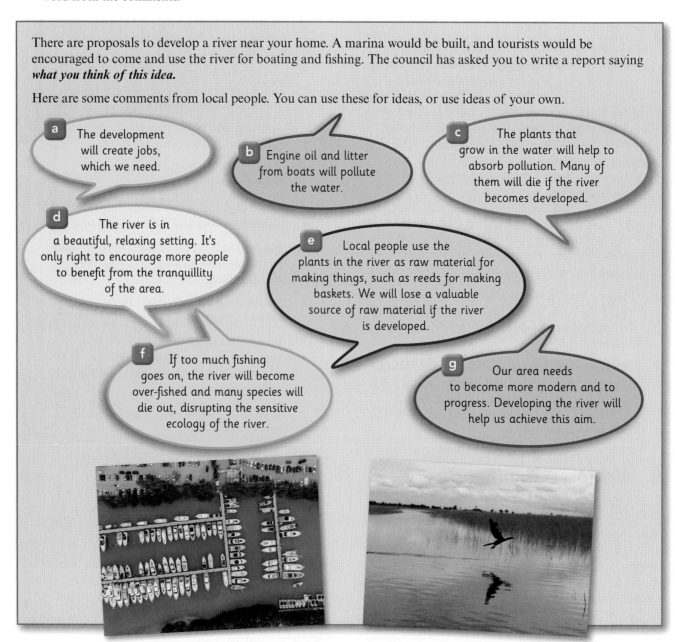

a The development will create jobs, which we need.

b Engine oil and litter from boats will pollute the water.

c The plants that grow in the water will help to absorb pollution. Many of them will die if the river becomes developed.

d The river is in a beautiful, relaxing setting. It's only right to encourage more people to benefit from the tranquillity of the area.

e Local people use the plants in the river as raw material for making things, such as reeds for making baskets. We will lose a valuable source of raw material if the river is developed.

f If too much fishing goes on, the river will become over-fished and many species will die out, disrupting the sensitive ecology of the river.

g Our area needs to become more modern and to progress. Developing the river will help us achieve this aim.

11 Writing your own report

Now write your report. Give it a suitable title.

Remember:

- Your report is for the council. Use appropriately formal language.

- Use paragraphing and logical connectors.

- Consider both the advantages and the disadvantages, but in the final paragraph make it clear what you think is the right thing to do.

GRAMMAR SPOTLIGHT

The future: making predictions

When we make predictions about the future, we use different words to express how certain we are.

Practice

1 Look at the examples below, taken from this unit, and put them in order according to how sure the writer is about their prediction. (Two of them are similar.)

   a Pollution *is likely* to decrease as so many new trees will be planted.

   b Attending a cycling training scheme *may* help you identify the less polluted routes.

   c There is no doubt that the motorway *will* really put Rosville on the map.

   d Many readers *might* be worried about pollution from increased traffic.

2 In the email in Section D2, the writer mainly uses *will*. What effect does this have?

3 Write three predictions using *be expected to*, *be (almost) certain to* and *be bound to*. Here are some examples to help you:

   *Flooding **is expected to** get worse as a result of global warming.*

   *Car use **is almost certain** to increase over the next few years.*

   *Climate change **is bound to** affect the way we live our lives.*

Complete the practice activities in your Workbook.

EXAM-STYLE QUESTIONS

READING AND WRITING

Reading and writing: multiple matching

Read the article in which four young people (**A–D**) share their thoughts on caring for the environment. Then answer questions (a)–(i).

Our environment and us

A Elizabeth

I used to take the wonderful planet we live on for granted but I don't now. I recently read a powerful novel called *Oxygen*, about life in the future where the air is so contaminated with carbon dioxide and other greenhouse gases you can't go outside. When I finished this disturbing book, I stepped out onto my balcony with my mind full of horrible images and a feeling that a natural catastrophe could occur any second. Then I felt the air on my skin and it was as if I had never felt air before. I could not stop breathing in the oxygen in our air and feeling that we should be thankful. We can't see the air we breathe, yet we can't survive without it. In a million, billion invisible ways, nature is looking after each one of us. When I went back inside, I felt calmer. If you think your carbon footprint does not matter, you should read *Oxygen*. It will change your life, like it did mine. I never drop litter now, always recycle all my family's rubbish, cycle rather than go by car and keep the air-conditioning to a minimum.

CONTINUED

B Antoine

If I see litter anywhere, I have to pick it up and dispose of it in an environmentally friendly way. Metal cans, bottles, cartons and plastic bags sometimes get washed up on the banks of our local river. These cause environmental damage to the plants growing in the water and are dangerous to the birds, animals and fish. When I walk past the river on my way to school, I feel a powerful wish to get rid of any horrible rubbish. I just can't stand by and see our beautiful environment being destroyed. Once, I took off my shoes and socks and walked into the middle of the river to pull out a supermarket trolley. I wheeled it all the way back to the shop. Even though I could feel the customers looking and secretly laughing at me in my wet and muddy school uniform as I walked in, I knew it was the right thing to do. While I am here on this Earth, together with the birds and the trees, the sun and sky, I feel part of it and want to love and cherish it.

C Mia

On our last school trip, we stayed on a remote island where we could study wildlife and nature. I fell in love with the wild, unspoilt landscape, which is an amazing habitat for plants and animals. All you could hear was birdsong and the wind rustling through the trees. I was heartbroken when we had to return home. I could not bear to think of going back to the reality of waking up and looking out on streets full of traffic, or breathing in carbon emissions from polluting factories on my way to college. The strange thing is, though, since having that magical experience on the island, I can now see the wonders of nature surrounding me in the city: there is life, colour and greenery everywhere – wild flowers bloom in little bits of soil and the trees are full of nesting birds. Whatever we do to harm nature, I sense it will still be with us, renewing and regenerating the world.

D Mohamed

Some people say it is down to the government to stop global environmental catastrophes, such as flooding, desertification and drought. Undoubtedly, international governments should meet to stop climate change, but why wait for them? Carbon emissions from human activities have already done a huge amount of damage to animals and humans, and, if the predictions about global warming come true and we destroy the planet, none of us will have anywhere else we can go. Each of us should help save the planet by recycling rubbish and using less water. These actions could have enormous benefits. We must choose renewable sources of energy, too, like wave and wind power. I persuaded my family to put in solar panels so we can use energy from the sun for our showers. Will you do the same? It is great for the planet, and mum and dad could not help smiling when they got the electricity bill.

For each statement, write the correct letter A, B, C or D on the line.

Which person gives the following information?

a	The positive view that nature can be harmed but never destroyed	____	[1]
b	A warning that, if people destroy the planet, we will have nowhere else to live	____	[1]
c	An account of doing something that others found weird	____	[1]
d	A request to readers to carry out a specific action in their family home	____	[1]
e	A description of how something the writer read influenced their family home	____	[1]

CONTINUED

f The belief that humans are capable of benefitting from the environment as well as damaging it _____ [1]

g A description of seeing a familiar place differently after visiting another place _____ [1]

h The idea that we should take care of nature because nature takes care of us _____ [1]

i The feeling that the writer has a deep sense of belonging in the natural world _____ [1]

[Total: 9]

Reading and writing: multiple choice

Read the blog written by someone who is concerned about global warming, and then answer the questions.

Saving the planet

By FutureHope

Back in March, you may have chosen to spend 60 minutes without electric light, perhaps dining sustainably by candlelight, in the name of Earth Hour. Earth Hour, just in case anyone is unfamiliar with it, was started in Sydney, Australia, in 2007 by the Worldwide Fund for Nature. It has grown to become a global environmental movement involving millions of people from across the world, switching off their lights annually on the same date in late March. You will have seen powerful images of iconic buildings, such as Beijing's Olympic Bird's Nest, the Colosseum in Rome and Dubai's Burj Khalifa, plunging from light into darkness. Its purpose is to inspire us to save the world's precious resources and address the climate crisis. But does it work?

Despite its popularity, Earth Hour is not without its critics. Some worry that offering such an easy 'solution' to our climate problems lets people off the responsibility of taking more meaningful action. An alternative concern is that we may come away from Earth Hour with the message that, in order to slow down climate change, we have to return to the 'darkness' of medieval times, turning our backs on the technology that has improved our lives in so many ways. People are hardly going to welcome changes that they see as so deeply threatening to their way of life, some would claim. The most common complaint, however, is that the energy saving from a single hour without electric lighting is tiny in the overall picture, and lots of us switching back on simultaneously afterwards could even increase emissions at power stations. But while these facts are hard to deny, it's a point of view that shows a misunderstanding of the primary aim of the event: to raise awareness and stimulate conversation across news and social media.

The key to tackling global warming is, surely, to get us to stand together, so that our individual actions combine into something much more powerful and impossible to ignore. If you are feeling helpless in the face of environmental destruction, then seeing millions of people taking part with you in an event such as Earth Hour may provide exactly the motivation you need to turn your anxiety into something more positive. Flipping the light switch may be a symbolic gesture (and a photo opportunity for the world's press), but it's also one that is gradually forcing changes in public policy.

Sending the right message is what counts, then. There has been some interesting research into what makes the link, for the average individual, between hearing about the climate crisis and doing something about it. It seems that we adapt our behaviour more readily if 'people like us' are doing the same; hotels report greater success getting guests to reuse their towels if they display a sign saying that three-quarters of other guests have done so, rather than one stating that reusing towels is good for the environment. Humans are also more influenced by personal advantages and opportunities than by threats, it appears. In a survey of residents of the Danish city of Copenhagen who had swapped their cars for bicycles to travel to work, saving time and money were revealed as more popular reasons than cutting car emissions; this was the case even amongst those who claimed to be 'very worried' about global warming. In general, encouragement has proved to be far more effective than 'eco-shaming' (criticising people's poor environmental choices). Thus, we should celebrate what we and others can do to help, rather than regret our failure to be perfect.

CONTINUED

1   How many of the people reading the blog know what Earth Hour is, according to the writer?

   A   Some of them   ☐

   B   Most of them   ☐

   C   All of them   ☐   [1]

2   Some people criticise Earth Hour because it makes people think:

   A   they are being asked to live without technology.   ☐

   B   technology is responsible for climate change.   ☐

   C   global warming is not real.   ☐   [1]

3   According to the writer, claims that Earth Hour doesn't save energy:

   A   are true but not important.   ☐

   B   have not been proved.   ☐

   C   are probably untrue.   ☐   [1]

4   The blog writer seems to be:

   A   neither in favour of Earth Hour nor against it.   ☐

   B   mainly against Earth Hour.   ☐

   C   mainly in favour of Earth Hour.   ☐   [1]

5   The evidence from hotels tells us that:

   A   most hotel guests care about protecting the environment.   ☐

   B   very few people reuse their towels.   ☐

   C   people tend to copy other people's behaviour.   ☐   [1]

6   Which of the following is *not* the writer's view in this blog post?

   A   It's OK to help save the environment for selfish reasons.   ☐

   B   We are doing far too little to tackle global warming.   ☐

   C   Lots of small actions can make a big difference.   ☐   [1]

[Total: 6]

Reading and writing: informal

You have recently decided to make a change to your lifestyle to help the environment.

Write an email to tell a friend about your decision.

In your email, you should:

- explain what change you are going to make
- say why you think it is important
- say how the change will affect your daily life.

Write about 120 to 160 words.   [15]

[Total: 15]

CONTINUED

Reading and writing: formal

You and your friends have been discussing whether people should buy fewer clothes. You want to write an article for your local newspaper to make more people aware of the environmental issues.

In your article, explain what the problem is <u>and</u> suggest what people could do to improve the situation.

Here are some comments from your friends:

> The clothing industry is terrible for the environment.

> People throw away lots of clothes they haven't used much.

> We should think before we buy.

> Second-hand clothes are great.

Now write an article for the newspaper.

The comments above may give you some ideas, and you should also use some ideas of your own.

Write about 120 to 160 words. [15]

[Total: 15]

LISTENING

Listening: sentence completion

You will hear a conservation volunteer called Chiara Moretti giving a talk about a process called rewilding.

For each question, choose the correct answer, **A**, **B** or **C**, and put a tick (✓) in the appropriate box.

You will hear the talk twice.

Now look at questions 1–8.

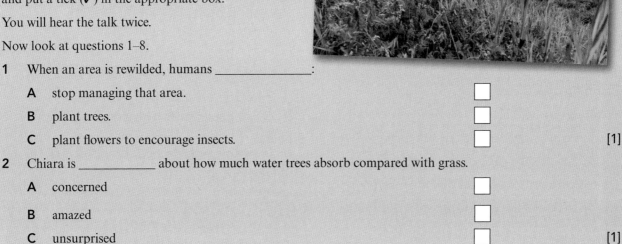

1   When an area is rewilded, humans _____:

   A   stop managing that area.   ☐

   B   plant trees.   ☐

   C   plant flowers to encourage insects.   ☐   [1]

2   Chiara is _____ about how much water trees absorb compared with grass.

   A   concerned   ☐

   B   amazed   ☐

   C   unsurprised   ☐   [1]

CONTINUED

3 Chiara says that birds and mice benefited in Yellowstone Park because _____:

   A new species of plants suited them better. ☐

   B elks were scared away from certain areas. ☐

   C wolves ate most of the elks. ☐ [1]

4 When bears were first brought to Abruzzo in Italy _____:

   A conservation workers were killed. ☐

   B farm animals were injured. ☐

   C farm workers tried to defend their animals. ☐ [1]

5 In Chiara's view, _____ is the most important way to protect Abruzzo's bears.

   A having the help and encouragement of local people ☐

   B keeping them away from road vehicles ☐

   C keeping hunters away ☐ [1]

6 For Chiara, the biggest benefit of rewilding by the sides of city roads is _____:

   A it improves the lives of car drivers. ☐

   B it encourages a population of living creatures. ☐

   C it saves public money. ☐ [1]

7 During 2020, there was a _____ percent increase in the size of Barcelona's butterfly population.

   A 74 ☐

   B 71 ☐

   C 28 ☐ [1]

8 Chiara says people who live in Barcelona want their council to _____:

   A tidy up their neighbourhood. ☐

   B expand the city. ☐

   C make the city more wildlife-friendly. ☐ [1]

[Total: 8]

SPEAKING

Warm-up questions

Warm-up questions help you feel more relaxed before you move on to answering assessed questions.

Take turns asking and answering the questions. Speak for 1–2 minutes.

- Tell me about a game or sport you like.

- Where do you usually do your homework?

- What do you like doing when you are with your friends?

CONTINUED

Interview

Read the questions. In pairs, decide who will play the interviewer and who will play the student. Then role-play the interview. Speak for about 2–3 minutes. Change roles and role-play the interview again.

Journeys

- What is the longest journey you have ever been on?
- If you could choose any vehicle, which would you most like to travel in?
- What do you like doing while you are on a journey?

Short talk

Read the options and compare them. You have one minute to prepare your talk. Now give a short talk to your partner. Speak for about 2 minutes. Change roles and listen to your partner's talk.

Forms of transport

Your local town wants to reduce the number of cars in town in order to cut pollution and reduce traffic jams. There are two suggestions for doing this:

- offering free bicycles to everybody
- cutting the cost of public transport by 50 percent.

Compare the two options and say which one you prefer, and why.

Discussion

Read the discussion questions. In pairs, decide who will play the interviewer and who will play the student. Then role-play the discussion. Speak for about 3 minutes. Change roles and role-play the interview again.

- Is it a good idea to ban cars from city centres?
- Some people have started to work or study from home more using modern technology. What is good or bad about this?
- Should we all give up air travel to protect the environment?
- Should we encourage people to spend their holidays in their own country rather than travel abroad?

SELF-ASSESSMENT CHECKLIST

Reflect on what you have learnt in this unit. For each area listed, decide whether you feel confident or need more practice. If you feel you need more practice, you will find some ideas to help you in Advice for Success. Come back to your self-assessment scores later in your course and see if your confidence has improved.

I can ...	Need more practice	Fairly confident
discuss issues related to our environment, using appropriate vocabulary		
scan for information in a magazine article		
understand detailed information in a formal talk		
use appropriate linking words to present my point of view		
write a report giving both sides of an argument		

ADVICE FOR SUCCESS

This section is to help you help yourself. Choose the suggestions you like and adapt them if you want to. Make notes about what you do and how it helped you.

Extending your skills

1   It is much easier to write an essay about a 'real world' topic like the environment if you have plenty of ideas about the topic. You can improve your understanding of controversial subjects, and your topic vocabulary, by listening to or watching current affairs programmes in English.

2   Offer to research a mini topic for your class and present your findings to everyone. Topics connected to the environment would be particularly relevant for this unit; for example, you could research the carbon footprint of different foods that we eat.

3   Learn how ideas are linked and expanded by reading opinion-based articles online or in magazines; for example, you could look for articles suggesting how we could solve the problems of traffic and pollution in our cities in the future.

Showcasing your skills

4   Take an active part in class discussions and school debates (in all subjects) to practise thinking logically and giving your opinions orally.

5   Have patience with your writing skills and practise them. Show your written work to someone you trust and listen to their comments.

6   When you are answering a writing question with a stimulus (as in Sections D10 and D11), don't just copy out the words you are given. Give reasons of your own to support your views.

7   Link your ideas with appropriate linking words.

8   Try to show some audience awareness when you write: read the instruction carefully so you know who will be reading it as well as the purpose for your piece of writing .

> Unit 5
Entertainment

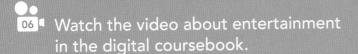 Watch the video about entertainment
in the digital coursebook.

BEFORE YOU START

Look at the photo on this page.

a   What kind of thing might these people be watching, and how can you tell?

b   Why might there be empty seats?

c   Do you think all forms of public entertainment are declining in popularity?

d   What could the venues do to encourage more people to attend?

A Cinema and other forms of entertainment

1 Introduction and discussion

1   How do you feel about each of these kinds of entertainment? The phrases in the box might be useful.

- Watching films or TV
- Playing computer games
- Going to the theatre to see a play
- Listening to the radio
- Listening to music by yourself
- Going to concerts
- Listening to buskers (street performers)

> It depends.
>
> I absolutely love . . . but I'm not really into . . .
>
> . . . when I'm in the mood
>
> I've never . . . (but I'd quite like to)
>
> (. . . ing) doesn't interest me at all
>
> I/We sometimes have it on in the background

2   If you watch films, how and where do you do it? Which method do you use most often? The phrases in the box might be useful.

- On television
- Using a streaming service
- By downloading them
- By renting DVDs
- At the cinema
- In an open-air cinema (e.g. a drive-in cinema)

> I/We tend to . . .   Once or twice
>
> Occasionally   Never

2 Film vocabulary

Complete the film review by filling the spaces with words or phrases from the box of *Mission in Space*.

> box office   scene   performance   cast
>
> plot   genre   played by   characters   film
>
> hero/heroine   directed by   Oscar   role

Mission in Space

Mission in Space won a film award, but Selina Summers didn't win a(n) **(a)** _____ for Best Actress despite her superb **(b)** _____ as Helena Page, the brave and intriguing **(c)** _____ who undertakes her first mission on board the space ship *Mission*.

The **(d)** _____ begins slowly, with Helena (grieving for the loss of her husband in a car crash) expressing her need to prove to herself that life still has a meaning and purpose. Her partner in outer space is Hudson Carr, **(e)** _____ Jasper Hunt, who is entirely convincing in

the **(f)** _____ of the experienced older astronaut. Things become more tense when Hudson has a heart attack, and Helena is left to cope entirely alone in a dark and mysterious universe. The final **(g)** _____, however, leaves no one doubting Helena's courage or will to live. The other members of the **(h)** _____ include Carlos Martinez as the voice of Mission Control, and Farley Harrison as the voice of the captain of *Mission*. They are both perfect as the calm but rather cold **(i)** _____, typical of space missions. The film is **(j)** _____ Hugo Bandera, who may be remembered for other **(k)** _____ hits such as North Star. The **(l)** _____ is a welcome addition to the growing science fiction fantasy **(m)** _____.

3 Film questionnaire

What we look for when we watch a film is very personal. To help you understand more about your preferences and attitudes to films, answer the questions.

What I want from a film

1 How do you choose a film to watch?

- [ ] Recommendation from friends.
- [ ] By reading film reviews.
- [ ] By watching the trailer.
- [ ] By seeing which actors are in it.

2 The following comments are often made about what makes a good film. How far do you agree with them? Mark each comment like this:

I agree strongly ✓ ✓   I agree to some extent ✓
I don't agree ✗

- [ ] There needs to be a lot of suspense.
- [ ] Fast-moving action is essential.
- [ ] The plot should contain surprising twists.
- [ ] The cast should include some famous actors.
- [ ] It should have been made recently.
- [ ] It should contain many emotional scenes.
- [ ] It should make a serious point.
- [ ] It should make you laugh.
- [ ] The special effects should be outstanding.

3 Besides the comments you have ticked above, what else makes a good film, in your view?

4 Select the statements you agree with:

- [ ] There is too much violence in films today.
- [ ] I prefer films that seem realistic and true to life rather than science fiction or horror movies.
- [ ] My favourite films are based on true stories.
- [ ] Seeing the film after you've read the book is usually disappointing.
- [ ] I'm sick of hearing about films in which evil people commit terrible crimes.

4 Asking for information

When you've finished the questions, swap answers with a partner. Read your partner's answers and pick out a few responses that interest you. Ask for more information in a friendly way, to show you're genuinely interested.

Examples:

- *May I ask* why you think fast-moving action is essential?
- *Would you mind telling me about a* film that has made you laugh?
- *What I'd like to know is why* you don't like films about evil people.
- *Could you explain in more detail why you think* films should contain emotional scenes?

Here are some more useful phrases for following up your partner's answers:

- *Something else I'd like to know is . . .*
- *Can you give me an example?*
- *What exactly do you mean by . . . ?*
- *Sorry, I don't quite understand why . . .*

5 Following a model discussion about films

🎧 5.1

You are going to hear a model conversation in which two students, Marta and Navid, tell their teacher about two films they have enjoyed. You will notice that the teacher asks for information and follows up the students' answers.

Which of these aspects of the films were mentioned by Marta and Navid?

- [ ] Characters
- [ ] Genre
- [ ] Hero
- [ ] Message of the film
- [ ] Plot
- [ ] Reasons for recommending
- [ ] Setting
- [ ] Music
- [ ] Special effects
- [ ] Suspense

6 Comprehension and overview

1 Read the following statements. Which statement does *not* reflect Navid's view of *The Way to the Sea*?

A He thought the main character was very convincing.

B It contained some spectacular special effects.

C It was interesting but taught him nothing memorable about life.

D He found the bleak city settings very atmospheric.

2 Which statement does *not* reflect Marta's view of *You After Me*?

A She identified with the setting.

B She found one particular scene very amusing.

C She thought the ending was very emotional.

D It made her realise how trust can be betrayed.

3 What verb tense do Navid and Marta mainly use when they are talking about the plot in the films? Do they use the past or present tense? Why do you think this is?

4 How successfully do Navid and Marta convey the qualities of each film, in your view?

7 Language study: *So . . . that* and *such . . . that*

These forms are often used to give emphasis when we say how we feel.

- *So . . . that . . .* can be used with an adjective without a noun.

  Example: *The film was so scary that I had to close my eyes.*

- *Such . . . that . . .* is used with an adjective and a noun.

  Example: *It had such a sad ending that we left the cinema in tears.*

In both cases, you can leave out *that* if you wish to.

Practice

1 Join these pairs of sentences using so . . . (*that*).

a I was keen to see the concert. I was prepared to pay a lot for a ticket.

b The death scene was badly acted. The audience actually laughed.

2 Join these pairs of sentences with such . . . (*that*).

a The film took a long time to make. The director ran out of money.

b The story was fascinating. The film company wanted to make a film about it. (Begin: *It was . . .*)

8 Involving your listener

People can read film reviews for themselves, but when you talk about a film, your listener is interested in *your* particular responses to a film.

The following sentences make your responses sound more personal and will engage your listener more effectively. Working with a partner, discuss how each of the sentences could end. Complete them appropriately, using a past tense.

Example: *The scene where the monster appears is so frightening that I jumped off my seat.*

a   The scene where the heroine dies is so sad that . . .

b   It's such an intriguing plot that . . .

c   The scene was so funny that . . .

d   The scene where we find out the true identity of the murderer is so compelling that . . .

e   The hero gives such a convincing performance as a blind man that . . .

f   The gangster scenes are so violent that . . .

9 Pre-reading: Sound effects

You are going to read about how sound effects are created for films. Answer the questions in pairs or small groups.

1   Do you think most films contain sound effects, or only certain ones? Can you think of any examples of sound effects in films or TV programmes you have viewed recently? How do you think the sounds might have been created?

2   Look at these words associated with particular sounds. Check their meaning using a dictionary if necessary. Match them with the description of the sound.

a	clang	1	long, high-pitched sound like young animals or car brakes
b	smash		
c	moan	2	low sound of somebody in pain
d	rustle		
e	flap	3	shout of terror
f	scrunch	4	loud, deep sound of metal being struck
g	crash		
h	squeal	5	sound of a bird's wings moving up and down
i	shatter		
j	scream	6	sound of something breaking into pieces as it strikes another object violently
		7	sound of something breaking suddenly into tiny pieces
		8	sound of a vehicle or person hitting something
		9	sound of making a piece of paper (for example) into a ball in your hand
		10	soft, dry sound (e.g. leaves or paper)

10 Scanning for information

You are going to practise the skill of finding specific information as quickly as possible within a long text in order to answer questions 1–6.

Question 1 requires a date. For questions 2–6, underline the key words that your eye should be looking out for. Then scan the text for a date and these words. When you find one of them, read that section of text more carefully to get the answer. Ignore other details at this stage.

1   When did films first include sound?

2   Why does the sound of a sword fight need to be recorded separately?

3   Why might the sound of crows be added to a soundtrack?

4   What does a foley pit consist of?

5   What might a foley artist use to create the sound of (a) a bird's wings and (b) a falling body?

6   Name two film series that have used the 'Wilhelm scream'.

FOLEY, THE ART OF SOUND

1   Most film buffs know a little about the roles of people involved in putting together a film: the casting director, producer, camera team, screenwriter, and so on. But how many of them know what a foley artist is?

2   Foley is the art of creating sound effects, whether for film, TV, radio or computer games. The skill is named after the American Jack Donovan Foley – who worked on the earliest films to include sounds, back in the 1920s. In those days, the microphone used **on set** could only record the dialogue, so all other sounds had to be created separately and added in to the film in editing. Recording techniques have, of course, become much more sophisticated in the intervening period, but the principle is essentially the same today.

3   During **a shoot**, the recording team's main focus is on the actors and their **delivery of the lines**. Other sounds may not be picked up adequately so they won't be heard, or they may be too intrusive and drown out the dialogue – for example, if filming in a factory beside working machinery or next to a plane with its engine running. Swords may actually be made of plastic or wood, so they won't create the necessary metallic clang as they strike each other during a fight, and breaking a car windscreen made of toughened safety glass may not create the satisfying smashing sound that an audience would expect. Recording sounds separately allows the sound mixer to adjust the levels of different noises to the correct balance within the scene. This also enables sounds to be added that were never in the original recording, perhaps to

create a particular mood. The sound of **crows** cawing or the wind moaning might add tension to a scene, while a background of gentle birdsong might have the opposite effect.

4   There is a further marketing-related reason for creating a separate sound effects track. Often, the film dialogue will need to be extracted and replaced with one in a particular foreign language – and obviously the **ambient** sounds must not be lost along with the original dialogue.

5   It is the responsibility of a foley artist team to create all the background noises to make every scene as believable as possible to the viewer. The foley sound should be entirely unnoticeable. One of the main aspects of their work is footsteps, which is a rather more complex area than it may at first seem. A good foley studio will have what is called a 'foley pit', consisting of samples of different surfaces that actors might walk on, from various kinds of wooden floors, to sand or loose gravel, carpet, ceramic tiles, to name a few. The studio will also keep a variety of shoe types, ranging from soft-soled indoor **slippers** to workman's metal-toed boots, which can be matched to the film characters' footwear. While watching the relevant section of **footage** on screen, the foley artist's task will be to precisely imitate the speed and rhythm of the footsteps as their owner wanders casually, tiptoes secretly or runs in terror, taking into account the actor's age, weight, and so on.

6   Another key task for the foley team is to record what is known as a 'cloth pass', which means reproducing the often very quiet and subtle sounds created by the characters' clothes as they move. A leather jacket, for example, sounds very different from a doctor's **scrubs** or the full-length silk dress worn by a princess. Foley artists will create and record sounds by rustling or waving fabric that makes sounds corresponding to those of the characters' garments, or sometimes even by wearing similar clothing themselves. As with the footsteps, they will **sync** the sounds with what they see in the film footage.

7   Recording **props** is the third and possibly most varied aspect of the foley process. While some

sounds, such as putting a glass of water down on a wooden table, might be straightforward to recreate, other sounds demand some imagination and experimentation. A bird's flapping wings might be produced by waving a pair of leather gloves up and down, a gently burning log fire by slowly scrunching up a sheet of **cellophane**, or a body falling from a height by dropping heavy old-fashioned phone directories onto a cushion. Very complex sound effects have to be created with layers of different sounds: a car crashing into a building might be a combination of squealing tyres, shattering glass and metal being slammed against brick.

8   Not surprisingly, sound libraries exist which offer a vast array of prerecorded sound clips. While foley artists do make use of this material, it may not quite fit the context in a specific film, not to mention the risk of duplicating sounds across films. An example of this is the infamous two-second 'Wilhelm scream', first used in a film in 1953 when a character called Private Wilhelm is shot through the leg by an arrow. Since then, the same sound effect has featured in more than 400 films, including *Toy Story* and several Star Wars films, having become a running joke among film producers as well as fans.

GLOSSARY

on set: in the place where a film is recorded

a shoot: a filming session

deliver a line: say aloud a line from the actor's script

crow: particular kind of large, black bird with an unpleasant cry

ambient: in the surrounding area

slippers: soft shoes for wearing indoors

footage: a piece of film

scrubs: loose clothes worn by nurses and doctors in hospitals

sync: short for synchronise: cause something to happen at the same time

props: objects used by actors in a film or performance

cellophane: thin, clear, plastic material for wrapping or covering flowers, etc.

11 Reading and making notes

Answer the questions below. Give your answers in notes.

1 Why are sounds recorded separately from dialogue when making a film? Write four bullet point notes.

2 What are the three main types of sounds that foley artists create and record? Give examples for each.

3 What factors affect the sound of different footsteps, according to the text? One factor is the type of surface. List another four or five factors.

4 List two reasons why sound libraries are not a perfect solution.

12 Vocabulary practice

Find a word or words from the text with the following meanings.

a Paragraph 1: people who love films and know a lot about them

b Paragraph 2: given the same name as

c Paragraph 3: a feeling of nervousness, as if something bad is about to happen

d Paragraph 5: copy, behave in a similar way

e Paragraph 5: walks very quietly so nobody will hear

f Paragraph 6: very difficult to notice

g Paragraph 7: easy

h Paragraph 8: a very large and impressive group of something

i Paragraph 8: well-known (for something bad)

B Describing and recommending films

1 Asking for and giving recommendations

In pairs, read aloud this short dialogue between two friends, Raj and Cara. Raj wants information which will help him decide which film to watch with his little sister. Underline the questions Raj uses to ask for recommendations.

Raj: I'd like to watch a film with Anila tonight. Have you seen any good ones lately?

Cara: What about a historical romance, like *The Golden Ring*? I saw it last week. It's set in <u>nice</u> countryside. It's got a really <u>nice</u> heroine, and the historical costumes are really <u>nice</u>.

Raj: Mmm, maybe . . . What else is worth watching at the moment?

Cara: *Lost in Time* is a <u>nice</u> children's movie. The animation is very <u>nice</u>.

Raj: Uh huh. Can you recommend a thriller?

Cara: *Shadow of the Wolf* is <u>good</u>. The acting is <u>good</u> too.

Raj: I'm not sure. It might be too frightening for Anila. Maybe a comedy might be more fun. Can you recommend one?

Cara: *Crazy Arnie* is a <u>nice</u> comedy. It's got some <u>good</u> dialogue.

Raj: Well . . . Anila and I like science fiction films because of the special effects. Any ideas?

Cara: *Planet Zero* is a <u>good</u> sci-fi film with <u>good</u> special effects.

Raj: Well, I'll think it over. Thanks for the help.

2 Adjectives for talking about films

As you probably noticed, the adjectives *nice* and *good* are overused in the dialogue.

1 Replace nice and good (where they are underlined in the dialogue) with adjectives from the box, which are more interesting and provide more useful information. There may be several possibilities.

amusing   appealing   attractive
breathtaking   convincing   disturbing
dramatic   engaging   enjoyable
gripping   hilarious   impressive
likeable   magnificent   memorable
mysterious   powerful   quirky
spectacular   stunning
thought-provoking

2 Now read the dialogue again, this time with the new, more varied adjectives. Swap parts.

3 Collocations

A collocation is a combination of words that sound natural when used together. For example, the performance of an actor can be described as *convincing*, but we would not describe the setting of a film in this way.

With a partner or in a small group, look again at the adjectives in the box above. Decide which can be used with the following nouns. Remember that some adjectives can go with more than one noun.

a plot

b characters

c costumes

d setting

e special effects

f performance

4 Understanding the style of short reviews

Short reviews are designed to be read quickly. They outline the plot, mention the people involved, often include a key fact about the production, and try to give the reader a sense of the style and themes of the work.

Check that you understand the following vocabulary:

nerdy   drought   masterpiece
organs (of the body)   spellbinding   creepy
CGI (computer-generated imagery)

Scan these eight short reviews and match them with statements 1–8 which follow them.

 A

Spider-Man: Into the Spider-Verse

In this fresh approach to a very familiar superhero character, we see nerdy but likeable mixed-race teenager Miles Morales transform into the one and only Spider-Man after being bitten by a radioactive spider in the New York subway. Fast-paced fun and adventure follow as Miles meets up with other Spider-people from parallel universes to fight the evil Kingpin, making use of his newly found super-powers along the way. This visually stunning masterpiece combines old-fashioned graphics and modern CGI effects magnificently to make you feel as though you have walked into the pages of a comic book.

135

B

Maleficent

Maleficent is a gorgeous young creature with beautiful black wings. She has a perfect life growing up in a forest kingdom until the day an army of humans try to invade her land. Maleficent becomes the protector of her people, but is betrayed. Desperate for revenge, Maleficent places a curse on Aurora, the infant daughter of the new king of the humans. However, Maleficent comes to realise that Aurora holds the key to peace in the kingdom.

C

Never Let Me Go

In the remote countryside, innocent children seem to be enjoying their education at a traditional boarding school, but there is a dark secret: when the children grow up, they will all be forced to donate their organs.

Inspired by Kazuo Ishiguro's award-winning novel of the same name, the film *Never Let Me Go* is not only a thriller but also a philosophical work about the choice we face between challenging our destinies or accepting them.

D

Touching the Void

Joe Simpson's account of a life-changing moral dilemma and heroic survival on a mountainside is horrifyingly unforgettable. Those who have seen the film or read the book will know that, of course – but they will also be wondering how on earth it could work on the stage. The answer is: brilliantly, thanks to the ingenuity of David Greig and Tom Morris, writer and director respectively, and a spellbinding series of theatrical tricks. Don't believe me? Buy a ticket and judge for yourself.

E

Man of Tai Chi

Tiger Chen is the sole student of the elderly Master Yang. While Tiger does well with the physical aspects of his Tai Chi training, Master Yang struggles to teach him the more philosophical side of the discipline. The Master worries about his student, but the ambitious Tiger doesn't listen, becoming determined to demonstrate the effectiveness of his personal style. Trapped by an organised crime gang, Tiger ends up taking part in a fight to the death. *Man of Tai Chi* is a multi-lingual narrative and is partly inspired by the life of the well-known stuntman, Tiger Chen.

F

Stranger Things

If you haven't yet discovered this multi-season TV show, you've been missing out. Set in the 1980s, this sci-fi horror-drama centres around a group of young teenagers threatened by mysterious forces released as a result of a science experiment gone wrong. Season 1 starts off with the disappearance of one of their friends while biking home through woods.

Stranger Things provides so much: a creepy atmosphere, inspiring and genuine characters, and a feast of 1980s features that will delight both teens and those old enough to have lived through those years.

G

The Boy who Harnessed the Wind

Set in rural Malawi in Africa, this is the remarkable but true story of William, a young boy whose parents were too poor to send him to school. Refusing to give up, and after teaching himself engineering, William eventually designs and builds a huge wind turbine to power a water pump, thus saving his whole farming community from the deadly effects of a terrible drought. Great credit should go to the whole cast, but in particular to lead actor Maxwell Simba, who perfectly expresses William's cheeky determination.

H

22 Jump Street

Two police officers go undercover at a college. But instead of chasing real criminals, their task is to look for key words spoken during lectures that might suggest illegal activities. They persevere, however, and uncover information about a criminal gang. Following on from the box office hit, *21 Jump Street*, this new comedy is just as silly but will make you laugh even more.

This review:

1   tells the reader this is a live performance.

2   explains that several languages are spoken.

3   praises the star's performance.

4   suggests the film will make you think about the meaning of life and death.

5   describes how lovely the film is to look at.

6   describes a plot in which the main character admits they were wrong.

7   says the film is the sequel to an earlier, less funny film.

8   mentions two different age groups that will enjoy watching it.

5   Choosing key words

Film reviews are designed to give readers a general impression of a particular film. For that reason, it is important that a reviewer chooses their words carefully in order to convey the most important information as effectively as possible.

1   Look at the first part of the review of *Never Let Me Go* (below).

   a   Highlight the adjective that tells us the school is cut off from the outside world.

   b   Circle the verb that shows there is a happy atmosphere in the first part of the film.

   c   Underline the adjective + noun that suggest that the film might be frightening.

d   Circle the verb which lets us know the children will have no choice about what happens to them.

In the remote countryside, children seem to be enjoying their education at a traditional boarding school, but there is a dark secret: when the children grow up, they will all be forced to donate their organs.

2   Examine the extract (below) from the review of *Man of Tai Chi*. Underline the word(s) that tell us:

   a   that Tiger has a very strong personality.

   b   that Tiger has not chosen to be part of the gang.

   c   that the fight is extremely dangerous for Tiger.

The Master worries about his student, but the ambitious Tiger doesn't listen, becoming determined to demonstrate the effectiveness of his personal style. Trapped by an organised crime gang, Tiger ends up taking part in a fight to the death.

6 Presenting a film or play to the class

> **Critical thinking** You are going to give a short talk to members of your class about a film (or play) you have enjoyed.

1 Before you begin, make a plan.

Introduction
- Mention the title and the type of film (genre).
- Say why you have chosen to talk about this film or play.
- If you want to, mention the director and main actors.

Plot, characters and setting
Give a brief outline of what happens, who is involved and where the story takes place. Plots can be complicated, so keep your description short, giving most attention to the beginning of the plot.

Conveying the quality of the film or play
Say why you thought the film or play was powerful. Aim to involve your listeners (see Section A8), and remember the importance of key words in giving information (see Section B5).

You may want to mention:
- the performance of particular actors
- the use of humour, suspense or special effects (provide examples)
- the underlying 'message' of the film or play.

Recommending the film or play
Say why you recommend the film or play and why your audience will like it.

2 Deliver your talk. Remember to describe the plot and characters in the present tense.

While other students are doing their talks, listen carefully and note down:
- at least one positive comment about the talk
- two questions to ask when they have finished speaking.

7 Pre-listening discussion

> **Critical thinking** Discuss the following with a partner.

1 Think about the last film or series you watched. Was it in your own language, or in English (or another language)?

2 Do you mostly watch films or series in your own language or in English? Is that out of choice, or because that is what's available?

3 Would you like to see more films made in your own country? Why / Why not?

4 When you watch films made in another language (not your own), do you watch them with subtitles, dubbed into your own language or neither?

5 Do you prefer foreign-language films with subtitles or with dubbing? How does it affect your experience as a viewer?

6 From the point of view of the film production company, do you think creating subtitles or dubbing is easier?

8 Listening for gist

You are going to hear a talk about dubbing (the process of changing the speech in a film to a different language).

Before you listen, check that you know (or can guess) the meaning of the following vocabulary.

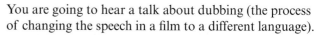

| lip-synching | utterance | frames (of a film) |
| camera angle | in sync with | multi-task |

Listen for gist. Does the talk mention any of the issues you have just discussed in Section B7? Which? As you listen, make notes to help you remember.

9 Comprehension check

Listen again and answer the questions.

1 When recording the dialogue in the new language, matching the screen actor's lip movements is _____ keeping the same meaning.

A more important than

B not as important as

C equally as important as

2   A dubbing actor needs to have a voice that:

   A   the audience will like listening to.

   B   seems to match the original actor's face.

   C   is higher or lower than the original actor's voice.

3   When selecting dubbing actors, it's very important to:

   A   avoid confusing the audience by using unusual voices.

   B   choose the most talented dubbing actors for the important characters.

   C   keep the same dubbing voice for the same actor.

4   Sometimes a dubbing actor may have to eat during the recording:

   A   to match what the original actor was doing.

   B   because of the tight recording schedule.

   C   to help them experience the same emotions as the on-screen actor.

5   Using subtitling rather than dubbing:

   A   improves the audience's language skills.

   B   may improve the audience's language skills.

   C   makes the audience prefer hearing the film's original language.

6   Which of the following is *not* given as an argument in favour of dubbing?

   A   You don't need to be able to read.

   B   Dubbed films work better on small screens.

   C   Viewers don't lose concentration and do other things.

7   Dubbing is being used more and more because:

   A   users of streaming services want more options.

   B   streaming services are having difficulty attracting new viewers.

   C   streaming services want to appeal to more people.

10 Language study: Viewpoint and evaluative adverbs

Look at these phrases from the talk you have just listened to.

***Unfortunately**, this can sometimes mean minor changes to the meaning of the words . . .*

***Clearly**, gender and age must be considered . . .*

***Obviously**, the same applies to other movies where the same character appears . . .*

*It's interesting to note, **incidentally**, that those countries which mainly show English-language films with subtitles . . .*

***Additionally**, young people in particular have a tendency to 'multi-task' . . .*

In each case, the adverb tells us something about the phrase that immediately follows it, so it can be helpful when you're listening. Speakers (or writers) use adverbs like this to guide us or to express their viewpoint.

***Unfortunately:** I'm going to tell you something negative*

***Clearly / obviously:** I'm going to tell you something you probably already know or could work out for yourself*

***Incidentally:** I'm going to mention something less important, or perhaps I'm changing the topic slightly*

***Additionally:** I'm about to add an extra point*

1   Look back at the example phrases at the start of this section. What punctuation do you need when using these adverbs to start a sentence or phrase?

2 Here are some further adverbs that are used in the same way. Match each adverb to the correct meaning.

a	presumably	1	I'm giving a direct and honest opinion that might upset someone.
b	personally		
c	luckily	2	I think this is fortunate.
d	surprisingly	3	I don't know for sure, but I think this is probably true.
e	frankly		
f	apparently	4	This is unexpected.
		5	This is just my opinion.
		6	I've heard or read that this is true.

3 Use a suitable adverb in each gap to link the following pairs of sentences (or sentence halves). You can use adverbs from the matching exercise above or the ones from the talk. There may be more than one possibility.

a Our local theatre offered free tickets for the play last week. _____, hardly anybody came.

b My friends watch movies on their phones but, _____, I find the screen too small.

c OK, so I think everything's organised for Meera's party on Saturday. _____, do you know if anyone's checked the weather forecast?

d My aunt's invited me to watch a TV programme about gardening. _____, I'd rather watch paint dry!

e It's a shame they've cancelled the concert. _____, we'll get a refund.

f I heard that the opening night of the play was a disaster. _____, the lead actor couldn't remember his lines!

g The concert was so popular it sold out straight away but, _____, we managed to get tickets!

4 Another adverb used in a similar way is *actually*. What does it mean and how is it used? Think of some examples.

C Reading and television

1 Reading habits questionnaire

1 Complete the questionnaire about reading for pleasure; it was produced by a bookshop to find out about people's reading habits.

1 Name the last book you read for pleasure. When was this? Did you finish it? Would you recommend it?

_____

2 Tick the types of books that you can remember reading during the last five years:

- ☐ YA (young adult)
- ☐ Action and adventure
- ☐ Classics
- ☐ Comic books or graphic novels
- ☐ Mystery or crime
- ☐ Science fiction or fantasy
- ☐ Historical fiction
- ☐ Horror
- ☐ Romance
- ☐ Suspense or thrillers
- ☐ Biography or autobiography
- ☐ 'How to' books
- ☐ Other non-fiction

3 Do you prefer to read an actual book or an ebook (on a tablet, e-reader, etc.)? Why?

_____

4 What was your favourite book when you were growing up?

_____

5 Do you read (or have you read) plays, novels or poetry at school? Would you say that this has (a) encouraged you to read more or (b) put you off?

_____

6 What is the longest book you have ever read for pleasure?

_____

7 Is there a book that you have read more than once? What was it?

_____

8 Have you ever met an author or been to a book signing?

_____

9 Where do you get your books from?
- [ ] School library
- [ ] Public library
- [ ] Bookshop
- [ ] Market or second-hand bookstall
- [ ] Purchase online
- [ ] Download from a website

10 What most influences you when you choose a book, from 1 (hardly at all) to 5 (very greatly)?
- [ ] The look of the book cover
- [ ] The blurb on the back of the book
- [ ] Recommendations from a friend
- [ ] Recommendations from a teacher
- [ ] Online reviewers (including Bookstagrammers, BookTubers or other online alternatives)

11 Have you ever been given a bad recommendation?

_____

12 If there is a film that came from a book, is it better to read the book or watch the film first, in your view?

_____

13 What is your favourite place to read?

_____

14 Name a famous author from your country. Have you read any of their books?

_____

15 Have you read (for pleasure) a novel in English? What was it and what did you think of it?

_____

16 If you hardly ever read for pleasure, why is that? Tick all that apply.
- [ ] No time
- [ ] Don't enjoy it
- [ ] Peer pressure
- [ ] No local library
- [ ] Don't know what to read
- [ ] Prefer computer games, films or TV
- [ ] Other

17 What might make you read more?

_____

_____

_____

2   Go back and circle the numbers of the eight questions that interest you the most.

3   Swap questionnaires with a partner. Take it in turns to talk about one of the questions with a circled number. If necessary, look back at Unit 2, Section A2 for ideas about keeping conversation going.

2 Listening: Strategies for interrupting

You are going to listen to a radio interview. Jonathan, a librarian, is concerned that young people are giving up reading because they are too busy watching films and TV programmes online.

1   Listen first for general meaning and note down why Jonathan thinks films and TV are intellectually less stimulating than reading.

2   The interviewer has some difficulty interrupting Jonathan. As you listen, tick the phrases he uses as he tries to interrupt.

☐ Just a minute, . . .

☐ With respect, . . .

☐ If I could just butt in here, . . .

☐ Excuse me, I'd like to say that . . .

☐ Hang on!

☐ If you don't mind my interrupting, . . .

☐ If I could get a word in here, . . .

3 Detailed listening

Listen again and answer the following questions.

1   What are children not getting when they watch TV and films rather than read? Give two examples.

2   What is the difference, according to Jonathan, between reading a novel and watching a film?

3   How, according to Jonathan, are children affected by watching violence on screen?

4   How can parents help their children to understand what they read? Give two examples.

5   Which best summarises the attitude of the interviewer to Jonathan?

A   Angry and sarcastic.

B   Bored and impatient.

C   Interested and concerned.

4 Post-listening discussion

1   > **Critical thinking** Do you agree with Jonathan that reading quality fiction helps intellectual development more than watching films?

2   In your view, does violence on-screen make people behave violently? Does the same apply to books, or not? Explain your answers, with reasons and examples.

5 Dialogue: Interrupting each other

Asif and Eleni are having a discussion about violence on screen, in films or TV programmes. They keep interrupting each other.

Read the dialogue aloud with a partner. Use a suitable phrase from Section C2 for interrupting each time you see the word '*interrupting*'.

Eleni: I agree with Jonathan that people are copying the violence they see in films, and it's time something was done about it. Even kids' programmes are much more violent than they used to be, and the crime rate is getting worse too. Children are being influenced to think that violence is all right and—

Asif: (*interrupting*) Children are very sensible. They can tell the difference between what happens on TV and what goes on in real life. It's rubbish to suggest that people watch a programme and suddenly become more violent. I don't think violent scenes in books are better or worse than violence on TV. There isn't that much violence on TV anyway.

Eleni: (*interrupting*) Some of the cartoons they are putting on even for very young children are really violent. They don't help children understand the terrible effects real violence has, or how it can destroy people's lives. TV makes violence seem exciting and—

Asif: (*interrupting*) Violent behaviour comes from your background and the way you're brought up. It has nothing to do with television. TV doesn't make people behave violently. If you see violence in your home or around you in your real life, that's the example you copy.

Eleni: (*interrupting*) Violent TV programmes will make children who are growing up in bad homes even worse. They're even more likely to act in an aggressive way. Jonathan said parents should help children read more, and I agree, but I think they should say what their kids are allowed to watch on TV, as well. They'll know if their children will be affected.

Asif: (*interrupting*) That would be a complete waste of time. And in any case, children don't want their parents interfering. Surely kids have the right to some privacy about what they choose to read or watch online?

Eleni: (*interrupting*) It's not only children who are influenced. Some adults just aren't able to discriminate about what they watch. They might think violence is fun, or even learn how to commit a crime. They find TV incredibly powerful and—

Asif: (*interrupting*) Most TV programmes are really boring, actually! They don't influence me to do anything except switch off and find something more interesting to do!

6 Spelling and pronunciation: The letter c

1   Have you noticed that *c* is pronounced in different ways? Say these words aloud to show the different ways *c* can be pronounced: as /k/ (hard c), /s/ (soft c), /ks/ and /ʃ/ (sh).

copying	cinema	accept	sufficient

2   Study these words, grouped according to the sound that *c* makes in the word. Then do the matching exercise below to complete the rules.

/k/	/s/	/ks/	/ʃ/
cartoon	publicity	accent	musician
commit	privacy	accident	precious
crime	concept	eccentric	special
discuss	incidentally		efficient
actor	bicycle		ocean
publicly	cellophane		

a   *C* is pronounced /k/ (hard c)

b   *C* is pronounced /s/ (soft c)

c   *Double c* (cc) is pronounced /ks/

d   *C* is pronounced /ʃ/ (sh)

1   before the vowels *e, i* or *y*.

2   before the vowels *a, o* and *u* and before most consonants.

3   before *ea, ia, ien* or *ious*.

4   before *e* or *i*.

3 With a partner, say the following words with the correct pronunciation for each letter *c*, following the rules above. Do you both agree that your pronunciation is correct?

a	process	j	incident
b	career	k	efficient
c	accelerator	l	discovered
d	principle	m	recipe
e	scenery	n	special
f	magnificent	o	successful
g	suspicious	p	ceiling
h	concentrate	q	racing car
i	accurate		

7 Using words in context

Make up five sentences using one or more words from the lists in Section C6. If you can, include other words containing the letter *c*. Write the sentences down, check your spelling, then swap them with a partner. Read your partner's sentences aloud.

Examples

My uncle had a special secret recipe for ice cream.

She had a successful career as an actor.

8 Spelling and pronunciation: The letters *ch*

The letters *ch* have three main sounds.

- In some words, *ch* is pronounced /k/.

  Examples: *chemist   technical   headache   chaos*

- In some words, *ch* is pronounced /tʃ/.

  Examples: *cheese   check   French   rich*

- In a few words in English, *ch* is pronounced /ʃ/.

  Examples: *chef   machine*

Practice

With a partner, read aloud the words in groups 1, 2 and 3. Find and underline the word in each group where *ch* makes a different sound from the other words.

Group 1	**Group 2**	**Group 3**
character	search	chauffeur
architect	watch	parachute
mechanic	achievement	brochure
synchronise	scheme	machinery
moustache	charity	chocolate
choir	butcher	chef

With a partner, practise saying each group of words. Use a dictionary to look up any unfamiliar words.

9 More practice of *c* and *ch* sounds

Read this dialogue with a partner. Check each other's pronunciation.

Alex: Our drama club is putting on a production of *Charlie and the Chocolate Factory* for the end of term.

Jamie: That sounds exciting.

Alex: It is! The club is in charge of everything. We've chosen the actors, written the script, created the costumes, painted the scenery and even designed the brochure to gain publicity. The school principal gave us special permission.

Jamie: Sounds like a recipe for chaos to me!

Alex: Well, we've had one or two headaches, but we've concentrated very hard on getting it right. There was one little slip, though. I play an eccentric character and I have to wear a ridiculous moustache. In our dress rehearsal, the moustache fell off just as I was about to speak!

Jamie: Never mind. I'm certain the audience will appreciate all the effort you've put in. How much are the tickets?

Alex: Actually, it's free but there's a collection at the end. Half the proceeds will go to the school fund and the other half will go to Children in Crisis, the school's charity.

Jamie: Well, I really hope it's a big success.

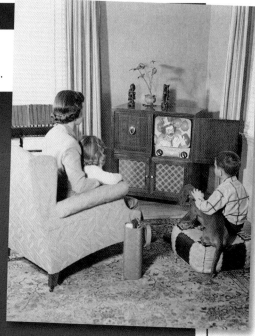

INTERNATIONAL OVERVIEW

Books, TV and cinema

In a small group, answer these quiz questions about books, TV and cinema.

1 In which of these countries do people spend the most hours per week reading books?

  India   China   United Kingdom   Australia   USA

2 The earliest known printed book (in 868 CE) comes from which country?

  USA   Germany   Italy   China   Saudi Arabia

3 The average reading speed is 200–250 words per minute. What do you think is the fastest reading speed?

4 Approximately when (in which decade) did people first watch television in their homes?

5 The word *tele-vision* comes half from the Greek language and half from the Latin language. *Vision* (from Latin) means *seeing*. What do you think *tele* means?

6 A study calculated how long an average UK citizen spends watching TV in their whole life. How long do you think this is? Give your answer as a total number of weeks, months or years.

7 Which country makes the most films per year?

  Japan   India   China   Nigeria   USA

8 In which country are Bollywood films made, and where does the name come from?

9 Which country makes *anime* films? What kind of films are they?

D Writing a book review

1 Preparing key points for a review

> **Critical thinking** Imagine that you have been asked to review a book for your school online magazine. Choose a book and write down the title. Ideally, it should be one you love or one that is memorable in some way. (If you are absolutely not a reader, you could write about a play, film or TV series instead.)

Prepare some brief notes under the following headings.

Plot

What happens, in a nutshell? Is it part of a series?

Note down one or two appropriate adjectives or phrases (e.g. *gripping, fast-moving, lots of twists and turns, minimalist*). Is character development more important than plot?

Setting

Where and when does it take place?

What is interesting about it? Does it create an appropriate atmosphere for the plot development?

Note down one or two appropriate adjectives or phrases (e.g. *depressing industrial estate, old-fashioned boarding school, futuristic city*).

Character(s)

Who is in it?

Do they change during the book, or cope with challenges? Did you identify with any of them? Is the relationship between them a key feature of the book?

Note down one or two appropriate adjectives or phrases.

Style and genre

For example, do we see the action through the eyes of a first-person narrator? Is it a graphic novel, typical dystopian novel, diary, 'whodunnit', or something else? Does it jump between present and past, with flashbacks?

Audience

Who would (or would not) enjoy it, and why?

2 Reading a review of a classic novel

Read the following review of a classic novel written by a student. Then answer the comprehension questions that follow.

Great Expectations

Reviewed by Gilang Cheung

Have you ever liked the hero in a novel so much that you wanted everything to turn out all right for him? I felt like this when I read *Great Expectations* by Charles Dickens. I'd
5 like to recommend it for the school library because I'm sure other students will identify with the main character, too.

Set in nineteenth-century England, the novel tells the story of a poor orphan called Pip,
10 who secretly helps an escaped prisoner – a good turn that has unexpected consequences. Pip meets the eccentric and bitter Miss Havisham, one of the most memorable characters I have ever **encountered**, and
15 becomes rich beyond his wildest dreams. I won't spoil the story by telling you how the plot twists and turns, but I can guarantee surprises!

In a style that I found painfully direct, Pip
20 shares his innermost thoughts and **aspirations** – even ideas he later becomes ashamed of. During the course of the novel, Pip changes a lot. He becomes more aware of his **shortcomings** and more **compassionate**.
25 He pays a high price for self-knowledge and, like me, I think you'll be moved to tears at the end.

One of the things I learnt from reading the novel is how **corrupting** money is. Pip, for
30 example, no longer cares about keeping promises he made when he was poor. The novel made me think about how loyalty and **integrity** are more important than wealth.

The novel provides a vivid and rewarding
35 insight into nineteenth-century Britain. Students of English language and literature will find it particularly fascinating.

GLOSSARY

encounter: meet (unexpectedly)

aspirations: hopes

shortcomings: personal failings

compassionate: feeling pity for others

corrupting: causing to become dishonest or immoral

integrity: honesty

Comprehension check

1   What is the title of the novel and who is the author?

2   When and where is the story set?

3   Which two characters are mentioned besides Pip?

4   How does Pip change during the novel?

5   How do we know Gilang identifies emotionally with Pip's suffering?

3   Reading a review of a contemporary YA novel

Read the following review of a contemporary YA novel written by a student. As you read, consider how the style and content are similar to or different from the one you have just read.

Then answer the comprehension questions that follow.

The Knife of Never Letting Go

Reviewed by Francesca Baldini

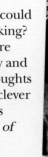

1   Wouldn't it be great if we could hear what others are thinking? Except that it's a nightmare because there's no privacy and no peace: everybody's thoughts make 'Noise'. This is the clever idea behind Patrick Ness's gripping novel *The Knife of Never Letting Go.*

2   In this first novel of the Chaos Walking **trilogy**, we meet the hero

Todd Hewitt a month before the birthday that will officially make him a man. Todd comes from Prentisstown, a small town with a dark history, which we will only discover later, and from which all women have mysteriously disappeared. We follow Todd as he runs away from town through a dangerous **swamp**, pursued by an army of hostile men from Prentisstown. Travelling with him is a weirdly silent girl called Viola – the only girl Todd has ever encountered – as they face heartbreaking challenges along the way. The cliffhanger at the end will leave you desperate to read the next book in the trilogy.

3   The author plays brilliantly with the horrifying concept of 'Noise' (hearing others' thoughts constantly). At several points, Noise is shown visually through sentences in **random fonts**, **scattered** over the book pages, adding to the sense of chaos. The thoughts of animals are part of the Noise, too; so we hear the thoughts of the little dog Manchee, who follows Todd around, adding some much-needed humour to break up the sometimes unbearable tension.

4   The development of the characters and their friendship in the novel is skilfully handled, with Viola and Todd learning to trust each other and to become tougher in a cruel world. One thing that may surprise you is the way the author uses Todd's rather rough and ungrammatical speech to convey his thought process. Don't worry; you'll soon get used to it, and you'll enjoy how it makes Todd's character feel genuine and relatable.

5   The novel encourages reflection about topics such as the dangers of information overload and the secrets kept by entire communities. In particular, it made me consider how one person can make a difference in the world by standing up for their values.

6   Whether you are already a fan of YA **dystopian** fiction or you just love fast-paced, intriguing storylines, I would highly recommend reading the whole trilogy – ideally before you see the film adaptations. The novels may be a little **bleak** and upsetting for sensitive tastes, but for others, they will be an unforgettable experience.

GLOSSARY

trilogy: set of three novels

swamp: an extremely wet area with trees growing (often inhabited by crocodiles)

random: not planned

font: a set of letters in a particular style

scattered: thrown in different directions without a plan

dystopian: relating to an imaginary society in the future, usually a bad one with lots of suffering

bleak: sad and hopeless

Comprehension check

1   What is the title of the novel and who is the author?

2   What does the review tell us about the setting?

3   The reviewer only tells us a little about the plot. From what we are told, can you guess in what way the girl is 'weirdly silent'?

4   Which words tell us that Todd and Viola's journey is difficult?

5   Do you know or can you guess what a 'cliffhanger' is (paragraph 2)?

6   What does the reviewer tell us about the mood of the book (paragraph 3)?

7   Which words tell us that the reviewer likes the way characters develop (paragraph 4)?

8   Why does the reviewer mention the film adaptations of the books (paragraph 6)?

4   Analysing example reviews

Answer the questions by studying both reviews (in Sections D2 and D3). Make brief notes, then discuss your answers in pairs.

1   The opening of each review begins with a question. In what way is this effective?

2   In their second paragraph, both reviews have to summarise a complicated plot.

   a   How does Gilang deal with this issue? Underline the relevant sentence.

   b   Underline examples of how Francesca avoids plot spoilers.

3   What did Gilang (paragraph 4) and Francesca (paragraph 5) learn from reading their book? Underline the phrases they use.

4   Gilang and Francesca recommend *Great Expectations* and *The Knife of Never Letting Go* for different audiences. Who are they?

5   Underline examples in each review of how the reviewer takes account of their readers.

6   Which review interested you more? Why?

5   Useful language for reviews

Here is some typical language used by reviewers of novels. Tick any expressions that you would like to use in a review of your own – you can adapt them if you wish. (If you are planning a film review instead, write B against any expressions that only apply to books.)

Style, pace, dialogue, and so on

It's beautifully written.

It has an elegant/poetic/chatty style, which . . .

It flows beautifully.

It moves along at a rapid pace . . .

The dialogue makes you feel as if you are in medieval times / in the aliens' world / in the dangerous world of lawless criminals . . .

Setting

It's set in . . .

It's set against the powerful background of . . .

The historical details are superb.

It's a wonderful re-creation of . . .

It has a marvellous sense of time and place.

Recommending

It's worth reading because . . .

You'll be delighted / kept in suspense by . . .

It's hard to put down.

It's a masterpiece /classic.

It's the best book I've (ever) read.

It's not to be missed.

You will be moved to tears / want to sleep with the lights on.

It will make you think about . . . in a different way.

There's an astonishing ending / plot twist that I'm not going to reveal.

I can't wait to read (the sequel / her next novel).

6 Criticising aspects of a book, film or play

It is possible to write a review that is entirely or mainly negative. However, if you are planning to *recommend* the book (or film or play), make sure that criticism is only a small part of your review.

Think back to the book you wrote notes for in Section D1, and write a sentence about one thing you *didn't* like so much about it. If you can't think of anything, write about a different novel (or film) that you would like to criticise.

It's a pity that (the ending felt so depressing / predictable / rushed / ridiculous).

I would have liked to see more . . .

I found the description of (scenery / battle scenes, etc.) rather too (long / detailed / violent, etc.) for my tastes.

I wasn't very convinced by (character, plot twist).

Despite the rather (slow beginning, over-long descriptions, unconvincing event), I really enjoyed . . .

7 Effective openings for book reviews

⟩ **Critical thinking** When writing an opening paragraph, remember the following tips.

- Immediately involve the reader.

- Make the reader want to read on.

- Convey the novel's special qualities.

- Keep it short.

- Don't give away the story ending.

In small groups, with these points in mind, read paragraphs A–F, taken from book reviews written by students. Rank them 1–6 from most to least effective. You can correct any structural errors you notice, but focus on the content and style.

A I want to try to explain to you about a very good novel which is also very long and which I recently read called 'In Our Stars'. Extremely, the writer did his best for this book and I couldn't leave any single moment in the book without reading it.

B I cannot always write to the school magazine but as I have been the one in my class that my teacher has asked me to do this as I have not done it before, I decided to write you about a book I read on holiday in France last week and I think you will really get surprised. I was I nearly fainted. I read a very long book called something like 'Twisters' or something, by Harry and whose other name I forget. It is about a band but then the band gets famous and it is going on for a very long time.

C Last week I read one of the most powerful and moving books ever, 'The Bellmaker' by Brian Jacques. In the novel, animals are given human personalities and motives. However hard-hearted you are, this compelling tale of how a courageous group of animals band together to defend their kingdom against, Foxwolf, will bring a tear to your eye.

D If you've been recently bored and willing to read a long book that I read about in someone's blog, I thought it was a true story but when I nearly finished it, I knew it was all made up and it was not true and I was disappointed. I recommend you read this book about Anna. It's a book about how a girl who lives in Alaska runs away from her boarding school into a worst place that she had never thought of before and she is trying not to stay there longer. But it is not a true story. When you finally get to finish this endless book, you will be sad about the people in it.

E Have you ever wanted to be the hero in a novel? No matter how you reply you'll love reading 'Dark Eye'. The hero is a likeable but naive trainee police cop who is on a hunt for a gang of criminals in New York. The suspense is great and the writing is just perfect.

F The book I thought was very long and want to explain you for my school website is 'Staying Alive' by Li Chang. I could read it more times too if I had time. I think the book has already sold a billion of them which is very scarce. I want to tell you about Jon (the detective in the book) who is very nice and the strange and unusual things that happened to him after gangsters put him in a cellar and are cruel to him but he is escaping. Jon is very funny and being surprising even when he is nearly dead but at the end he is alive.

8 Writing an opening paragraph

> **Critical thinking** Write the opening paragraph for your own review of a novel based on your notes in Section D1. Follow the tips in Section D7.

Share your completed paragraph with others in a small group. Swap feedback on each other's paragraphs.

9 Building a review of a thriller from prompts

Do you enjoy reading novels with exciting plots? If so, then you might enjoy *The Kidnapping of Suzie Q* by Martin Waddell.

Build up a complete review of the novel from the following prompts.

The Kidnapping of Suzie Q

The Kidnapping of Suzie Q / Martin Waddell / be / most thought-provoking / atmospheric novel / have read. It be / set / modern urban Britain / it tell / story / through eyes / courageous heroine Suzie. One day / she be making / ordinary trip / supermarket / buy groceries / when supermarket be / raided. In the confusion / criminals / kidnap Suzie / she be standing in / checkout queue.

The criminals / keep Suzie / captivity. Suzie recount / ordeal / graphic / painful detail. I be / impress / Suzie's courage / determination / refusal / panic / give up. Several incidents / novel / reveal Suzie's ability / cope / when she be threatened / them.

The story make / think / ordinary life / be changed / one incident. It be also / inspiring / make me realise / inner strength / ordinary people can have / cope with / disaster.

The novel be / skilfully written. Martin Waddell's style be / direct / witty / characters be / strong / convincing. The plot be / intriguing / never predictable. If you like / tense novels / you find this hard / put down.

10 Completing your own book review

Write two further paragraphs to add to the opening paragraph you wrote for your own review in Section D8. Refer back to the notes you made in Section D1, and look back at all the reviews in this unit if you need ideas.

When you have finished, swap reviews with other students. Give feedback as follows:

- Does the review give you a good idea of the genre, plot, setting and characters?

- Does it tell you what is special about the book/film and who it is suitable for?

- Does it use suitable language from the unit (for example, from Section D5 or from the example reviews)?

11 Look, say, cover, write, check

1 Learn these commonly misspelt words using the 'look, say, cover, write, check' method (see Unit 1, Section B12 if you need a reminder).

suspicious	moustache	receive
succeed	access	chauffeur
except	special	conscious
defence	technology	conscience

2 Ask a partner to test you when you are confident you have learnt them correctly.

3 Choose six of the words and put each one into a sentence to show its meaning.

GRAMMAR SPOTLIGHT

Use of the present perfect tense to talk about experiences

1 We use the present perfect tense when we are referring to experiences up to the present time. In particular, we often use it with adverbs such as *ever* or *yet*.

With a partner, study the following example sentences from this unit. Identify the two different verb tenses used in the underlined phrases. Try to explain why we switch from one to the other.

a **Raj:** I'd like to watch a film with Anila tonight. <u>Have you seen</u> any good ones lately?

Cara: What about a historical romance, like *The Golden Ring*? <u>I saw it</u> last week.

b <u>Have you ever liked</u> the hero in a novel so much that you wanted everything to turn

out all right for him? <u>I felt like this</u> when I read *Great Expectations*.

c <u>Have you read</u> a novel in English? <u>What was it</u> and <u>what did you think</u> of it?

2 We form the present perfect tense with the appropriate form of the verb *have* + the past participle of the main verb. Past participles can be regular (ending in -*ed*) or irregular. Your dictionary will tell you the past simple form and past participle of irregular verbs.

Write the present perfect form of each verb.

a I (*watch*) quite a few episodes of that drama. The final episode is next week.

b As a journalist, my sister (*meet*) and (*speak*) to several famous actors.

c You (*hear*) the theme song from that new movie?

CONTINUED

3 What is the difference in meaning between the following sentences?

    a My mum has been to that new theatre in town.

    b My mum has gone to that new theatre in town.

Practice

Complete the sentences with the correct form of a suitable verb. Decide whether it should be in the present perfect or simple past tense. Include the word in brackets, if one is given.

a I don't think I _____ (ever) such a boring evening. That film _____ absolutely awful!

b I _____ (rarely) the opportunity to go to a play when I lived in the countryside, but since we moved here, I _____ to about 20!

c How many times _____ (I) you to put your phone down and stop watching videos? You _____ (not) your homework yet!

d As a child, I _____ books all the time. It's such a pity that I _____ when I got a bit older. Last year I _____ a new book club, though, and since then I _____ several novels with the group. I'm so glad I _____ reading again!

e Over the years the rock group _____ at venues all over the world, but since their lead singer's accident, they _____ (not) outside their home country.

Complete the practice activities in your Workbook.

EXAM-STYLE QUESTIONS

READING AND WRITING

Reading and writing: multiple matching

Read the article about four young people (A–D) who have views on reading in the digital age. Then answer questions **(a)–(i)**.

Reading in the digital age

A Ibrahim

Books and I have a long history together. Ever since I can remember I've had a book with me. I read anything and everything, but my favourite things are novels – I read one a week, at least. But I'll admit that these days the way I read is different. Now I do almost all my reading on my tablet, and I tend to read often and for short periods. What I like about ebooks is that they are so convenient. You can carry hundreds around with you at once in the ereader. When I go on holiday, however, I always buy a paperback guidebook. I like to turn down the pages of places I want to go to. I can also make my own notes on places I visit. Some people say that reading on the screen is not the same experience and the internet is a distraction. Well, the internet can be a distraction whether you're reading an ebook or a printed book. People resist change. But we must accept that the ebook is not only the present, but the future.

B Samorn

It's supposed to be the younger generation that's into everything new and the older one that thinks that life was better in the past, but we need to remember that people are individuals. My mum and dad start using any new technology as soon as they can get their hands on it. Long before ebooks became popular, my parents were reading them, ignoring the old books on the shelves. They've downloaded thousands of titles onto their tablets and they sit on the sofa, gazing at their screens, faces lit by the bright light of the display. They keep telling me I have to get one. I still haven't given in. I prefer physical books. I like the colours and the feel of them. The only time I read an ebook is when I download one for the reading discussion group I go to after school sometimes. My friends and I like to read the latest bestseller, share our views and give the novelist a mark out of ten. But otherwise, I am a fan of the real book!

C Logan

Although I like reading, particularly books about history, I'm a very active person. If I sit around for too long with a book in my hand, I have a sudden urge to go for a swim or play a quick game of football in the park with my mates – anything to burn off some energy. I'm probably not the best person to write about all of this, then, but my view on reading in the digital age is this – it's the content that matters, not how we read it. We haven't always printed books. The ebook may be just the next stage in the evolution of the technology. It won't end here, there'll be more changes in the future: who knows how we'll be reading in 2050? Personally, I prefer physical books. Not so much because of how it feels to hold one, or anything romantic like that, but just because it's good to pick up a book now and again and get away from apps, social media updates and the blinking lights on my smartphone notifying me of another message.

D Marta

You can't move for blog posts entitled 'Young People and the Crisis of Reading', and that sort of thing. OK, I would love it if more of us were readers, but whether we enjoy it or not has got nothing to do with the internet or digital technology. There have always been people who don't like reading. My point is simple – you can like ebooks and books, just as you can enjoy talking to your friends face to face or only on social media. We don't have to decide if we want one but not the other. Ebooks are great for travelling because you can take hundreds of them at once, but reading a printed book in bed is a more relaxing experience than reading on a screen. My parents bought me an ereader a few years ago for my birthday. The next day, when they saw me reading a printed book, they were a bit disappointed. I had to explain to them that the ereader was great, but that I wouldn't stop reading physical books just because I had an ereader.

CONTINUED

For each statement, write the correct letter A, B, C or D on the line.

Which person gives the following information?

a   Advice not to assume everyone is the same _____ [1]

b   The idea that we don't have to choose between ebooks and printed books _____ [1]

c   A reflection that the writer's approach to reading has changed _____ [1]

d   The fact that the writer was given an ereader by someone else _____ [1]

e   A feeling that printed books provide an escape from modern technology _____ [1]

f   The idea that the writer has been resisting the demand to read ebooks _____ [1]

g   A personal preference not to get travel tips from an ebook _____ [1]

h   The wish for reading to be more popular _____ [1]

i   The suggestion that ebooks might not be with us forever _____ [1]

[Total: 9]

Reading and writing: informal

You and a friend recently made a video and uploaded it to a video-sharing site on the internet.

Write an email to tell your cousin about it.

In your email, you should:

*   explain what the video was about

*   say why you decided to upload it

*   describe how you felt about the experience.

Write about 120 to 160 words. [15]

[Total: 15]

Reading and writing: formal

You recently went with your family or friends to an open-air concert or another kind of musical event near where you live. The organisers of the event have asked you to write a review for your local community online news page.

In your review, say what was good about the event and what you thought was less successful.

Here are some comments from other people who attended:

> The atmosphere was great.

> It was too short.

> The refreshments were very expensive.

> The place where it was held was ideal.

Write a review for your community online news page.

The comments above may give you some ideas, and you should also use some ideas of your own.

Write about 120 to 160 words. [15]

[Total: 15]

CONTINUED

LISTENING

Listening: short extracts

You will hear five short recordings. For each question, choose the correct answer, **A**, **B** or **C**, and put a tick (✓) in the appropriate box.

You will hear each recording twice.

You will hear two friends talking about a film one of them has seen.

1   Which part of the film did Zeynep find most frightening?
    A   The beginning ☐
    B   The middle ☐
    C   The ending ☐

2   The actor that impressed the girl:
    A   has dark hair. ☐
    B   can't hear. ☐
    C   has won a prize. ☐

You will hear two friends talking about visiting an art exhibition.

3   What does the girl like about the art gallery?
    A   Its suitability for young and old ☐
    B   Its original ideas ☐
    C   Its café ☐

4   What will people be able to see at the gallery next month?
    A   Photos of city scenes ☐
    B   Sculptures ☐
    C   Nothing ☐

You will hear a tour guide talking to a group of students.

5   What will the students *not* be doing during the tour?
    A   Seeing where sound effects are made ☐
    B   Learning about visual effects ☐
    C   Visiting the museum ☐

6   Which of the following are they allowed to do?
    A   Take photos of celebrities ☐
    B   Talk about who they have seen during the tour ☐
    C   Go away from the tour group without telling the guide ☐

You will hear a teacher talking to the mother of one of her students, Jin.

7   Jin's mother:
    A   hasn't met the teacher before. ☐
    B   has tried to stop Jin playing computer games. ☐
    C   doesn't know how much work Jin is doing. ☐

CONTINUED

8 How does Jin's teacher feel about Jin's school work now?

   A Worried ☐

   B Disappointed ☐

   C Hopeful ☐

You will hear a woman leaving a voicemail message for her adult daughter.

9 What is the problem with the things Oksana's mother was looking for?

   A She couldn't find either of them. ☐

   B She could only find one of them. ☐

   C One of them was damaged. ☐

10 What has Oksana's mother offered to do to help with the school play?

   A Make clothes ☐

   B Prepare refreshments ☐

   C Help with publicity ☐

5.5

LISTENING

Listening: multiple matching

You will hear six people talking about film-making.

For questions **1–6**, choose from the list (**A–H**) which idea each speaker expresses. For each speaker, write the correct letter (**A–H**) on the answer line. Use each letter only once. There are two extra letters, which you do not need to use.

You will hear the recordings twice.

Now look at the information **A–H**.

Information

A I sometimes change my views during the film's development.

B Disagreements make the atmosphere during filming unpleasant.

C Things have to be returned to normal after filming.

D I like to seem confident.

E I protect my public image.

F Lack of time for the job puts pressure on me.

G The audience should believe in the character.

H I generally find actors challenging to work with.

1 Speaker 1 _____ [1]

2 Speaker 2 _____ [1]

3 Speaker 3 _____ [1]

4 Speaker 4 _____ [1]

5 Speaker 5 _____ [1]

6 Speaker 6 _____ [1]

[Total: 6]

SPEAKING

Warm-up questions

Warm-up questions help you feel more relaxed before you move on to answering assessed questions.

Take turns asking and answering the questions. Speak for 1–2 minutes.

- Tell me about your friends.
- What do you usually do when you get home after school?
- Where would you like to go for your next holiday?

CONTINUED

Interview

Read the questions. In pairs, decide who will play the interviewer and who will play the student. Then role-play the interview. Speak for about 2–3 minutes. Change roles and role-play the interview again.

Leisure time activities

- Can you tell me how you choose which films to watch?
- Do people your age read for pleasure?
- Would you ever give a book to somebody as a present?

Short talk

Read the options. Think about the advantages and disadvantages of each option. You have one minute to prepare your talk. Now give a short talk to your partner. Speak for about 2 minutes. Change roles and listen to your partner's talk.

Finding out about a book

Your teacher wants to inspire students to read a famous novel. She has two ideas for how to do this:

- show the class the film based on this book
- invite the author to come and give a talk.

Compare the two options and say which one you prefer, and why.

Discussion

Read the discussion questions. In pairs, decide who will play the interviewer and who will play the student. Then role-play the discussion. Speak for about 3 minutes. Change roles and role-play the interview again.

- When learning a language, is it more useful to watch films in that language or to read books in that language?
- Do actors have the right to a private life or is it okay for newspapers to publish articles about them?
- Some film stars get paid up to 20 million dollars per film. How do you feel about that?
- Some people say films don't represent everybody in our society, for example, only using good-looking actors. How far do you agree?

For even more speaking practice, watch the videos about technology in the digital coursebook

SELF-ASSESSMENT CHECKLIST

Reflect on what you have learnt in this unit. For each area listed, decide whether you feel confident or need more practice. If you feel you need more practice, you will find some ideas to help you in Advice for Success. Come back to your self-assessment scores later in your course and see if your confidence has improved.

I can ...	Need more practice	Fairly confident
discuss issues related to entertainment, using appropriate vocabulary		
scan for information and take notes on key concepts		
understand gist and then detail in a formal explanation		
prepare and deliver a structured talk		
interrupt someone politely		

ADVICE FOR SUCCESS

This section is to help you help yourself. Choose the suggestions you like and adapt them if you want to. Make notes about what you do and how it helped you.

Extending your skills

1 Read or listen in English to reviews about films, books, plays, concerts, and so on, that you have been to or read, or ones that interest you. You may find reviews in online (or print) newspapers or magazines, on video-sharing platforms or on apps that allow people to post photos and recommendations, or in the 'Customer reviews' next to books or DVDs for sale online.

2 In your school or local public library, ask for information about book forums, book clubs, or similar, with an international following that would allow you to share or read book tips in English.

3 Use a search engine to find recommendations for 'books that changed my life', 'best books of the year', and so on. Make a note of any interesting recommendations, but also note any useful language that you could recycle.

4 Online film- or book-related quizzes in English can be fun and a good way to pick up useful (sometimes more colloquial) language, for example, there's one on the BookBrowse website – find 'Personality quiz' on the drop-down menu on the 'Fun' tab.

5 Read or watch English-language videos on video-sharing platforms about aspects of film-making, such as visual effects, costumes, cartoon-making, or similar. Or try the following feature film about sound effects: *Making Waves: The Art of Cinematic Sound.*

6 Investigate the options to choose foreign-language subtitles or dubbing next time you watch a film via a streaming service. If you can, choose English! Watch a film at the same time as a friend, and practise discussing your opinions in English afterwards.

7 Prepare a short talk on a different film from the one you presented in Section B6. Take into account any feedback you were given after your first talk. Record yourself as you deliver the talk, then listen back to yourself. What could you improve?

8 Practise reviewing a live performance (e.g. a play, dance performance or music concert). Use the skills you have learnt in this unit, but also think about:

   – the costumes, special effects, lighting, and so on, if appropriate

   – the audience's reactions to the performance

   – relevant details that added to the atmosphere – for example, weather, numbers of people, location

   – where you were sitting: could you see/ hear well? Who were you with? (This might not be appropriate in a formal review – it depends on the context in which you are writing.)

Showcasing your skills

9 Practise using interrupting strategies (see C2–5) next time you are having a conversation in English.

Travel and the outdoor life

In this unit you will:

- Explore the topics of travel and tourism

- Scan for detailed information in a brochure and an article about travel

- Write a description of an outdoor activity and a place using vivid and engaging language

- Identify detailed information in a conversation and take notes from a lecture

- Use a range of vocabulary and grammar for talking about blame and responsibility

- Plan, prepare and give a short talk about tourism

08 ◀ Watch the video about travel and the outdoor life in the digital coursebook.

BEFORE YOU START

Look at the photo on this page.

a   Choose three adjectives to describe the landscape in the photo.

b   Why do you think someone chose to set up their campsite here?

c   What makes people travel to unusual places?

d   What's the most unusual place you have ever visited?

A Holiday time

1 Holiday quiz

What do you really like doing on holiday? With a partner, rate the following points on a scale of 1 (unimportant) to 4 (very important). Add anything else you or your partner like doing.

		Myself	**My partner**
a	Staying in a comfortable, well-equipped hotel / holiday home	☐	☐
b	Seeing beautiful scenery and new places	☐	☐
c	Making new friends	☐	☐
d	Doing outdoor activities, e.g. hiking, climbing, swimming	☐	☐
e	Learning a new skill, e.g. sailing, cooking, windsurfing	☐	☐
f	Going to theme parks	☐	☐
g	Having time for reading and quiet thought	☐	☐
h	Exploring city attractions, e.g. art galleries, museums	☐	☐
i	Learning more about local culture and customs	☐	☐
j	Lazing on a sunny beach listening to favourite music	☐	☐

Share your ideas in your group. What are the most popular things to do on holiday? What are the least popular?

2 Pre-reading discussion

The web page describes a programme for teenagers to volunteer abroad during the summer holidays. In pairs, look carefully at the photos without reading the text. Who can you see? Where are they? What are they doing? How do you think they are feeling? What is the atmosphere like?

Home | Volunteer holiday programmes | Thailand

Exciting volunteer programmes in Thailand

Learn to dive, collect data on marine life and plant trees

Our qualified instructors will teach you how to scuba dive safely so that you can help staff collect and record data about marine life in the Andaman Sea. This will help us to improve the health of the ecosystem.

The huge increase in the amount of plastic washing up on the beaches is endangering birds, fish and turtles. Join our amazing team of volunteers walking along the coastline to collect rubbish and protect wildlife.

Mangrove swamps are habitats for thousands of species of birds, fish and reptiles. We help protect these creatures by planting trees to prevent the destruction of these valuable ecosystems. Plant trees with us and learn to understand these beautiful habitats.

At weekends, we organise exciting cultural and sightseeing trips so that you can learn about Thailand's fascinating culture and traditions. We'll also visit an elephant sanctuary and a marine biology centre. All day trips are included in your programme.

There will be plenty of time for relaxation, too. Enjoy swimming and surfing on one of the beautiful sandy beaches nearby. For an extra fee, our friendly local guides can take you trekking or hiking to learn about the plants and animals of the forest.

Our hostel accommodation is quite simple, but comfortable and clean. This is a great place to meet other volunteers and share experiences. Our volunteers come from countries all over the world. This is a unique opportunity to make international friends!

Our volunteer projects are for 15 to 18 year olds only and there is a minimum stay of two weeks. Prior swimming skills are required for all diving activities. Download our application form. Write to us with your questions or take a look at our FAQ page.

3 Brainstorming

> Critical thinking What do you think might be the good points and bad points of this kind of holiday? In pairs, write down any ideas you can think of. Try to add at least another two or three good and bad points.

Good points
- Trying new skills
- Helping the environment

Bad points
- Not enough time to learn a new skill properly
- Difficult to communicate with teenagers from other countries

Share your ideas in a group. Add any new ideas to your own list.

4 Reading for gist

> Critical thinking Read the web page quickly for general meaning. Don't worry about understanding every word. As you read, underline any *opinion* adjectives that try to persuade you to apply for this programme.

5 Comprehension check: Scanning the text

Scan the web page to find answers to these questions.

1 Identify three new skills you can learn on this holiday.

2 Identify three ways that volunteers will help the environment.

3 Can non-swimmers take part in this programme?

4 Suggest three reasons why you might need good communication skills on this programme.

5 Find one negative point mentioned in the web page.

6 You are 16 years old and a good swimmer. You want to stay for one week. Why would you be unable to attend the programme?

7 What information is not included in the brochure? List three points.

8 Write a question to the website about one of your points in Question 7.

6 Identifying persuasive techniques

What type of audience is this web page aimed at? What persuasive techniques are used to influence the reader? Consider:

- evaluative language, including opinions

- the choice of photographs (who is in them and what they are doing)

- the layout.

7 Analysing the message

> Critical thinking Do you think this kind of programme really helps the environment? Or is it more about the benefits for volunteers? Has the web page convinced you that taking part in this volunteer holiday is worthwhile? Why / Why not?

8 Language study: Using modifiers before adjectives

We can use modifiers before adjectives to make them stronger or weaker. Modifiers such as *very, really* and *extremely* make adjectives stronger. Modifiers such as *a little, slightly, fairly* and *rather* make them weaker.

The website says that the accommodation is 'quite simple'. *Quite* is a modifier that usually means 'moderately' (more than 'a little' but less than 'very'). But it can also mean 'completely' when used with certain adjectives. Which do you think it means in the following sentences?

a I was quite surprised by the friendliness and hospitality of all the staff.

b Qualified staff accompanied on all diving trips, so we were quite safe.

9 Shifting stress

The pattern of stress in some words alters when they are used as different parts of speech. For example, the words 'record' and 'increase' can have different stress depending on whether they are used as nouns or verbs:

*The **in**crease in the amount of plastic is endangering birds and fish.* (noun)

*We will help to in**crease** the number of beaches where it is safe for turtles to nest.* (verb)

*A **rec**ord number of turtle eggs hatched on this beach this year.* (noun)

*You will be able to help staff collect and re**cord** data about marine life.* (verb)

Practice

Mark the stress in the words in italics as you listen to the sentences.

a You'll make good *progress* on the course.

b You can *progress* to a higher level.

c The farmers sell their *produce* in the market.

d The factories *produce* spare parts for cars.

e I *object* to people checking their phones during a meal.

f She brought many strange *objects* back from her travels.

g Black and red make a striking *contrast*.

h If you *contrast* his early work with his later work, you will see how much it has changed.

i The teacher does not *permit* talking in class.

j I can't get a work *permit*.

k I bought Dad a birthday *present* yesterday.

l The artist will *present* his work at the next exhibition.

Now practise saying the sentences aloud to a partner. Do you both agree about the stress?

Where does the stress fall when the word is a noun and when it is a verb? What is the rule?

B Outdoor activities

1 Asking questions

What is your favourite outdoor activity? Use the prompts below to make questions. Then talk in pairs about your favourite outdoor activity. If you prefer, one of your group can go to the front of the class to reply to the questions.

What / you like / do / your free time?

Where / you do it?

What / you feel like / when you do it?

What special equipment / you use?

How good / you be / at it?

How / you feel / after / activity?

Why / you recommend it?

2 Reading: Identifying leisure activities

1 Describe the photos. What leisure activities do they show?

You can choose the level of difficulty of the trail that you want to try. In some ways, it's easier than skiing because your hands are free. It feels like you're flying through the air!

C   It's really good exercise for your upper body, but best of all is the sense of calm and relaxation you can get from being out in the open by yourself. I love pushing off from the shore and taking the first stroke. It's as if I leave all my worries behind me on land. I think people of any age can enjoy this activity. There's no noise and no stress. Plus, you can go to places that are hard to reach by land. One of my best memories is enjoying a beautiful sunset from the middle of a volcanic lake!

D   There's a park near my home where I meet up with friends after school. It's fun to learn new styles and tricks. Not only is it physically demanding – you definitely burn lots of calories this way! – it's also mentally challenging because you have to persevere and not give up. When you learn a new flip or twist, you feel like a champion! Safety can be an issue, though – that's why I always wear a helmet.

E   I was tired of the same roads around town and decided to try something different. I joined a club that goes out to the hills every weekend. The main difference is that you're not on a paved road. The trail is often rough and covered with branches or roots and stones, so you need to be very aware of your path and constantly scan for obstacles, and you need strong shoes. You need to take shorter steps, especially when the route takes you up or down hills. It's a good activity for someone who enjoys something active that's not competitive.

F   I first tried this when we went on holiday to Italy. I had been swimming in the sea since I was tiny, but that was the first time I had tried any kind of diving, and I loved it! It feels like you are entering a whole new world. The colours are different. They're much clearer and more vivid. You can see fish and coral in their natural habitat. You learn to observe nature more carefully. I've learnt a lot about marine life and want to study it in the future. Maybe I'll be an underwater photographer one day!

2   Match the photographs with the descriptions below. What key phrases help you to decide? Find at least four key phrases in each extract below.

A   I like going to a different place every weekend. I usually go with one or two friends and we plan our route the day before. We work together and help each other reach the summit. Some people don't use any gear, but I always take rope, good shoes and a helmet. It's an activity where you just focus on the physical challenge and don't think about anything else. You need to be quite fit to do this activity. The best thing is the feeling of satisfaction when you get to the top – and the amazing views!

B   I enjoy testing my own limits and overcoming challenges. It's not all about going fast, although that's part of the fun! It's also about skill and balance and coordination. You can be part of a team and take part in competitions.

3 Scan the descriptions to answer these questions. Which activity:

a appeals to someone who likes being alone?

b gives someone an aim for the future?

c can be done in a town or city?

d develops strength in the hands and arms?

e involves cooperating with others?

f would appeal to someone who finds speed thrilling?

3 Developing your writing style

Many students can write a simple description of an outdoor activity they enjoy. However, writing in a way that engages your readers as well as giving facts demands more skill. Certain language structures can help you.

- The *-ing* form (gerund) is often used when describing how much you like something. Remember that *love, like, enjoy, prefer, hate*, and similar can be followed by *-ing* forms.

  Examples: *I like going to a different place every weekend.*

  I enjoy testing my own limits.

- Clauses (beginning *which, where*, etc.) can link two ideas and provide extra information.

  Example: *There's a park near my home where I meet up with friends.*

- *Since* can be used to indicate the point in time something began.

  Example: *I had been skiing since I was tiny.*

- *Like, as, as though, as if* are used to compare one thing to another.

  Examples: *It feels like you're flying through the air!*

  You feel like a champion!

- Using **precise adjectives and adverbs** gives your writing more clarity.

  Examples: *It's mentally challenging. It's physically demanding.*

  You learn to observe nature more carefully.

4 Identifying language structures to engage readers

Study the descriptions of activities in Section A2. Underline any structures or expressions you would like to use in writing about your own favourite outdoor activity.

5 Describing a favourite activity

Write a description of an outdoor activity you enjoy. Use a wide vocabulary and range of structures. Write at least 100 words. You need to mention:

- why you like the activity

- the skills and equipment you need (check any technical words)

- when and where you can do it

- any other personal responses to it

- why other people might enjoy it too.

6 Reading aloud

Read your description to your group. If you like, you can substitute the word 'blank' instead of naming the activity. Let the group guess what you are describing.

Discuss which descriptions were most successful at persuading you to try the activity.

7 Pre-listening discussion

1 › **Critical thinking** Have you ever been camping? Talk to your partner about what it was like. If you have never been, look at the picture and tell your partner what you think it would be like.

2 What qualities do you need to be a good camper? Do you think you have them?

3 Camping holidays are good fun but can sometimes be stressful. What might people find stressful or argue with each other about on a camping trip?

 # 8 Listening for gist

Omar and Natasha have just come back from their first camping holiday with a youth club. What did they find difficult about the holiday? Note three things.

Overall, do you think they enjoyed the trip despite the difficulties?

 # 9 Listening for detail

Now listen for detail and choose the best ending for each statement.

1 The teenagers had difficulty getting the tent up because:

A   the weather was bad.

B   they were in a hurry.

C   there weren't any instructions.

2 The boy felt guilty because:

A   he made a mistake in setting up the tent.

B   he had forgotten part of their camping gear.

C   he didn't bring the right clothing.

3 The girl blames herself for:

A   not helping to make breakfast.

B   not putting the food away correctly.

C   forgetting to bring the bread.

4 The girl says it was a problem that:

A   she hadn't brought her phone.

B   her phone battery ran out.

C   she couldn't check her phone.

5 The teenagers' attitude to going on a camping trip in future is:

A   Negative: There are too many discomforts and problems.

B   Cautious: OK, but there are risks involved in this kind of trip.

C   Enthusiastic: They would look forward to going camping again.

10 Post-listening discussion

1 › **Critical thinking** Omar and Natasha mention the uncomfortable aspects of camping, like *stone-cold showers*. What do you think they might have enjoyed about their trip that they did not mention? Try to think of three things.

2 If you went camping, where would you prefer to go? In your own country or abroad? Try to explain why.

11 Blame and responsibility

Omar blames himself for forgetting the waterproof sheet. Natasha blames herself for letting the bread get soggy. Below are some expressions people use to blame each other, admit responsibility or tell each other they are not to blame. Pick the ones you heard in the conversation. Which expressions sound most critical? When would it be acceptable to use them? When would it be inappropriate?

Blaming

- *It's your fault.*
- *You're responsible.*
- *I blame you for it.*
- *It was down to you.*

Admitting responsibility

- *It's my fault.*
- *I do feel guilty.*
- *I feel bad about it.*
- *I'm responsible.*
- *I should have been more careful.*

Telling someone they are not to blame

- *Don't blame yourself.*
- *It wasn't your fault.*
- *It was just one of those things.*
- *You shouldn't feel bad about it.*

12 Comparing cultures

> **Critical thinking** What do you say in your language when you want to blame someone, admit responsibility or tell someone they are not to blame for something? How does it compare with what is acceptable in English?

13 Functional language: Writing a dialogue

Imagine you have gone on a hiking trip with a group of friends and one of you forgot to bring the bottled water. What would you say to each other?

Write out this or a similar dialogue. Remember to refer back to Section C11 for suitable expressions. Practise the dialogue in pairs. Finally, exchange dialogues with another pair and practise their dialogue.

14 Colloquial expressions: Adjective collocations

On the audio recording you heard showers described as '*stone cold*', the night as '*pitch dark*' and the water as '*crystal clear*'.

In colloquial language, the meaning of an adjective is often emphasised by the addition of a noun or another adjective before it.

Examples: *stone cold* (*noun + adjective*)

   icy cold (*adjective + adjective*)

Practice

Complete the gaps in the following sentences with an adjective or noun from the box. You will need to use one word twice.

boiling	bone	brand
fast	freezing	wide

a   This jacket is ruined and it was _____ new! I only bought it last week.

b   Let's start a fire. It's _____ cold in here.

c   Oh no! The carpet got wet when it rained last night. Someone left the window _____ open.

d   I was exhausted after our long trek back to the campsite. As soon as my head hit the pillow, I was _____ asleep.

e   The temperature's very high today. It's _____ hot in the sun!

f   It had been weeks since the last rainfall, and the vegetation was _____ dry.

g   I went to bed early and tried to sleep, but at 1 a.m. I was still _____ awake.

15 More colloquial expressions

Instead of 'getting up very early', you heard Omar talk about 'getting up at the crack of dawn'. Complete the following sentences with these colloquial phrases:

a bite to eat	a hair out of place
at the last minute	from time to time
hear a pin drop	a drop of rain

a   We stopped at a café on the way home to have
   _____.

b   The farmers are very worried about their crops. There hasn't been _____ for months.

c   The library was so quiet that you could
   _____.

d   Her appearance is immaculate. She never has
   _____.

e   Dan never plans ahead and made all the arrangements for his holiday _____.

f   You shouldn't study all day long. It's good take a break _____.

Now work in pairs to create some sentences of your own with these expressions. You need to use the whole expression – you can't use just part of it.

16 Word building: Adjective suffixes

Many adjectives are formed by adding suffixes to the end of other words. Below are some examples from the audio recording.

waterproof (water + proof)

childish (child + ish)

enthusiastic (enthusiast + ic)

In groups of two or three, discuss how you could form adjectives from the following words by adding suitable suffixes. In some cases, more than one suffix is possible.

Notice the way the spelling changes in some words. Check your ideas in a dictionary. Then create sentences using the adjectives.

bullet	fool	heat	irony
nomad	panorama	pink	scene
sound	style	twenty	warm

17 Punctuating direct speech

In written English, inverted commas (also called quotation marks) must be put around all the words someone actually says. You open inverted commas at the beginning of the speech and close them at the end.

Study the following examples of the way direct speech is punctuated. Focus in particular on:

- the use of capital letters

- the position of other punctuation marks (commas, question marks, etc.)

- the correct way to punctuate quoted words within direct speech.

1   Tariq said, 'I don't have any money. Do you?'

2   Mum paused and reached into her bag for her phone. 'Do you want to see our holiday photos? I took some on my phone,' she said.

3   'Have another piece of cake,' urged Leila. 'I baked it specially.'

4   Costas shouted, 'You tell me, "Don't worry about it," but I can't help worrying.'

5   'Look out!' screamed Maria. 'Can't you see that lorry?!'

Practice

Complete the punctuation in the following conversation. You need to add commas and inverted commas.

What was the best part of your holiday in America? Juliana asked when she saw Paulo again.

Going along Highway One from Los Angeles to San Francisco said Paolo without hesitation. I wouldn't have missed it for the world.

What's so special about Highway One? Juliana asked. Isn't it just another dead straight American highway?

Well replied Paolo the road runs between mountains on one side and the Pacific on the other. The views are beautiful. Seagulls fly over the waves. There are great cliffs full of redwood trees. Yes he paused for a moment it's truly magnificent.

What was the weather like? Juliana asked. Every time I checked the international weather forecast there was one word hot.

In fact Paolo laughed we had stormy weather but when the sun broke through it created fantastic rainbows. We visited a cove where you can hunt for jade. Anything you find is yours and I'd almost given up looking when I found this. He reached into his pocket and pulled out a tiny green fragment. Here he said it's for you.

C Tourism: The pros and cons

1 Brainstorming

> **Critical thinking** Tourism is now probably the world's biggest single industry.

Work in groups of three or four and jot down anything you can think of under the following headings. Pool your ideas with other groups and add any new ones.

1   What are some of the pleasures and drawbacks of being a tourist? Write three more pleasures and three more drawbacks.

    Pleasures
    You can see a different way of life.

    Drawbacks
    Your holiday is too short to get a real understanding of the country.

2   What are the advantages and disadvantages to the host country of a rise in tourism? Write three more advantages and three more disadvantages.

    Advantages
    It creates jobs.

    Disadvantages
    Foreign companies take the profits from tourism back to their own countries.

3   How can tourists behave responsibly when they go abroad? Write four more points.

    They can buy from local traders.

2 Introducing eco-tourism

1   You are going to hear the introduction to a lecture about tourism and complete some notes about the talk. Read through the notes first and predict what kind of word you will need in each gap. A number? A noun? A verb?

2   Listen to the introduction and complete the notes. Write one or two words in each gap.

Tourism

Tourism definition: Travel to other places for fun; for example, beach holidays, **(a)** _____, outdoor activity holidays.

Make use of commercial services; for example, transportation, **(b)** _____ tour companies and tourist attractions.

2019 – tourism generated **(c)** _____ dollars globally, there were **(d)** _____ tourist arrivals.

2030 – **(e)** _____ tourist arrivals.

Local economies suffer when there is a **(f)** _____ or a pandemic.

Too many tourists can cause damage; for example, **(g)** _____ or Pompeii.

Eco-tourism aims to minimise **(h)** _____, emphasises **(i)** _____ for local cultures and the environment.

One example of an eco-tourism project is in **(j)** _____.

3 Post-listening discussion

1 Do you think that some types of holidays are more eco-friendly than others? Tell your partner about one of your holiday experiences and say how it was or was not eco-friendly.

2 Work in pairs. Discuss what makes a hotel or resort more eco-friendly. Write a short advertisement for an eco-friendly hotel.

4 Pre-reading discussion

1 You are going to read an article about tourism in Sicily and Sardinia, two islands off the Italian coast. Before reading the article, describe what you can see in the pictures. Tell your partner.

2 In pairs, discuss the following questions. What do you think a holiday on these islands would be like? What do you think you would enjoy? Would you find anything difficult to get used to? Would you like the opportunity to go? Why / Why not?

> Critical thinking

3 What do you think foreign visitors expect your own country to be like? Are their perceptions correct, do you think? How do foreign visitors to your country usually behave? If you get a lot of visitors, does the atmosphere in your area change? How? Try to explain your views.

5 Vocabulary in context

Match the following words from the article with their definitions.

a whiff
b gilded
c glow incandescently
d pastures
e enigmatic
f soar
g gorges
h lush
i secluded
j robust
k mosaic

1 to shine with a warm, bright light
2 growing thickly and strongly
3 strong
4 to fly high
5 covered or decorated with gold
6 grassy fields
7 a picture made of small coloured pieces of glass or stone
8 a brief smell
9 private, hidden away
10 mysterious
11 steep, narrow valleys

6 Identifying descriptive language

Read the article carefully, underlining the descriptive language as you read. For example, the following sentence uses descriptive adjectives. *We want <u>unspoilt</u> landscapes, markets, traditions and cuisine, and <u>distinctive</u> architecture.*

OFFSHORE ITALY

Sicily – mosaics, ruins and churches

Unspoilt, even wild, the Italian islands of Sicily and Sardinia give an unexpected flavour to holidays in the Mediterranean.

What most of us want is to visit a 'real' country. We want unspoilt landscapes, markets, traditions, cuisine and distinctive architecture. We want people who are welcoming yet different from us.

Historically, there are two ways in which local character is preserved. The first is a poor economy; the second is physical separation from the mainland – the key reason why Sicily and Sardinia have stayed unspoilt.

I recently went to Taormina, Sicily's best-known seaside resort. Located on Monte Tauro, Taormina can be reached via **funicular** from its two bays below. Although its streets are traffic-free, they become crowded with holiday-makers in high summer. Even with so many people, nothing can take away the magic of this medieval town. After all, what other major holiday resort has a backdrop that includes a world-class Graeco–Roman amphitheatre, wonderful hills and a 3323-metre volcano, Mount Etna?

Graeco-Roman amphitheatre in Sicily

Here, in the east of Sicily, there's a link with southern Italy, but move further west and the influence is decidedly more Arabic. By the time you enter the Sicilian capital, Palermo, with its street market similar to a souk and couscous cafés, there's an exciting whiff of North Africa.

In Palermo, this mix of the two traditions has produced some of the most beautifully decorated buildings in this part of the world. There's the Cappella Reale, the chapel that King Roger II built for himself in the 12th century. When entering from the central courtyard, it takes a while for your eyes to adjust to the darkness. But gradually the gilded mosaics which line the walls come alive; while overhead, wonderfully carved ceiling paintings of exotic gardens and hunting scenes glow incandescently against a deep blue sky. The chapel is the supreme jewel of the city, yet a few kilometres away, on the hilltop at Monreale, is a cathedral where the mosaics are equally beautiful.

Sicily may not have as much mountain wildness as Sardinia, but it has a lovely broad landscape with rolling plains and corn-coloured hills. Life is taken at a relatively slow pace, and sleepy hilltop towns come to life only for a festival or wedding. In some of this lovely country, farmers are waking up to the possibilities of agriturismo, boosting an income by offering hospitality (converted cottages and, sometimes, country food) to enthusiastic tourists.

Visiting Sicily now, it is easy to forget that for nearly 3000 years, it was the most fought-over island in the Mediterranean. The ancient Greeks loved it as one of their richest colonies and left behind a marvellous collection of temples to prove it.

Sardinia has some of the most astonishing countryside in Europe. Much of the population is concentrated in its two main towns, Cagliari in the

Sardinia – wild at heart, with glamorous resorts

south and Sassari in the north, so in the centre of the island, shepherds still herd sheep and goats to remote valleys, visiting pastures used in Roman times. The land is dotted with mysterious stone
65 buildings called nuraghi, which were left behind by the Sardinians' prehistoric ancestors.

Eagles and black vultures soar over the mountains; pink flamingos flash their wings by the coast – everywhere you look, there are gorges, caves, wild
70 boar, deer and flowers. All this makes Sardinia a terrific destination for fishing, cycling, walking and riding.

Yet, despite extensive areas of wilderness, the island has some of the best resort hotels in all
75 Italy. One of the most successful of the tourist developments is Forte Village. It is set in 55 acres of lush garden with a wide range of sports on offer, and there are three hotels to choose from, plus a selection of secluded cottages, entertainment
80 and childminding services. It may not be the 'real' Sardinia, but it's hard to find a better quality holiday resort.

GLOSSARY

funicular: a mountain railway where the cars are operated by cable

7 Comprehension check

Now try to answer the following questions:

1 What, according to the writer, is the main reason that Sicily and Sardinia have remained unspoilt?

2 Why is the writer reminded of North Africa? Give two examples.

3 How has the combination of Arabic and Italian influences affected the architecture?

4 Which activities does the writer suggest Sardinia is well-suited to? Give two examples.

5 Which island, according to the article, would be:

   a   a good destination for a keen birdwatcher?

   b   attractive to someone who likes mountain views?

   c   a good choice for a tourist who prefers traditional, rural accommodation?

   d   appealing to a tourist who admires ancient Greek architecture?

   e   of interest to someone who is curious about volcanoes?

   f   a good destination for someone who enjoys evidence of prehistory?

   g   suitable for a family who want to stay in modern accommodation with childcare facilities?

6 Which statement best summarises the author's view?

   A   Overall, Sicily is a higher quality destination for tourists.

   B   Sardinia has the most to offer tourists choosing a holiday.

   C   Each island is unique with different benefits for tourists.

8 Post-reading discussion

Imagine you are going on a holiday. Which of these places would you prefer to stay in? Discuss the advantages and disadvantages of each place with a partner.

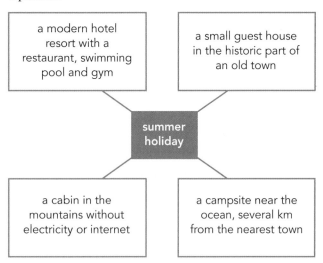

| a modern hotel resort with a restaurant, swimming pool and gym | a small guest house in the historic part of an old town |

summer holiday

| a cabin in the mountains without electricity or internet | a campsite near the ocean, several km from the nearest town |

9 Language study: Adverbs as modifiers

We can use adverbs before adjectives to add to the meaning of the adjective. There are several examples in the article:

beautifully decorated (line 31)

wonderfully carved (line 38)

relatively slow (line 47).

Combining adverbs with adjectives appropriately is a matter of practice. There are no hard and fast rules.

Choose adverbs from the box to complete the sentences below. After you have finished, compare your answers with a partner's. Sometimes more than one answer is possible.

alarmingly	fully	strikingly	badly
painstakingly	surprisingly	dazzlingly
seriously	utterly	faintly	strangely

a   I found the standard of service in the hotel _____ bad.

b   He has _____ recovered from his accident.

c   The temple is a _____ attractive building.

d   The buildings were _____ bombed in the war.

e   I was _____ ill in hospital.

f   The beggar was _____ destitute.

g   You'll need sunglasses as the midday sun is _____ bright.

h   They expected prices to be high on holiday, but everything was _____ cheap.

i   The ancient relics in the museum had been _____ restored.

j   Even after washing, the coffee stain on that white tablecloth is still _____ visible.

k   We held our breath as the coach went _____ fast around steep mountain bends.

l   The disco, which was usually very noisy, was _____ quiet.

10 Imagery in descriptions

Striking images convey a lot of information in a few words.

The writer describes Sicily as '*a lovely, broad landscape with rolling plains and corn-coloured hills*'.

1 Does the writer describe everything about the Sicilian countryside, or select a few key features? What kind of image does the phrase '*rolling plains and corn-coloured hills*' convey?

2 What kind of images of Sardinia come to your mind when you read that '*shepherds still herd sheep and goats to remote valleys, visiting pastures used in Roman times*'?

or

'*Eagles and black vultures soar over the mountains; pink flamingos flash their wings by the coast*'?

3 Study the examples carefully and underline key adjectives or images that suggest the area is still wild and untouched by modern life.

11 Adjectives: Quality not quantity

It's far better to be selective. How many adjectives have been used before the nouns in the following examples? How successfully do they evoke a particular atmosphere ?

exotic gardens (line 39)

sleepy hilltop towns (line 47)

Choose an example of descriptive writing from the text that you think contains pleasing images. Comment on it in the same way.

12 Comparing two styles

> **Critical thinking** Compare the following two descriptions of the same place. How do the styles of the extracts differ? Which do you prefer? Why?

A

> The village is very, very nice. Tourists like going there but there is not a lot of new development, crowds or traffic or things like that. There are stone houses near the harbour. The buildings are not painted in dark colours. They are painted white or cream. The buildings have blue, grey or brown shutters. There are hills around the village. There are many pine trees on the hills. The view from the top of the hills is very good. You can see the whole area.

B

> The village is strikingly pretty and unspoilt. The houses, rising up from the harbour, are pale-coloured with painted shutters and made of stone. The village is surrounded by hills covered with pine trees, which provide panoramic views of the area.

13 Developing your writing style

There are a number of ways you can improve your writing style:

- Choose your adjectives with care and use them precisely.

- Remember that you can create adjectives by adding suffixes to nouns or adjectives, for example *panoramic*, *colourful* (see Section B16).

- You can make adjectives more emphatic by using adverbs as intensifiers, for example *staggeringly*, *exceptionally*.

- Adjective collocations, such as *crystal clear*, are another way of adding impact to your descriptions (see Section B14).

- Use clauses to link ideas beginning with *which, where, when* and phrases beginning with *made of, with*, and so on.

- Use comparisons: *like, as, as though, as if*.

All the above techniques will help you to write more concisely – using fewer words to greater effect.

Practice

Now use the ideas in the list to help you rewrite the following description.

> The town developed around a marketplace. The marketplace is very, very old. It is in the shape of a rectangle. In the town, the people live in the way that they used to live hundreds of years ago. They like visitors. They will always help you. You do not need to be afraid of them. They wear clothes that are very simple. They wear long, loose, white cotton robes. The town has many very, very old buildings. The buildings were built in the 13th century. It also has many restaurants. There are many different kinds of restaurants. You can eat nice food. The food is from different cultures.

14 Writing your own description

1 Think about your last holiday or day out. Try to recall what was distinctive about the experience. Was it the people's way of life? The landscape? The food? The places of interest? Where you stayed? Or a combination of all of these? What particular images come to your mind? When you are ready, write them down. Don't worry about trying to write neatly or accurately. Just let the words flow out onto the page.

2 Re-read what you have written and select the best images. Concentrate on those that convey the atmosphere and feeling of the experience. Don't try to describe everything.

3 Now try to write a description. Use the techniques you have learnt in the unit so far. Write about 100 words.

15 Giving a short talk

Prepare a talk of about five minutes on the topic: '*More tourists = more economic and social benefits.*'

Planning the talk

Use the notes you made earlier to help you produce a list of key points under main headings.

Give your talk depth by adding examples of your own. Try to think of specific ways tourism affects your country. What have you noticed about the behaviour of tourists and the effects they have on the local atmosphere and environment?

If you have travelled, you could compare tourism in your country with tourism abroad. What was your own experience of being a tourist in a foreign country? How were you treated? What did you learn about the treatment of tourists in your own country?

INTERNATIONAL OVERVIEW

International tourism

International tourism is always popular. Discuss the questions with a partner.

1 From the countries on this list, guess the top four international tourist destinations in order of popularity.

> Australia   Brazil   China
>
> Egypt   France   India
>
> South Africa   Spain
>
> UK   USA

2 Which country on the list would you most like to visit? Why?

3 Which country would you most like to visit if you could choose anywhere in the world? Why?

4 Which places in your country would you most like to visit? Why?

5 Which holiday destinations abroad and at home are popular with people from your country?

Presentation

Use your notes to help you give your talk to your group. Avoid just reading your notes out as that will not engage your listeners. Make eye contact, speak clearly and be prepared to answer questions.

Being a good listener

Remember, it is polite to show an interest in what the speaker is saying. Listen attentively to other group members' talks and have at least one question or comment ready to ask at the end.

16 Words from names

The island of Sardinia gave its name to the small oily fish called *sardines* (also known as pilchards). Many words in English are derived from the names of people or places.

1   Try to match these names to the people and places in sentences a–h. Check the meaning of any unfamiliar words.

Denim	Diesel	Fahrenheit
Marathon	Morse	Pasteur
Rugby	Sandwich	Volta

a   Lord _____ didn't have time for a proper meal, so he devised a way of eating meat between two slices of bread.

b   The Battle of _____ in Ancient Greece gave its name to a long-distance running race.

c   Gabriel _____ developed a thermometer which showed boiling and freezing points.

d   The city of Nîmes in France gave its name to a robust fabric called 'serge de Nîmes'. This was eventually shortened to _____, which is used to make jeans.

e   Samuel _____ invented a code of dots and dashes which could be used for sending messages over long distances.

f   Alessandro _____ invented the electric battery.

g   A boys' school in _____, England, gave its name to a type of sport where players carry the ball instead of kicking it.

h   Rudolf _____ devised a special type of oil-burning engine.

2   Are any words in your own language derived from names of places or people? Compare ideas with your classmates.

17 More homophones

Problems with homophones are the root of many spelling errors. Remember that homophones have the same sound but different spellings. (Look back at Unit 1, Section C11.)

1   Work with a partner to try to find a homophone for each of these words. The words have come from the texts you have read in this unit so far.

blue	boar	deer	flower
herd	meet	real	route
scene	sea	soar	wear

2   Put each homophone into a sentence.

D Personal challenges

1 Reading an example email

Read the email, which describes an activity holiday.
How good a description do you think it is?

> Hi Lucia,
>
> Wow! I've got so much to tell you. The activity holiday was really great. I loved Tasmania. You would too. Do you remember how scared I was before I went? I didn't think I'd find it easy to go away by myself, especially as I'd never done it before, but the group leaders were so kind to me and I never once felt alone.
>
> So we stayed in a converted boarding school in this really beautiful area. I had to share my room with two other girls, but we got on well and we've been Skyping each other since I got back. We were lucky with the weather as well! The guides said it could be unpredictable, but we only had one heavy downpour.
>
> Each day we did different things – there were so many activities to choose from! My favourite was canoeing. Didn't you do that somewhere a couple of years ago? Our instructor was really funny and made us relax. He even made the safety demonstration fun! He took us out on this lovely calm river near the school to practise our techniques, and I'm not trying to say that I'm a master canoeist or anything, but I'm pleased with what I learnt in a week.
>
> Right, I'd better bring this to an end now – this is a long email for me, isn't it? I just wanted to say that I think you'd love it there, Lucia – the place, the people, all the things you can do, everything. Tell me if you ever think of going because I might come with you!
>
> Email soon.
>
> Love,
>
> Fatima

2 Comprehension check

1   Where did Fatima go on holiday?

2   How did she feel before she went? Were her feelings justified?

3   What was her favourite activity? Why?

4   Why does she think Lucia would like the same type of holiday?

5   How does she feel overall about the trip?

3 Analysing the email

1   What is the main topic of each paragraph?

2   Analyse the language Fatima uses to describe:

- the place
- the activities
- the instructor
- her feelings.

3   How does she close the email? Consider the last sentence of the final paragraph and the closing phrase.

4 Vocabulary check: The weather

The weather, particularly on holiday, is a popular topic of conversation. Decide whether the following statements about the weather are likely to be true or false. Use a dictionary if necessary.

a   The blizzard made driving home easy.

b   The weather was showery so we had to water the garden every day.

c   Early in the morning, the grass is wet with dew.

d   At home, we switch on the lights at dusk.

e   I needed to put on my sunglasses because the sky was overcast.

f   The weather was so mild last winter that we hardly wore our coats.

g   The gale blew several trees over.

h   It's not worth hanging out the washing to dry as it has begun to drizzle.

i   Constant low temperatures and hard frosts meant there was no chance of a thaw.

j Farmers are very pleased to have a long period of drought.

5 Spelling revision

Some adjectives are formed from nouns by adding the suffix -y. You need to remember the rules for doing this.

A final -e in a word is usually dropped when adding -y.

Example: *ice – icy*

The rule for one-syllable words is that we double the final consonant if the word ends in one vowel and one consonant.

Examples: *sun   sunny   BUT   cloud   cloudy*

6 Writing about the weather

Choose an appropriate noun from the box and change it into an adjective to fill each gap in the postcard. Take care with your spelling.

```
storm   chill   mud   mist   fog

        haze   rain
```

POSTCAR

Hi everyone,

We're having a good time here but the weather isn't great. Every day starts _____ or even _____. This clears up by midday and we usually get a little _____ sunshine. We had a _____ day yesterday and the ground was too _____ for walking. It's generally _____ and I'm glad we brought warm clothes. Our boat trip was cancelled because it was _____. We're hoping for calmer weather tomorrow.

Love,

Cheng

7 Discussion

> Critical thinking Spending time in a developing country as a volunteer in a school, hospital or a charity project is very popular with young people. However, it is sometimes claimed that young, inexperienced students from affluent nations have little to offer the world's poorer countries. They enter a difficult situation with little training or worldly knowledge. They might have ideas that are inappropriate for the country. In addition, they might be very homesick – almost an extra burden on the charity.

How far do you agree with these ideas? Is there any way problems like these could be overcome? Discuss your views with your partner.

8 Building a blog from notes

Basima is working in a nursery school in Ecuador. She has started a blog so she can tell her friends back home about her new life. Use the notes to build up a complete blog entry.

At first / be very busy / but now / have time / update my blog/. I / enjoy myself here. The weather be warm / sunny / except for / last night / there be / big storm / which turn / paths / into rivers.

The family / I stay with / be very kind. The house be / three-bedroomed / and be quite comfortable. I be very close / my 'sisters' / who tell me off / if I do anything wrong! Each morning I wake up / sound / exotic birds / dart / among trees.

Yesterday I take / bus / through breathtaking countryside / to local city. I go / bustling market. Everywhere / people sell things / but I be not sure / was buy!

I help / look after / young children / nursery school. The children be delightful / and be very polite. The work be demanding / rewarding.

I miss everyone / home / but I feel / grow up quickly / and I be / more confident now.

I going to / upload / photos tomorrow and would love / read your comments.

9 Look, say, cover, write, check

1 Learn these commonly misspelt words using the 'look, say, cover, write, check' method (see Unit 1, Section B12 if you need a reminder).

Mediterranean	restaurant
accommodation atmosphere	glamour
separation jewel jewellery	pleasure

2 Ask a partner to test you when you are confident you have learnt them correctly.

3 Choose six of the words and put each one into a sentence to show its meaning.

10 Discussion

1 Talk to your partner about what you can see in the photograph.

2 Study these comments made by tour guides working in the tourist industry. Discuss each of them with your partner and decide if this work attracts either of you.

a It's essential that you like travel and, above all, have a lot of patience with people.

b Although the clients are on holiday, you've got to remember you're not on holiday and you must always be prepared to be responsible.

c Touring a country with a group makes it hard to keep up friendships at home.

d You have to be able to live for two weeks out of a suitcase or rucksack.

e You're with the group 24 hours a day on a tour. There's not much privacy.

f You've got to be well organised and methodical at all times. The arrangements you are in charge of can be very complicated.

11 Reordering a magazine article

The following article was uploaded onto a school website. Reorder the sentences logically and divide the article into three paragraphs. Underline the words and phrases that help you to link the text.

Life as a tour guide in Rhodes

a   Initially, they relied a lot on me to explain about the banks and shops and to recommend local restaurants and the best sightseeing trips.

b   Finally, I hope this has given you some idea of what life as a tour guide is all about.

c   The work itself is very varied, and I have the opportunity to meet new people and see interesting places.

d   I have groups of all ages.

e   In addition, there are many stunning, unspoilt beaches and peaceful villages.

f   It is the first time they have been abroad.

g   Although it gives you the chance to have lots of fun, it's not all glamour.

h   Now, however, they are much more relaxed.

i   However, if any of you are keen to get involved, I would definitely recommend it!

j   It's got an impressive old town and a new town with graceful, modern buildings.

k   In fact, they are more independent than many much younger tourists.

l   First of all, let me give you an idea of what Rhodes is like.

m   Next, I'd like to tell you a bit about my job.

n   At the moment, for example, I'm looking after a group of elderly people.

GRAMMAR SPOTLIGHT

Adverbs of frequency

- The adverbs of frequency *always, usually, often, seldom, rarely, hardly ever* and *never* show how often something happens.

  They usually go immediately before the main verb:

  *I **always take** too many clothes on holiday.*

  *You **never have** time to be bored on our activity holidays.*

  So if the verb has two parts, the adverb goes before the second (main) verb:

  *She **had never enjoyed** camping.*

- The word *sometimes* is another common adverb of frequency. It is different because it can go in three positions:

  ***Sometimes** I **eat** toast for breakfast.*

  *I **sometimes eat** toast for breakfast.*

  *I **eat** toast for breakfast **sometimes**.*

- With the verb 'be', adverbs of frequency go after the verb:

  *I **am usually** hungry after school.*

  *Joel **was sometimes** late for class.*

*Students **are always** met and escorted by holiday camp staff.*

Practice

1   Look at the descriptions in question 2 below. Find the frequency adverbs and underline them.

2   Correct the mistakes in these sentences by putting the adverb in the correct position. One sentence is already correct!

   a   I ride always my bike to school.

   b   Maria often goes swimming with her friends.

   c   He prefers usually the buffet-style breakfast.

   d   Visitors to the Taj Mahal seldom are disappointed.

   e   We play sometimes tennis after college.

   f   Lewis hardly ever is on time – it's so annoying!

   g   The children go rarely to the cinema.

   h   She never has been on holiday abroad.

Complete the practice activities in your Workbook.

EXAM-STYLE QUESTIONS

READING AND WRITING

Reading and writing: note-taking

Read the blog post about the ancient world of the Incas, and then complete the notes.

Hi to everyone who's interested in travel and adventure! I'm delighted to share my experiences as an archaeologist with you and hope they will inspire you to explore, travel and learn!

Ever since the age of 11, when I dug up a bronze statue in the garden and my parents found that it was 600 years old, I have been fascinated by the secrets of the past. My curiosity has taken me all over the world, and I have just returned from an expedition to Peru. I have been working with an international team in the Andes Mountains excavating to uncover remains of an old Inca city, Machu Picchu.

The Inca were an American Indian people who arrived in the central Andes about 1250 CE. They built up an empire in South America that stretched across modern Peru and Ecuador to parts of Bolivia, Chile and Argentina.

The Incas were ruled by an emperor, who had absolute power. They developed a rich and complex civilisation and had skills in engineering and architecture. They also studied astronomy – the movements of the planets. Ordinary people ate simple food – mainly vegetables, grains and dried fish. The capital was Cuzco. Like all Inca cities, it was beautiful, with paved roads and a magnificent palace. Quechua was the Inca language, but there was no system of writing. Although the empire was damaged by civil war and then conquered by the invading Spaniards in 1532 (who were attracted by Inca gold amongst other things), the Quechua language has survived. Thirteen per cent of the population of modern Peru speaks Quechua and it is also spoken elsewhere in the Andes.

When I was in Peru, I spent quite a bit of time working in the ruined city of Machu Picchu. You may have already heard of it because it is a World Heritage Site and attracts tourists and experts from all over the world. It is an amazing place, and the remains of the city are fascinating. Machu Picchu was built in a remarkable position. It was constructed on the side of a mountain high up in the Andes, about 2430 metres above sea level. It was a truly astonishing achievement to build the city in such a challenging mountainous location. It was made from stone, cut without iron tools. Some stone was cut from a quarry on site. Other rocks came from further away and – because wheeled vehicles were unknown - were pushed up the steep slope by hundreds of builders.

Beautiful houses, stunning temples and even fountains were constructed. More than a hundred stone staircases were made to connect different levels in the city. Perhaps most impressive of all, an observatory was built so astronomers could watch the movements of the sun, moon and stars. What better place to do stargazing than on a crystal-clear night high up in the mountains?

Archaeologists and historians have wondered why the city was built in such a remote and difficult position. One theory is that the site was chosen for religious reasons. The Incas believed that the gods they worshipped lived in the mountains and in water, so the landscape of Machu Picchu was perfect for honouring them.

The area was also a good place for the Incas to gather for ceremonies – especially for the winter and summer solstices, the shortest and longest days of the year. A temple in Machu Picchu was designed at a particular angle so that when the sun shone through the window on the winter solstice it lit up a stone shrine.

CONTINUED

Today, this historic site is a magnet for tourists. Around 1.5 million tourists visit the site every year, which has caused damage to some of the structures and the surrounding natural habitat. As a result, there are now restrictions on how many people can visit in a day and some areas are closed to visitors in an effort to preserve them for future generations. It is so important for all of us – tourists and visitors, as well as archaeologists – to help preserve the beauty and mystery of this fascinating site for future generations.

Imagine you are going to give a talk about the world of the Incas to your classmates. Use words from the blog post to help you write some notes.

Make short notes under each heading.

1   Unique features of Inca civilization:

Large empire in South America
_____

_____

_____

_____   [3]

2   Challenges faced by the Incas when building the city of Machu Picchu:

_____

_____

_____

_____   [4]

[Total: 7]

Reading and writing: informal

A friend has emailed you complaining that he/she is bored and asking you to recommend a new leisure activity.

Write an email to respond to your friend.

In your email, you should:

* suggest an interesting leisure activity
* explain why you think he/she would enjoy it
* say if any special equipment or training are required.

Write about 120 to 160 words.   [15]

[Total: 15]

CONTINUED

Reading and writing: informal

You have just arrived home from an adventure holiday climbing in the mountains.

Write an email about your holiday to a friend.

In your email, you should:

- explain why you chose that particular holiday
- describe exciting things you saw and did
- say why you would recommend this holiday to other people.

Write about 150 to 200 words.

[15 marks]

Reading and writing: formal

You have just returned from a week's activity holiday. Write a review of the holiday for a magazine.

In your review, describe the place, say what activities you enjoyed and suggest why other people would enjoy the holiday.

Here are some comments from teenagers on the same holiday:

> Ziplining across the river was the most exciting thing I've ever done.

> The hiking trip was too difficult for me – I was exhausted.

> The hostel was comfortable and everyone was very friendly.

> I really enjoyed learning how to kayak on the lake.

Now write a review.

The comments above may give you some ideas, and you should also use some ideas of your own.

Write about 120 to 160 words.

[15]

[Total: 15]

LISTENING

Listening: sentence completion

You will hear a museum tour guide giving a talk about Viking history and culture.

For each question, choose the correct answer, **A**, **B** or **C**, and put a tick (✓) in the appropriate box.

You will hear the talk twice.

CONTINUED

Now look at questions 1–8.

1   The guide starts his talk with reasons why the Vikings were impressive _____:

   A   warriors   ☐

   B   traders   ☐

   C   travellers   ☐   [1]

2   Their longships _____ because they were narrow and light.

   A   were easy to make   ☐

   B   travelled quickly   ☐

   C   could adapt easily   ☐   [1]

3   Some of their ships have been _____ the river.

   A   taken out of   ☐

   B   destroyed by   ☐

   C   returned to   ☐   [1]

4   Viking children learned to _____ and fight at an early age.

   A   find food   ☐

   B   make weapons   ☐

   C   sail ships   ☐   [1]

5   Not many shields and crossbows have been found because they _____:

   A   were lost at sea   ☐

   B   burned in fires   ☐

   C   decayed in the ground   ☐   [1]

6   The guide mentions that Vikings used bearskins _____:

   A   to keep themselves warm   ☐

   B   to scare their enemies   ☐

   C   to make clothes for fighting   ☐   [1]

7   The Vikings thought it was important that their weapons should be _____.

   A   attractive   ☐

   B   valuable   ☐

   C   heavy   ☐   [1]

8   When a Viking warrior died, his _____ was buried with him.

   A   bearskin   ☐

   B   sword   ☐

   C   helmet   ☐   [1]

[Total: 8]

CONTINUED

SPEAKING

Warm-up questions

Warm-up questions help you feel more relaxed before you move on to answering assessed questions.

Take turns asking and answering the questions. Speak for 1–2 minutes.

- Can you tell me about your school?
- What subject do you most enjoy at school?
- What kind of sport do you like?

Interview

Read the questions. In pairs, decide who will play the interviewer and who will play the student. Then role-play the interview. Speak for about 2–3 minutes. Change roles and role-play the interview again.

Your holidays

- Can you tell me about your favourite kind of holiday?
- Where do you usually go for your holidays?
- Where did you go for your last holiday?

Short talk

Read the options and compare them. You have one minute to prepare your talk. Now give a short talk to your partner. Speak for about 2 minutes. Change roles and listen to your partner's talk.

Holiday plans

You and your family are planning to go on holiday this summer and are considering the following options:

- a holiday in a small village in the countryside where you can go kayaking in a nearby lake and hiking
- a holiday in a large hotel with a swimming pool which is near the beach where you can go snorkelling and surfing.

Discuss the advantages and disadvantages of each option. Say which option you would prefer, and why.

Discussion

Read the discussion questions. In pairs, decide who will play the interviewer and who will play the student. Then role-play the discussion. Speak for about 3 minutes. Change roles and role-play the interview again.

- Many people think it is important to travel and visit other countries and cultures. What do you think?
- What factors should people consider when planning a holiday to a national park or place of natural beauty?
- Should people be discouraged from taking long flights to visit other countries for their holidays?
- What factors are most important to you when choosing a holiday destination?

For even more speaking practice, watch the videos about holidays in the digital coursebook

SELF-ASSESSMENT CHECKLIST

Reflect on what you have learnt in this unit. For each area listed, decide whether you feel confident or need more practice. If you feel you need more practice, you will find some ideas to help you in Advice for Success. Come back to your self-assessment scores later in your course and see if your confidence has improved.

I can ...	Need more practice	Fairly confident
discuss issues related to travel and tourism, using appropriate vocabulary		
scan for information in a brochure and an article		
write a description of an outdoor activity and a holiday destination, using vivid and engaging language		
identify detailed information in a conversation and take notes from a lecture		
express blame, admit responsibility and tell someone they are not to blame		
plan, prepare and give a short talk		

ADVICE FOR SUCCESS

This section is to help you help yourself. Choose the suggestions you like and adapt them if you want to. Make notes about what you do and how it helped you.

Extending your skills

1 Many students have difficulty concentrating on a topic for very long. In the modern world of the internet, smartphones and tablets, sustaining attention on a topic for a long time can be quite hard. Try to strengthen your powers of concentration. Time your ability to concentrate on a topic without getting distracted or having a break. Gradually try to extend the length of time you can do this. If you find yourself getting distracted, take a break and walk around the desk or get a drink of water. Then come back to your work.

Gradually, you will build up the length of time you can concentrate.

2 To increase your vocabulary, look up words in a collocations dictionary. This will help you identify words that frequently go together. Then try to use these words together in your writing.

3 At the end of each lesson, make notes of the main points and key words that you have learnt. Review them again a few hours later. Re-activating your knowledge at frequent intervals can help you to remember and retain new information.

4 When you finish reading an article or story, try summarising the main ideas in one or two sentences. Summarising helps you to identify key points and remember them better.

CONTINUED

Showcasing your skills

5   Read a composition question carefully and underline what you have to do. If you are given a detailed stimulus, such as a printed text from a magazine, be extra careful. Make sure you only write what is expected of you.

6   Make a very brief plan before you begin. Students sometimes panic at the thought of planning because they think it will use up valuable time. However, it is essential if you are to have a clear structure for your writing. If there is no time to write a complete essay, a clear plan will show what you were going to write.

7   Try to draw on personal experience in developing ideas for a description. This will make your writing sound more authentic and persuasive.

8   Aim to produce a mature style by using some of the techniques you have developed in this unit. Avoid lots of plain, short sentences with bland words like 'nice' or 'good'. Use clauses, comparisons, unusual adjectives and images to make your descriptions interesting and distinctive.

9   Description alone is not enough. You will have to explain your reasons for liking something. You usually have to say why you think other people would enjoy whatever it is, too. Try to give clear, interesting reasons that relate sensibly to your topic.

10 As always, check through your work for mistakes in spelling, grammar and punctuation.

11 Make sure you have written in paragraphs. If you haven't, the next best thing is to indicate where they should be. Aim to leave enough time to do this.

12 Always scan the text for factual detail. Look first for clues to meaning from pictures, headings, and so on. Then read the information quickly to get the gist before you try to answer questions. It is usually possible to 'spot' the information in the text.

13 Remember that, even if a text gives information about prices, and so on, you need to showcase your ability to read information carefully, not your mathematical skills.

>Unit 7
Student life

LEARNING INTENTIONS

In this unit you will:

- Explore the topic of study and student life

- Identify ideas, opinions and attitudes in a magazine article about exam stress

- Give advice in an email, using appropriate register and style

- Identify factual details and understand what is implied in a talk about student counselling

- Use a range of vocabulary and grammar for talking about problems and giving advice

10 Watch the video about student life
in the digital coursebook.

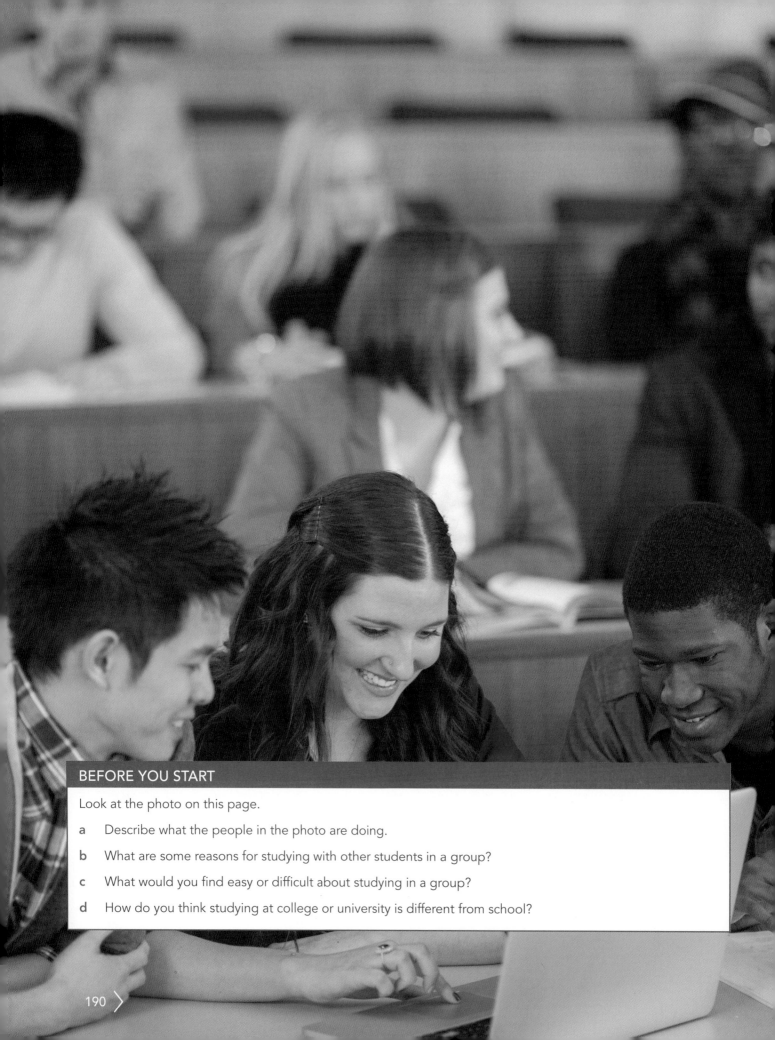

BEFORE YOU START

Look at the photo on this page.

a   Describe what the people in the photo are doing.

b   What are some reasons for studying with other students in a group?

c   What would you find easy or difficult about studying in a group?

d   How do you think studying at college or university is different from school?

A Challenges of student life

1 Completing a checklist

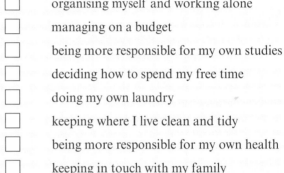

Checklist

- ☐ having my own place
- ☐ shopping for food and other essentials
- ☐ making sure I eat regularly and sensibly
- ☐ cooking for myself
- ☐ finding new friends
- ☐ organising myself and working alone
- ☐ managing on a budget
- ☐ being more responsible for my own studies
- ☐ deciding how to spend my free time
- ☐ doing my own laundry
- ☐ keeping where I live clean and tidy
- ☐ being more responsible for my own health
- ☐ keeping in touch with my family and friends

In many countries, it is traditional for students to leave home and attend a college or university in another city. This is usually an exciting and challenging time. If you left home to study, what do you think you would look forward to? What do you think you might find difficult?

Work by yourself. To help focus your thoughts, copy and complete the checklist. Mark the ideas on the checklist like this:

> ✓✓ I'd really look forward to this.
>
> ✓ I wouldn't mind this.
>
> ? I'm not sure how I'd feel about this.
>
> ✗ This would definitely worry me. I don't know how I'd cope.

If you have already left home to study, mark the checklist according to what you know about your ability to cope from your actual experience.

2 Pre-listening task

You are going to analyse the way two teenagers talking about starting university interact with each other.

Before you listen, answer these questions with a partner.

1   What do you think makes a good listener?

2   What makes a conversation lively and interesting?

3   What makes it dull or boring?

4   A good conversation may be likened to a game of table tennis. Why?

Improving communication

Here are some strategies people use to improve communication. Extend the list if you can.

Using good body language

- Looking and sounding interested

- Making eye contact

- Smiling and nodding

Asking open questions

- *How/What do you feel/think about . . . ?*

- *Why . . . ? What . . . ? Where . . . ? How . . . ? Is there anything else . . . ?*

Giving encouragement/reassurance

- *That's interesting. Tell me more.*

- *That's amazing. I'm really impressed.*

- *Don't worry! I'm sure you . . .*

Paraphrasing

- *You mean . . . ?*

- *Are you saying that . . . ?*

- *In other words, you feel . . . ?*

Asking for more information/clarification

- *What do you mean exactly? Can you explain a bit more?*

- *I'm not sure I follow you. Can you give me an example?*

Empathising/asking for empathy

- *I can see you're excited/anxious/upset.*

- *I know what you mean. / It's the same for me.*

- *Do you see what I mean? / Do you feel the same?*

Making suggestions / offering advice

- *Maybe you could . . .*

- *If I were you, I'd . . .*

- *It might be a good idea to . . . .*

- *Have you considered / thought about . . . ?*

- *Why don't you . . . ? / What about . . . .?*

3 Reading and listening at the same time

7.1

Now follow the conversation. As you listen, underline examples of interactive techniques.

Luke: How do you feel about starting university this autumn?

Malika: Oh, you know, I'm excited, but a bit anxious, too.

Luke: Really? What are you anxious about?

Malika: Well, I've never had to organise my timetable before and manage my study time. My teacher or my parents always remind me to study. I'm just not sure if I'll be able to stay motivated. Do you know what I mean?

Luke: But you always seem such an independent person! I think you're underestimating yourself. I'm sure you'll get the hang of it once you start. Is there anything else worrying you?

Malika: Well, I'm worried about making friends. I don't think I'm very good at meeting people and—

Luke: Oh, don't worry about that! I'm sure there will be plenty of opportunities to socialise and meet new people. Anyway, everyone'll be in the same boat!

Malika: That's true. How about you? Do you feel anxious about starting university?

Luke: Yes, I'm a bit anxious about finances. My parents are paying the tuition fees for me, but I'll also have a part-time job to help pay for my food and accommodation.

Malika: You mean you've already found a part-time job? I'm impressed!

Luke: Yes, it's in student services so I'll be on campus all the time.

Malika: That sounds excellent! Maybe you could start with just a few hours and increase them later when you have a better idea about your studies?

Luke: That's a very good idea. I'll try that! I'm also a bit worried that I won't be able to keep up with coursework.

Malika: What do you mean exactly? Can you give me an example?

Luke: I mean, what if I'm not clever enough to write all the essays and pass the exams? My parents have really high expectations of me!

Malika: I know exactly how you feel. It's the same for me. My parents want me to be a professor one day! Have you thought about talking to some of the students in the previous year and asking them for some tips?

Luke: No, but my mum's friend has a daughter who started there last year. Maybe I'll ask her for some advice.

4 Conversation study

Does the conversation between Luke and Malika sound friendly? With a partner, try to work out the tone of the conversation. To help, circle an example in the dialogue that illustrates each of these points.

a   The speaker shows a desire to understand.

b   The speaker offers advice in a friendly way.

c   The speaker tries to reassure and encourage.

d   The speaker tries to show empathy.

5 Developing your own conversation

1   Look back at the list you marked in Section A1 about the challenges of going to college or university. Think about the reasons for your answers.

2   Work in pairs to develop a conversation like the one above. You can base the conversation on starting college or university, or any other situation you find challenging, such as going away to stay with friends, starting a new school, or going on a group holiday without your family.

Remember:

- Explain your ideas clearly. Give reasons and examples.

- Say things that are true about yourself.

- Be good listeners to each other – interact well.

- Try to offer appropriate advice.

- Don't forget your body language.

6 Recording your conversation

Why not record your conversation and listen to it carefully? How well did you interact? Does it sound friendly and supportive? Have you helped each other explain your ideas?

7 Comparing languages

> Critical thinking You might like to record an informal discussion in your first language and compare the similarities and differences in interactive patterns with those of English. How do these affect the tone of the conversation?

8 Reading and discussing an email about problems

1   > Critical thinking Read this email written by Sheryl, a young university student, to a friend. What does she enjoy about university? What is she finding difficult? Did you note any of these points in your own discussion?

2   What advice would you give in reply? Share your ideas with your partner. Use suitable advice phrases, such as:

She should . . .

She could consider . . .

If I were her, I'd . . .

To... Bianca

From Sheryl

Subject: Hi

Hi Bianca,

I can't believe I'm already in my sixth week of **uni**. It took me a while to settle in, but now I'm starting to feel quite at home here. I'm attaching a photo of myself outside the university.

I meant to write earlier but there's so much going on all the time – lectures to go to, interesting people to meet, clubs to join – that I seem to be in a permanent state of confusion! I know organisation has always been my weak point, but it's getting ridiculous. I keep forgetting or losing things, or being late for lectures and **tutorials**. I'm behind with my assignments as well. Sometimes I think I'll never learn to cope with it all!

Is there any way I can get my act together? What do you think?

GLOSSARY

uni: university

tutorial: class where students are taught in a very small group

9 Reading an email offering advice

With a partner, read Bianca's reply. What do you think of the advice offered? How does it compare with your own ideas? Underline the advice phrases as you read.

Hi Sheryl,

1 It was great to hear from you. We miss you here – you're such a special person. Thanks also for the photo – what an impressive building!

2 I'm not surprised you feel chaotic and a bit overwhelmed. After all, only a few weeks ago you had your parents' routine and expectations, and a strict school timetable as well. Now you're suddenly expected to be completely responsible for yourself. When I started university, I remember things were a bit scary, but I found planning ahead was the key to getting organised.

3 One thing you might find helpful is to make a list each morning of things you have to do that day. Try to include everything on your list, from attending a lecture to returning your books to the library. Keeping on top of the assignments is challenging, too, but all you really have to do is draw up your own study timetable and stick to it. I know you're a 'morning' person, so why not schedule demanding intellectual tasks then? When you've got a minute during the day, don't forget to tick off things you've done.

4 The uni social scene sounds brilliant. You seem to be having a good time. I remember how popular and outgoing you were at school, so it must be tempting to say 'yes' to every social invitation. It's not a good idea to go out every night, though! You won't forget to pace yourself and save some time for **recharging your batteries**, will you?

5 I'll definitely be able to make the weekend of the 22nd. I'm really looking forward to seeing the college and meeting some of your new friends. I'm sure by the time we meet, you'll be super-organised ,and my advice will be irrelevant!

Love,

Bianca

GLOSSARY

recharging your batteries: resting after effort

10 Analysing the advice email

1 How does Bianca achieve an appropriate tone in the opening of the email? Which details are included to develop the opening paragraph more fully?

2 Paragraph 2 shows that Bianca understands why Sheryl feels confused. How does she define the problem for Sheryl? What link does she make with her own experience? How does this affect the tone?

3 Paragraph 3 offers Sheryl advice on being organised. Bianca doesn't sound bossy or superior – how does she achieve this? How is the advice linked to the writer's knowledge of Sheryl? How does this affect the tone of the email?

4 Paragraph 4 shows Bianca's attitude to Sheryl's social life. Her recognition of Sheryl's enthusiasm for parties is balanced by a note of caution. How is this expressed? Do you think Sheryl is going to be annoyed when she reads this, or is she likely to accept the advice?

5 The last paragraph confirms an invitation. How? Does Bianca manage to round off the email appropriately? How?

6 Circle the words and phrases in the email that create a warm and informal tone and register.

11 Advice phrases

> **Critical thinking** Here are some typical advice phrases. Which phrases are stronger and which are more low-key? Which phrases appeal to you?

> You need to . . .   You'd better . . .
>
> You really should . . .   If I were you, I'd . . .
>
> Why not . . . ?   Remember . . .
>
> You could always . . .   You could consider . . .
>
> Maybe you could . . .   All you have to do is . . .
>
> Try to . . .   You may like to try . . .
>
> How about . . . ?   You really ought to . . .
>
> You absolutely must . . .
>
> Have you ever thought of . . . ?

> Perhaps you need to . . .
>
> You know best, but perhaps you could . . .
>
> It's a good idea / not a good idea to . . .
>
> One thing you might find helpful is . . .

12 Expressing problems and asking for advice

1 The way people express their problems or ask for advice in English varies according to the seriousness of the situation and the formality of the context. Discuss the following statements and questions with a partner and suggest a context in which you might use each one.

a I'm frantic.

b I hope an acceptable solution can be found.

c I'm not sure what to do.

d I don't know what to do.

e What do you think would be best?

f I'd like some advice about this, please.

g I'm out of my mind with worry.

h What on earth should I do?

i I would be grateful for any suggestions you can make.

j Do you have any ideas about this?

2 How do you express problems in your own language and culture? What might be a problem in your country that isn't one in other English-speaking countries?

13 Listening to students' problems

1 You are going to hear six students talking about their problems. Based on the audio recording, choose the most appropriate opinion (A–G) for each speaker (1–6). There is one extra opinion that you do not need to use.

Speaker 1 ☐
Speaker 2 ☐
Speaker 3 ☐
Speaker 4 ☐
Speaker 5 ☐
Speaker 6 ☐

A I think I made the wrong choice.

B I don't know what subject to study.

C I'd like to have more friends.

D I have to make a difficult choice.

E I need to be more creative.

F I'd like to be more confident.

G I sometimes misunderstand instructions.

2 Listen again and think of one more piece of advice for each student.

14 Tone and register in students' emails

1 〉 **Critical thinking** Oliver has just moved to a new town and started going to college. Working in groups of three or four, choose one person to read out this extract from an email he wrote to a friend at his old school.

> The tutors are very helpful at my new college but it's hard to make friends. I spend all my spare time watching TV. How can I meet some friendly people?

If you were in Oliver's shoes, how would you be feeling? What would you hope to hear in reply? Share your ideas in the group.

2 The following are openings to emails that students wrote in reply. In your group, take turns reading them aloud. Decide whether the tone and register sound right or not, and why.

a I received your email of 1 December explaining that you are not satisfied with your new life. If people don't like you, you must face the situation and solve it. There are many suitable activities you should take up, which would help you overcome this feeling.

b It was great to hear from you – knowing you had problems really made my day. The way I see it is that you're glued to the TV. All I can say is you should join a sports club. It will be useful for your health and good exercise for your legs.

c You might want to know why I haven't written. I have been working in my grandfather's shop. I get paid even though I'm working for my family. I meet lots of new people and the work is interesting too. What is your ideal career?

d I hope you're happier now since writing me that awful email. Why do you feel lonely? Don't you have friends there? You said how bored you are at your new college. I think there are many places of entertainment which you haven't looked for. Don't always be sorry for yourself. You ought to adapt yourself to your new world.

e I was sorry to hear that you're not enjoying your new college as much as you deserve to. I know how you must be feeling because we had to move a lot with Dad's job. However, have you considered joining the college drama club? You used to give some brilliant performances in the school theatre society. With your acting talent and sociable personality, I'm sure it won't be long before you're striking up new friendships.

15 Rewriting a paragraph

1 Choose one of the paragraphs you thought was inappropriate and rewrite it.

2 When you are ready, read out your new version to the group, explaining the reasons for any alterations you have made.

B The pressure of exams

1 Pre-reading task

Studying for exams can be stressful. You are going to read interviews with three students, their mothers and an education expert, about some of the problems that students say they have with exams.

Read through the problems in pairs or groups of three. Can you suggest any solutions? Share your ideas with other groups.

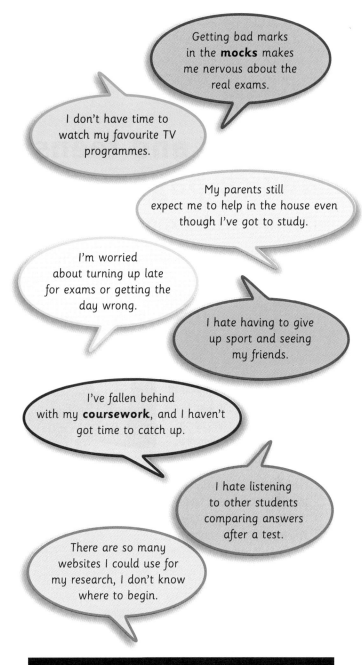

Getting bad marks in the **mocks** makes me nervous about the real exams.

I don't have time to watch my favourite TV programmes.

My parents still expect me to help in the house even though I've got to study.

I'm worried about turning up late for exams or getting the day wrong.

I hate having to give up sport and seeing my friends.

I've fallen behind with my **coursework**, and I haven't got time to catch up.

I hate listening to other students comparing answers after a test.

There are so many websites I could use for my research, I don't know where to begin.

GLOSSARY

mocks: tests that are set by teachers in preparation for the real exams

coursework: work such as projects, assignments and classwork done during the school year, which are marked by the teacher as part of the final exam mark

2 Reading for gist

Skim-read the following magazine article. Does the advice given include any of the ideas you thought of? Try to work out the meaning of any unfamiliar words from the context.

Parents and teens advice page:

Dealing with exam stress

Ask our counsellor for advice on common study problems.

Radek: When it gets near to exam time, I start getting headaches and stomach pains. I find it difficult to get
5 to sleep and sometimes I get panic attacks in the middle of the night. It's really hard to get down to revising and doing practice questions, which is
10 what I know I should be doing.

Radek's mum: I always know when exams are approaching because Radek starts to get very withdrawn. He often doesn't come down for dinner or finish his food. When I ask what's wrong, he just mumbles that he's busy
15 with schoolwork and doesn't have time to eat. I wish he'd talk to me more about what he's going through.

Counsellor: It's clear that Radek is aware of the signs of stress and realises that they are preventing him from doing his best. His mother also mentions mood and personality
20 changes. Radek should be encouraged to open up about the reasons for his anxiety, which can help to keep things in perspective. Creating the right conditions for a supportive conversation is definitely a good way to move forward. Make sure to listen carefully to each other, without judging,
25 and offer as much support and encouragement as possible. If you feel that you can't achieve this by yourselves, perhaps think about asking another family member or friend to help start a dialogue about ways to stay calm and reduce anxiety.

30 **Fauzia:** When it comes to revising for exams, I've so many different subjects that I just don't know where to start. It's really overwhelming.
35 Just looking at the pile of books on my desk makes me start to stress out! Sometimes

I'm up until three in the morning and it seems like I haven't done very much at all. I often get a mental block and I'm
40 constantly worried that I'm going to fail.

Fauzia's dad: We've always encouraged Fauzia to work hard and do her best, and that's all we expect from her. But I know she feels under emotional pressure from us and suffers from exam nerves. I'd like to help her organise her
45 time better, but at the same time, I don't want to discourage her from studying because that is what's going to help her get ahead in the future.

Counsellor: It is true that some stress can motivate you to study harder. Too much stress, on the other hand, can have
50 a detrimental effect. The fact that Fauzia is always thinking about the exams means that she can never rest or relax. Encourage Fauzia to plan a timetable for revision and tick off tasks that have been completed. This can help her to set realistic goals. A regular home routine with time for breaks
55 and a chance to relax is also a good way to help Fauzia achieve her best. Another suggestion might be for her to find a quiet place to study away from her bedroom, so that she won't think about exams when she is there.

Kenzo: I think I'm quite
60 good at dealing with exam stress. If I feel stressed, I just go for a run or out on my bike to chill out. But I tend to leave exam prep to
65 the last minute! Sometimes I'm up all night before an exam. I usually do OK though, except sometimes I run out of time in the exam and can't
70 answer all the questions. My favourite subjects are maths

and computer science, and I usually get top marks in those without having to revise too much.

Kenzo's dad: I don't think Kenzo takes exams seriously
75 enough, to be honest. He thinks he can just sail through
with a pass and that's fine. That's not the way I studied
when I was young. I'd like him to be a bit more ambitious
and think about the future. If he works hard now, he can
get into a good university and, ultimately, that will affect
80 his career.

Counsellor: It's a good idea to sit down together and try to
understand each other's point of view. Obviously, you and
Kenzo have different priorities right now but if you are open
to discussion, perhaps you can find some common ground.
85 One idea could be to help Kenzo by working with him on his
revision or finding some fun and attractive web tools that
will engage him and increase his motivation.

Ayesha: My parents are
always nagging me about
90 spending too much time on
social media. They've said I
can't go out with friends during
the week, which I'm OK with,
but then I end up having to stay
95 in touch with them on social
media instead. Sometimes we talk about schoolwork, and we
also help each other out if we're feeling stressed. But it's true
that I get too easily distracted and start swiping through lots
of messages and other websites to see what's going on.

1003 **Ayesha's mother:** I don't like nagging, but she really
should put the phone away when she wants to concentrate
on her schoolwork. I keep telling her, but she won't
listen! There's so much peer pressure nowadays to post
messages and share photos all the time. I don't know what
105 I can do about it really. Maybe I should really put my foot
down and take her phone away.

Counsellor: I don't think that taking her phone away will
help. Ayesha really needs to learn how to manage her
own time. Why don't you sit down together and design a
110 compromise plan, where Ayesha takes a one-hour break
from using the phone to do some revision and then takes a
ten-minute break to check her messages. Using her phone
needs to be seen as a reward for making progress with her
revision. If you can agree on a short-term plan to start off
115 with and then gradually increase the time between breaks,
it might help Ayesha to find the right balance between
study time and social media time.

3 Comprehension check

For each question, identify the speaker in the article.
Which student:

a   is not good at sticking to a revision plan?

b   needs to cut down on chatting with friends?

c   has no trouble avoiding exam nerves?

d   experiences physical and mental symptoms
of stress?

e   feels stressed by parents' expectations?

f   asks friends for help with reducing exam anxiety?

g   needs to practise timed exam-style questions?

h   should try to discuss negative feelings more?

i   needs to break down a revision plan into
smaller chunks?

j   needs to set boundaries between study time and
free time?

4 Post-reading discussion

〉 **Critical thinking** Work in pairs to discuss the
following questions:

1   Who do you think is the most hard-working of the
students? Try to say why.

2   Which students do you sympathise with
most? Why?

3   Do you agree with the counsellor's advice for each
student? Do you think the counsellor was generally
helpful or too critical?

4   What do you think, in general, of the attitudes of
the parents?

5   Are there any other ways these students could help
themselves? What do you think?

6   What are the methods you feel work best for
you when you are studying for exams? Share
your thoughts.

7   The counsellor suggests making a revision
timetable. How useful are timetables?

8   Imagine you are going to revise for an important exam. Which do you think would be the best place to study? Work in groups of three. Discuss the advantages and disadvantages of each place.

5   Vocabulary: Colloquial words and phrases

1   The following colloquial words and phrases were used in the article. Use them to replace the words in italics in the sentences below.

exam nerves	nagging	open up
sailed through	stick to	stressed out

a   It's a good idea to *talk honestly* about your feelings.

b   Luckily, I don't suffer from *anxiety before a test*.

c   I have a study timetable and I am determined to *persevere with* it.

d   My parents are constantly *telling* me *off* for staying up late.

e   I always get *really anxious* before a music exam.

f   He didn't do any work before the exam but *passed without any effort*.

2   Do you know any other verbs to describe anxiety or relaxation? Look up the meanings of these words: *chill out, calm down, wind down, be laid back, get worked up, panic, burnt out*. Use these verbs to ask your partner questions.

Example: *What do you do when you want to chill out?*

6   Word building

Building nouns from verbs

The counsellor advises Radek's mother to offer '*support and encouragement*'. The suffix -ment can be added to some verbs to make nouns.

1   Add -*ment* to each of the following verbs to make a noun.

2   Use each one in a sentence to show its meaning.

achieve	appoint	arrange
astonish	disagree	entertain
improve	manage	

Building adjectives from nouns

Fauzia was described as being under '*emotional pressure*'. The suffix -*al* can be added to some nouns to make adjectives.

1   Add -*al* to each of the following nouns to make an adjective.

2   Use each one in a sentence to show its meaning. Be careful, as the spelling sometimes changes, too.

magic	culture	music	function
classic	mathematics	person	nature

7 Language study: Giving advice

Here are some expressions used in the article to give advice.

A   Radek should be encouraged to open up about the reasons for his anxiety.

B   Encourage Fauzia to plan a timetable for revision and tick off tasks that have been completed.

C   Using her phone needs to be seen as a reward for making progress with her revision.

D   Ayesha really needs to learn how to manage her own time.

1   Which advice sounds most direct? Which is least direct?

2   Which advice verb is followed by *to + infinitive*? Which verbs are followed by the infinitive without *to*?

3   How would you change statements A, B and D into questions?

4   How would you make B, C and D into negative statements?

5   Can you replace *should, need(s) to* and *must* with any other expressions of similar meaning? What are they?

8 *Should/shouldn't have*

Using *should/shouldn't + have + past participle* has a different meaning from giving advice. With a partner, try to work out the meaning from these examples.

a   She should have taken an umbrella with her. I told her it was going to rain!

b   You shouldn't have bought her chicken-flavoured crisps when you knew she was a vegetarian.

c   He should have checked the exam timetable before he took the day off to play football.

d   I shouldn't have lost my temper about something so unimportant.

e   You should have telephoned to cancel your appointment if you couldn't come.

Practice

Join each pair of sentences to make one sentence containing should have or shouldn't have and a suitable linking word.

a   Joseph took a part-time job. He had exams coming up.

b   Indira went to the concert. She had an exam the next day.

c   He didn't check his bank balance. He spent a lot of money.

d   I shouted at my brother. He was trying to be helpful.

e   I borrowed my sister's jacket. I didn't ask her first.

f   Why didn't you buy some extra bread? You knew we needed to make sandwiches.

9 Using a more informal tone

Rewrite these sentences to make them sound more informal. Use the verbs *should, ought, need, must* or *had better*.

a   It isn't necessary for me to cook. Bruno is taking us out for a meal.

b   It is necessary to do your homework at a regular time each evening.

c   It was unwise to make a promise you can't keep.

d   It was wrong to leave all my revision to the last minute.

e   It's vital that Abdul gets more rest or he will fail his exams.

f   I regret not having listened to her advice.

g   It was wrong of him to play computer games instead of revising for the exam.

10 Spelling and pronunciation: Silent letters

Many English words contain silent letters. They can be at the beginning of words, as in:

wrinkle   knitting

psychology   honour

in the middle, as in:

salmon   foreigner

cupboard   listener

or at the end, as in:

comb   autumn

Sometimes a pair of letters is silent, as in:

right   daughter

Practise saying the words above with a partner. Check each other's pronunciation.

11 Identifying silent letters

1 The following words contain silent letters. Work with a partner to cross out the letters that are not pronounced.

a	design	g	should
b	answers	h	calm
c	what	i	circuit
d	law	j	assignment
e	night	k	weight
f	science	l	hours

2 Now practise saying the words correctly with your partner. Do you both agree that your pronunciation is correct?

12 Adding silent letters

Complete the following sentences with the correct missing silent letters. Choose from the letters in the box.

c	h	k	p	u
g	gh	l	t	w

a Lena must be the bri_ _test toddler in the nursery because she already _nows how to ta_k and say the alphabet.

b He wou_dn't lis_en to the expert's advice.

c He goes to the gym to do circ_it training after college.

d W_ereabouts do you go to college?

e Do you want a ha_f or a _hole bag of sweets?

f Can you _rite your ans_ers here?

g We turn on the li_ _ts when it gets dark.

h He hurt his _rist and his _nee when he fell over.

i Snow is always w_ite.

j _onesty is the best policy.

k These flowers have a lovely s_ent.

l The referee blows the w_is_le if something is _rong.

m She _rote under a _seudonym as she wanted to keep her identity secret.

n Their queen rei_ned for over 30 years.

o She is _sychic and can tell the future.

13 Detecting patterns

1 Can you see a regular pattern for any of the silent letters? Discuss your ideas with a partner and note any patterns you can detect.

2 Are there any silent letters in your own language? Share some examples in your group.

14 Idiomatic expressions

Try to work out the meaning of the idiomatic expressions in italics below from the context. (They each contain silent letters.)

1   I find the countryside too quiet and prefer the *hustle and bustle of city life*.

2   I thought the suitcase would be very heavy, but when I picked it up it was *as light as a feather*.

3   He *risked life and limb* to save the baby from the burning car.

15 Look, say, cover, write, check

Silent letters often cause spelling mistakes. Students say they sometimes forget to include them in a word. Here is a list of words with silent letters that often cause spelling problems.

1   Check the meaning of each word.

2   Try to identify the silent letter(s) in each word.

3   Use the 'look, say, cover, write, check' method to learn each word correctly (see Unit 1, Section B12 if you need a reminder).

sign	height	honour	yacht
listener	knock	scene	yolk
daughter	rhyme	rhythm	doubt
lightning	psychiatrist	overwhelming	

4   Ask a partner to test you when you are confident you have learnt them correctly.

5   Choose six of the words and put each one into a sentence to show its meaning.

C   Studying effectively

1   Punctuation reminders

Correct punctuation is important because it helps make meaning clear.

Full stops and capital letters

Remember, full stops are used to end a sentence. A capital letter is needed at the beginning of a new

sentence. Capital letters are also used for the names of people (*Ayesha, Pepe*), place names (*Cairo, the Amazon*) and acronyms (*BBC, DNA*).

1   Here is a description of how one student does homework. Punctuate it correctly. Remember to read it first to get the correct sense.

> *I need a few quiet moments to myself when i get in from school i have a drink and relax for a while then i get out my homework i work at a desk in the corner of the living room it is peaceful but not silent i like French and maths homework the best*

Apostrophes

Remember, apostrophes are used to indicate possession (*Zina's pen, the girls' coats*) and to show that a letter is missing (*it's hot*).

2   Punctuate the next part of the description.

> *ive got a few reference books which i keep on a shelf above my desk i borrow my brothers paints for artwork and i use my sister's laptop for essays ive used my dad's tools for some technology projects too they dont mind me borrowing their things as long as i look after them*

Commas

Commas are used in the following ways.

*   To separate things in a list:

    Example: *I need pens, pencils, rulers and a rubber.*

*   To separate a non-defining clause or an extra phrase from the main sentence:

    Example: *Mr Rivers, our geography teacher, comes from Nigeria.*

- To separate a participle phrase from the main clause:

  Example: *Having run all the way to the station, we were disappointed to find the train had just left.*

- After certain linking words and phrases:

  Example: *On the other hand, . . . ; Nevertheless, . . . ; However, . . .*

These are just some of the uses of commas. Remember, we generally put commas where we would pause in speech.

3 Now punctuate the rest of the extract correctly.

> our school has a homework link on the school website this means that you can use the homework page to check the homework youve been set it also prevents students getting too many subjects for homework at once about two years ago i had english history german physics biology maths and technology homework on the same night it was a nightmare the homework page prevents these problems however it also means teachers refuse to accept silly excuses for not handing in homework

2 Rewriting an email

Read the following email, which was written to a student who is not able to join his friends on holiday as he needs to retake an examination.

1 First, read it carefully to get the sense.

2 Then discuss it with a partner and rewrite it as necessary. Expect to make at least two drafts. You should consider:

- The paragraphing – Remember, a new paragraph is usually needed for a change of topic.

- The tone and register – Are they right for this situation? If not, think of alternative expressions you could use.

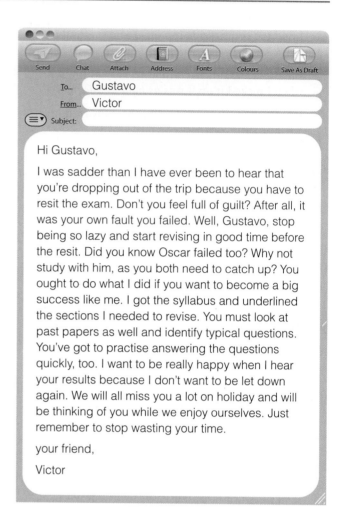

To... Gustavo
From... Victor
Subject:

Hi Gustavo,

I was sadder than I have ever been to hear that you're dropping out of the trip because you have to resit the exam. Don't you feel full of guilt? After all, it was your own fault you failed. Well, Gustavo, stop being so lazy and start revising in good time before the resit. Did you know Oscar failed too? Why not study with him, as you both need to catch up? You ought to do what I did if you want to become a big success like me. I got the syllabus and underlined the sections I needed to revise. You must look at past papers as well and identify typical questions. You've got to practise answering the questions quickly, too. I want to be really happy when I hear your results because I don't want to be let down again. We will all miss you a lot on holiday and will be thinking of you while we enjoy ourselves. Just remember to stop wasting your time.

your friend,

Victor

3 Reading aloud

Read your new version to your group.

4 More idiomatic expressions

The idioms in italics in the following sentences express feelings and attitudes. Discuss each with a partner and choose the definition you feel is correct:

1 At the party, the other students *gave her the cold shoulder.*

    A They ignored her.

    B They offered her cold meat.

    C They told her they disliked her.

    D They made her promise to keep a secret.

C   I always expect to do well in exams.

D   I believe I'll fail the next one.

5   When I told her she'd won the scholarship, she thought I was *pulling her leg*.

A   She didn't like the way I explained it.

B   She was convinced I was joking.

C   She thought I wanted something from her.

D   She was angry and walked away.

6   I thought this training programme would be right for me, but now I feel that I'm *out of my depth*.

A   The programme is generally too difficult for me.

B   The programme is working out more expensive than I expected.

C   The other trainees dominate the discussions.

D   The instructor gave me the wrong idea about the course.

5   Increasing your stock of idioms

Select the idiomatic expressions you would like to remember from Section C4. Use each in a sentence of your own to show its meaning.

6   Sentence correction

The following sentences from students' emails contain mistakes of grammar and vocabulary.
Try to rewrite them correctly.

a   If you be wisdom one, you follow your teacher advice.

b   You should build up a correct concept of mind to your work.

c   The qualities of good friend is invisible but uncountable.

d   You shouldn't never tell no one your password, or they can be accessible to your personal information.

e   Your email talking ideas many people thinking too.

2   When I read the exam paper, *I couldn't make head or tail of it*.

A   I realised I could not finish in the time.

B   I could not understand any of the questions.

C   I found the second part of the paper very difficult.

D   I could do only half the total number of questions.

3   He's *set his heart on* becoming a doctor.

A   He's sure he'll be a successful doctor.

B   He's very emotional about becoming a doctor.

C   He's very realistic about his prospects.

D   He really wants to qualify as a doctor.

4   I've never failed an exam, *touch wood*.

A   It's due to my careful preparation.

B   I really hope my good luck continues.

INTERNATIONAL OVERVIEW

Most popular countries for international students

Study the information in the bar graph and then answer the questions with a partner.

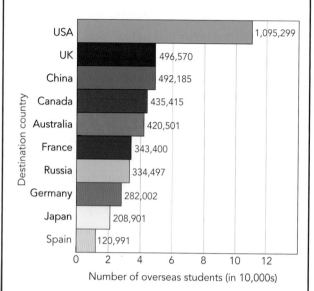

Numbers of overseas students (in 10,000s)

Numbers of overseas students studying in ten different countries, 2020

1   How many countries are being compared?

2   Which is the third most popular country for international students?

3   Which country has just under half the number of international students as Australia?

4   If you were choosing to study abroad, where would you like to go? Share your ideas with a partner, explaining why that country would appeal to you.

D Advising and helping

1 Pre-listening tasks

1   Some people turn to professional counsellors if they have problems. The following points are sometimes made in favour of counsellors. In groups of three or four, discuss how far you agree with them.

- Counselling is a real skill, and the counsellors are properly trained and qualified.

- Their advice is objective.

- It's not embarrassing to see a counsellor because you won't have to deal with them in any other role (e.g. employer, friend).

2   Can you see any disadvantages in going to a counsellor? Would you consult one? Why / Why not?

3   You are going to listen to a university counsellor talking to a group of new students about the counselling services available at the university. Her talk will cover the following topics:

- different areas of counselling

- different types of resources.

What would you like to find out about each of these? Write a question of your own on each topic. Compare your questions with those of a partner.

2 Listening for gist

Listen to the talk. Which of your questions are answered?

3 Detailed listening

Now listen to the talk again and complete the notes below.

Inference

What can you infer from the talk about the reason why students might not always take advantage of personal counselling services? Try to think of at least two or three reasons. (Remember, *inference* means drawing reasonable conclusions from the information given when it is not explicitly stated.)

4 Rewriting an email giving advice

1 You know that a friend of yours, Roberto, has difficulty getting on with his younger brother. He says that his brother scribbles on his posters, plays with his phone and starts arguments with him. What kind of advice would you give? Note your ideas.

2 Now read the advice that was written to Roberto by a fellow student. Do you think the tone and register sound right for the situation? Try to work out why or why not.

Rewrite the email, making any changes you think are appropriate.

Where? Who? What?

The counselling centre is located on the **(a)** _____ floor of the student services building.
It provides:

- a team of trained counsellors

- a resource centre

- talks and **(b)** _____

- walk-in visits and individual **(c)** _____ .

What kind of services?

- academic support

- **(d)** _____

- advice on mental health and and **(e)** _____ (information is not given to anyone without **(f)** _____)

- help for students with disabilities to **(g)** _____ or do examinations, help for students with learning difficulties

Where to get more information?

- open every weekday from 9 a.m. to **(h)** _____

- drop in for **(i)** _____

- phone or email

- website, which is updated every **(j)** _____ .

Send | Chat | Attach | Address | Fonts | Colours | Save As Draft

To... Roberto

From... Daniel

Subject:

Hi Roberto,

I was devastated to hear of this tragic problem. It seems as if your brother has ruined your life. I know that you have always been untidy and careless. The result of this behaviour is that your little brother can find your things and spoil them. It seems as if you are bad-tempered and impatient with him too. Of course he will not like you if you are unkind to him. You must learn to put away your things and control your moods. I also have a younger brother, so I am very careful to put my things away in a place where he cannot reach them. My younger brother and I have a close relationship. We play football together and I help him with his homework. We no longer quarrel because I am not selfish and have tried to understand him. We discussed the problem calmly with my parents. I did not shout or get angry which, as I see it, would be your reaction. It is a pity you cannot do the same.

Please write to me telling me that you have resolved your horrible problem. I hope to hear that there is a better atmosphere in your home.

All the best,

Daniel

5 Building a letter from a list of points

Planning

You read about this problem in your school newsletter:

I never seem to be in the right mood for homework or have the right stuff with me. I end up on websites that have nothing to do with anything! I am always getting distracted by my phone, too. My parents are fed up with me. Any ideas?

Polly

1. Discuss this problem with a partner and write down your thoughts about what could help Polly.

2. Read the following list of helpful homework tips, then add any ideas of your own to the list.

- Have something special to look forward to when you finish your homework.

- Don't leave it too late in the evening to start your homework.

- Make sure you understand what homework you have to do before you leave school.

- Put your phone on silent or put it away in a drawer.

- Keep the equipment you need for your homework (pens, reference and books) where you can find it at home.

- On the internet, be selective and avoid clicking on links that are not relevant.

- Plan your time: short, concentrated sessions are better than one long session.

- Save useful website addresses for research topics in your 'favourites' list.

- Use a clear surface to work on.

- Keep a homework diary to help you keep a check on the homework you have done.

Writing

Write a reply to Polly that will be published in the newsletter. Offer her some advice about doing homework. Choose ideas from the list of tips. Develop the points into three paragraphs. Use a friendly tone and register. Remember to add an opening and closing sentence.

6 Pre-writing discussion

> Critical thinking

1 Do you think bullying is a common problem? What are the differences between bullying in person and online bullying? Why do you think some people become bullies? Discuss these questions in groups of three.

2 A younger friend of yours emails you, saying:

> A boy in my class is bullying me. He keeps sending me horrible emails and makes sarcastic comments about my appearance and clothes on social media. If I report him to a teacher, it'll just get worse. What can I do?

What advice would you give to help your friend? Write down a few ideas.

7 Email completion

Now try to complete this email giving advice about bullying.

Send   Chat   Attach   Address   Colour Save As Draft

To... Leroy
Cc...
Subject:

Dear Leroy,

Thanks for your email, which I got this morning. It's always good to hear from you. I was really upset to hear that you are going through a hard time at your new school. Online bullying is a very common problem, and I'm sure you're not the only one. There are a number of things you could do to improve the situation . . .

From

Me

GRAMMAR SPOTLIGHT

'Text speak'

A text message is a concise form of writing. It is usually very informal and written in 'text speak' instead of proper sentences. As you already know, 'text speak' is not appropriate for formal situations.

Typical features of text messages are:

- missing pronouns, e.g. *Will try to call* = I will try to call.

- missing articles, e.g. *Bus is late* = The bus is late.

- missing capital letters, e.g. *saw maya at meeting in dubai* = I saw Maya at the meeting in Dubai.

- missing prepositions, e.g. *Train arrives madrid 8pm* = The train arrives in Madrid at 8 p.m.

- very little or no punctuation, e.g. *cant talk now will call later* = I can't talk now. I'll call later.

- special 'text speak' abbreviations and unusual spellings, e.g. *b4* = before, *2day* = today, *l8r* = later, *c u soon* = (I'll) see you soon, *yr* = your, *y'day* = yesterday, *2moro* = tomorrow.

All these features are used in order to save time when texting.

Some people use a lot of these features when they are texting, while others don't. You can, of course, make up your own 'text speak', if you think the other person will understand what you mean. There are no rules – it's up to you!

Practice

Study these extracts from text messages and then try to rewrite them in full sentences, with correct grammar, spelling and punctuation. You also need to make the style of one of them more appropriate to the situation.

a   hi libby! hope yr w/end in dublin went well

b   sorry but cant come 2nite. will fone u when i get home.

c   on way but gonna b 20 min late lotta traffic plse w8 4 me

d   hiya mr poulos! yeah gr8! i definitely want 2 take the job. thanks!

e   wl txt b4 i come round 2 make sure u r in

Complete the practice activities in your Workbook.

EXAM-STYLE QUESTIONS

READING

Reading and writing: open response

Read the following information from the University of Sydney website, and then answer the questions.

The University of Sydney

A history of thinking forward

Since 1852, when the doors of Sydney University opened for the first time, our founding principle as Australia's first university was that we would be a modern and progressive institution, supporting students of all backgrounds to further their education. The first degrees were given in 1856 and, in 1881, we became one of the first universities in the world to admit female students. Our university has produced pioneers in medicine, sport, the arts, politics and science.

From the start, we believed that financial issues should not stop students from learning. Students from lower income families, for example, have been given the chance to access further education through grants and scholarships, enabling them to benefit from the excellent educational opportunities we offer.

Study in our famous city

As a student at Sydney University, you're never far from Sydney's famous harbour, the Opera House or its beaches. The city abounds in culture and café life. If you head to the eastern suburbs, you can spend a lazy Sunday afternoon, and it won't cost you anything at all.

To get the most out of your time at university, you should also explore the clubs and societies on offer. The University of Sydney Union (USU) runs more than 200 clubs and societies in which you can make new friends. The clubs and societies are student-run, which means that you can get leadership experience if you help organise a club.

A place to live

We offer accommodation in college environments on campus and we also have self-catering accommodation off campus. College accommodation on campus is a great way to make the transition to independence.

Some students prefer to live off campus in the nearby suburbs instead of staying in university residences or colleges. This type of accommodation can book up fast, so be sure to start looking early and use our off-campus housing database to find rental accommodation that suits your needs.

Most students settle down quickly and easily to university life, but we do provide a one-on-one counselling service to support students who may be struggling to learn effectively due to psychological or emotional factors that affect their well-being. The service is completely confidential and staffed by trained personnel.

Our student card

The student card provides many benefits. As well as being proof of identity, it allows you to access buildings, borrow from the library, print and photocopy documents, and gives you access to a wide range of travel and student discounts. To access our 24-hour Study Centre after hours, tap your student card on the reader by the door.

The first semester

Use the first week of semester to get organised. While most students adapt to independent learning readily, others can find it problematic. If you are confused or worried because you do not know how to organise your study time effectively, do seek advice from our student mentors who can help you structure your schedule and give you study tips.

CONTINUED

1 When did students first graduate from Sydney University?

_____ [1]

2 In what way did the university change after 30 years?

_____ [1]

3 Which area of Sydney offers leisure opportunities free of charge?

_____ [1]

4 What skills can you gain by helping to organise the University's clubs and societies?

_____

_____ [1]

5 How can you get into the Study Centre at midnight?

_____ [1]

6 How does the University help students overcome potential barriers to learning?

Give **three** details.

_____

_____

_____ [3]

[Total: 8]

WRITING

Reading and writing: informal

You have a friend who is very nervous before exams. She has some important exams coming up and you would like to help her to be successful.

Write an email to your friend to offer advice.

In your email you should:

- describe some ways she could revise effectively
- suggest some things that would help her relax
- explain the importance of following the exam instructions.

Write about 120 to 160 words. [15]

[Total: 15]

CONTINUED

Reading and writing: informal

Your grandparents, who are both quite elderly, live in another town and would like to visit you at your school or college. They would like to stay in a modestly priced guesthouse.

They can stay for only three days and are anxious to see as much as possible. Write them an email in which you:

- welcome them

- offer advice about accommodation and travel

- suggest ways to make the most of their trip.

Write about 120 to 160 words. [15]

[Total: 15]

Reading and writing: formal

You recently went on a school trip to a science museum. Your headteacher has asked you to write a review of the trip for the school website.

In your review, say what you learned, what you enjoyed most and what you would change next time.

Here are some comments from students in your class:

> We didn't have enough time to try out all the science experiments.

> I learnt a lot about microchips and circuits.

> The robot-building laboratory was really exciting.

> We spent too much time waiting to go into the planetarium.

Now write your review for your headteacher.

The comments above may give you some ideas, and you should also use some ideas of your own.

Write about 120 to 160 words. [15]

[Total: 15]

7.4 LISTENING

Listening: dialogue

In Listening exams, exercises like this may have more recordings and questions than given below. Your teacher will be able to give you more examples.

You will hear three short recordings. For each question, choose the correct answer, **A**, **B**, **C** or **D**, and put a tick (✓) in the appropriate box.

You will hear each recording twice.

CONTINUED

1 Where is the boy going to study?

A   B   C   D

2 What did the boy do on Saturday?

A   B   C   D

3 What is the girl going to do first?

A   B   C   D

7.5

Listening: interview

You will hear an interview with a student counsellor. For each question, choose the correct answer, **A**, **B** or **C**, and put a tick (✓) in the appropriate box.

You will hear the interview twice.

Now look at questions 1-8.

1 What is a common problem for college students?

     A They are not able to finish college.

     B They cannot manage their money.

     C They don't ask for help.   [1]

2 What does the counsellor advise them to do?

     A Analyse their expenses.

     B Talk to friends.

     C Move outside college.   [1]

3 When advising students on how to study, she suggests that they should…

     A study for short periods of time.

     B use a wide range materials and books.

     C study earlier in the day.   [1]

CONTINUED

4   What advice does she give for exam stress?

    A   Spend more time on studying.   ☐

    B   Reduce time on social activities.   ☐

    C   Talk about their problems.   ☐   [1]

5   The counsellor sometimes speaks to a student's parents in order to …

    A   make sure a student's description is accurate.   ☐

    B   help students communicate with their parents.   ☐

    C   find ways for a student to live away from home.   ☐   [1]

6   What does the counsellor say is an essential part of the counselling process?

    A   The counsellor gives an objective opinion of the problem.   ☐

    B   The student knows that their information will not be shared.   ☐

    C   The student should follow the counsellor's advice.   ☐   [1]

7   How does the counsellor describe her approach to counselling?

    A   She offers clear and constructive advice.   ☐

    B   She empathises with students' problems.   ☐

    C   She helps students understand themselves.   ☐   [1]

8   How does the counsellor feel about her job?

    A   It is busy and stressful.   ☐

    B   There is a lot of responsibility.   ☐

    C   It is difficult to have an impact.   ☐   [1]

[Total: 8]

SPEAKING

Warm-up questions

Warm-up questions help you feel more relaxed before you move on to answering assessed questions.

Take turns asking and answering the questions. Speak for 1–2 minutes.

- What do you like doing in your free time?
- What kind of music do you like?
- What is your favourite kind of TV programme?

Interview

Read the questions. In pairs, decide who will play the interviewer and who will play the student. Then role-play the interview. Speak for about 2–3 minutes. Change roles and role-play the interview again.

Studying online

- Can you tell me how you use the internet for your learning?
- What are the advantages and disadvantages of studying online?
- How is online study different from studying in a classroom?

CONTINUED

Short talk

Read the options and compare them. You have one minute to prepare your talk. Now give a short talk to your partner. Speak for about 2 minutes. Change roles and listen to your partner's talk.

Choosing a course

You are planning to study a foreign language and you are considering the following options:

- a one-week course in the country where the language is spoken, staying with a host family
- a two-week course learning online with videos, online coursework and homework but no in-person teaching.

Discuss the advantages and disadvantages of each option. Say which option you would prefer, and why.

Discussion

Read the discussion questions. In pairs, decide who will play the interviewer and who will play the student. Then role-play the discussion. Speak for about 3 minutes. Change roles and role-play the interview again.

- Many schools and colleges have online courses. What do you think about them?
- Do you think online learning is better for some students than classroom learning?
- Some people think that teenagers spend too much time online. Do you agree?

 For even more speaking practice, watch the videos about education in the digital coursebook

SELF-ASSESSMENT CHECKLIST

Reflect on what you have learnt in this unit. For each area listed, decide whether you feel confident or need more practice. If you feel you need more practice, you will find some ideas to help you in Advice for Success. Come back to your self-assessment scores later in your course and see if your confidence has improved.

I can ...	Need more practice	Fairly confident
discuss issues related to study and student life, using appropriate vocabulary		
identify ideas, opinions and attitudes in a magazine article		
give advice in an email, using appropriate register and style		
identify factual details and understand what is implied in a talk		
talk about problems and give someone advice		

ADVICE FOR SUCCESS

This section is to help you help yourself. Choose the suggestions you like and adapt them if you want to. Make notes about what you do and how it helped you.

Extending your skills

1 Listening to English radio, watching TV or videos online, and reading printed and online magazines, newspapers and books can help you understand more about the way people adapt their language to different occasions and for different target groups. For example, an article for adults about ways of studying will be written in a different tone and register from an article on the same topic for 12-year-olds.

2 Speaking or writing on the same topic in a variety of tones and registers will also develop your writing ability.

3 Make the most of every opportunity to improve your spoken English. Try to answer questions as fully as possible. Avoid *Yes/No* replies or *I don't know*. Don't be afraid to take a little extra time to think of replies that will be helpful in keeping an interesting conversation going. Use expressions such as *That's an interesting question* or *I've never thought about that before . . .* to give yourself time to think.

4 Students often say they would like to improve their grammar. Here are some suggestions:

- Study the errors you frequently make. Use your knowledge of regular grammar patterns and the exceptions to try to work out the differences between your version and the correct version.

- Use a good grammar book or website to check explanations of points you usually make mistakes with. You need a book or website that gives lots of examples, not just the rules and their exceptions.

- Study with a friend who speaks your first language. Work together to analyse your mistakes. As always, investigate the grammar pattern and think about exceptions, too. See if you can work out a rule for that particular grammar point before looking it up online or in your grammar book.

- Apply your new knowledge of grammar in different situations. This will help you remember the point and also understand when the grammar is correct and when it has to be adapted to fit new situations.

- Exploring meaningful patterns and their exceptions will help your spelling and vocabulary work, too. In fact, you can detect patterns in all the subjects you're learning (maths, science, art, etc.) if you look for them.

Showcasing your skills

5 Don't worry too much about making mistakes when speaking. Remember, communicating effectively in a natural and lively way is much more important than having perfect grammar or pronunciation.

6 Ask for clarification, if necessary, with questions such as 'Could you repeat that? I didn't quite understand.' You can also paraphrase what the other person has said to make sure you have understood correctly, using phrases such as, 'Do you mean . . . ?' 'Are you saying that . . . ?' 'Are you asking me about . . . ?'

7 When you discuss a topic, try to think about it from many different angles and points of view. Illustrate your ideas with interesting examples from your own experience.

> Unit 8

The search for adventure

LEARNING INTENTIONS

In this unit you will:

- Explore the topic of adventure, exploration and the sea

- Understand the sequence of events in a story and a newspaper article about adventures at sea

- Write a narrative with effective use of tenses and engaging opening and closing paragraphs

- Identify and understand key points in an interview and a lecture

- Use appropriate stress and intonation for expressing surprise, consoling and sympathising

12 Watch the video about the search for adventure in the digital coursebook.

BEFORE YOU START

Look at the photo on this page.

a   What is happening in the photo, and what is the person doing?

b   Why do you think someone would choose to explore this place?

c   What do people find fascinating about deep-sea diving?

d   What can you experience underwater that is different from on land?

A The call of the sea

1 Visualisation

Close your eyes and think of the sea. What sights and sounds come to your mind? What do you feel when you think about the sea? Now open your eyes and spend a few minutes writing down whatever came into your mind in your own language or English.

2 Discussion

> **Critical thinking** Discuss the following remarks about the sea with a partner. Give each remark a comment, A, B or C.

A I identify strongly with this idea.

B This idea is interesting but I don't identify closely with it.

C I don't identify in any way with this idea.

☐ The sea is a place of great adventure. When you set sail in a boat, you never know what you are going to find.

☐ I love swimming. Being in water, especially the sea, is one of life's great pleasures.

☐ I live by the sea and love the way it changes. On hot days, it's cool and restful. On winter days, there are dramatic storms.

☐ When I go out in my boat, I feel free. I leave all my worries behind.

☐ Below its surface, the sea is full of life. I'd love to explore its depths and see the underwater world for myself.

☐ I think the sea is mysterious. Huge ships have disappeared in it, never to be seen again.

☐ I live far away from the sea. My dream is to see the ocean and hear its wonderful sounds.

☐ I admire anyone whose employment is connected with the sea. There are so many risks and challenges.

☐ Sailing presents a great spiritual challenge. In a storm or crisis, I discover unknown aspects of myself.

3 Sea vocabulary

> Critical thinking

1 In pairs or small groups, circle the word that does not belong in each of the following groups. Use a dictionary to help you. You'll need many of the words later in the unit, so make a note in your vocabulary book of any that are unfamiliar.

a Sea associations
   Which word is not associated with the sea?
   spray   tides   waves   ocean   cliffs   bay
   shore   rocks   hive   current   port   horizon
   channel   shipwreck   voyage   cargo   dock
   jetty   surf

b On the beach
   Which item would you not expect to find on the beach?
   pebbles   shells   rocks   starfish   sand
   spanner   sand dunes   seaweed   driftwood
   turtle

c Sea creatures
   Which creature is not associated with the sea?
   porpoise   turtle   lobster   whale   shark
   seal   dolphin   puffin   penguin   crab
   squirrel

d Words for boats
   Which of the following is not a word for a kind of boat?
   yacht   dinghy   raft   tram   speedboat
   liner   vessel   canoe   barge   car ferry
   catamaran   oil tanker   trawler

e Occupations connected with the sea
   Which is the odd one out in this group of occupations?
   captain   coastguard   solicitor sailor
   fisherman   skipper   lighthouse keeper
   mariner   smuggler   pirate

f Watersports
   Which of these sports is not connected with water?
   scuba diving   surfing   rowing   canoeing
   swimming   diving   sailing   windsurfing
   jet-skiing   abseiling   snorkelling

2 Now match the four photographs with four of these words. Describe anything else you can see in the photos.

4 Writing a descriptive paragraph

Yesterday, you made a trip to the coast. Write a paragraph describing what you saw, the sounds you heard and the way you felt.

Write about 80 words.

5 Reading aloud

In small groups, read your paragraphs aloud to each other. Listen well and make comments on what you hear.

6 Pre-reading discussion

1 For countries with a coastline, the sea may provide useful defence in war, a source of wealth from trade or fishing, and a way of maintaining separation from other countries. The sea is usually an important part of such nations' national identity. What part, if any, has the sea played in the history of your country?

2 There are many stories about the excitement and drama of the sea. Do you have any favourites?

3 What do you know about famous explorers of the oceans and of the Arctic and the Antarctic?

7 Reading and sequencing

Read the true story about Ernest Shackleton's voyage to the Antarctic. Guess the meaning of unfamiliar words.

As you read, number these events in the order in which they happened:

a   They set up camp on an island. ☐

b   The ship is trapped in ice. ☐

c   They row to another island. ☐

d   They set sail for the Antarctic. ☐

e   They are rescued from the island. ☐

f   They leave their ship. ☐

g   They camp on the ice. ☐

h   They trek across an island. ☐

i   They find help. ☐

j   They land in the wrong place. ☐

The Story of Ernest Shackleton and the *Endurance*

Crushed by the ice, the ship was gradually sinking beneath the surface of the sea. The men salvaged what they could and set up camp on the ice as they watched the ship disappear. This was not how they
5 had imagined their voyage would end when they had set out on their expedition to explore one of the most remote regions of the Earth.

The sea has always been a magnet for adventurers seeking to test the limits of human endurance. For
10 explorers of the early 20th century, crossing the ocean to explore the remote icefields of Antarctica was one of the fiercest and most tantalising challenges.

The famous Norwegian explorer, Roald Amundsen,
15 had already reached the South Pole in 1911 with his team of 4 men, 52 dogs and 4 sledges. But other challenges of the Antarctic still remained. In August 1914, Ernest Shackleton became the leader of a British expedition team of 27 men whose goal was
20 to cross Antarctica from coast to coast via the South Pole. Their ship was named the *Endurance*.

The team intended to establish a base on the shore of the Weddell Sea, but the ship never reached its destination. In January 1915, after battling through
25 a six-day gale, they became trapped in the ice. For nine long months, they drifted in the glacial waters, unable to navigate, until the ship was finally surrounded and crushed. The men had no choice but to abandon their ship.

30 They camped on the ice in temperatures below minus 20°C, salvaging
35 supplies and lifeboats from the ship. For five months, they drifted on **ice**
40 **floes** until finally, at the beginning of April, the ice began to crack. It took them seven days of rowing through storms and glacial waves to reach Elephant Island, where again they set up camp and managed to survive by eating seal meat and penguins.

45 The island was uninhabited and so remote that there was almost no chance of anyone ever landing there to find them. Shackleton decided to take one of the boats and sail to a whaling station on the island of South Georgia, about 800 miles away. They
50 left on 24 April, battling storms, massive waves and icy gales, until on 10 May, they finally reached land. But the storms had pushed their boat off course and they had landed on the other side of the island. So Shackleton and two other men, already exhausted
55 by their gruelling voyage, climbed over mountains and glaciers to get across the island – a trek of 36 hours in freezing conditions – until they finally reached the whaling station.

After rescuing the three other members of their
60 team, they started the attempt to get their men back from Elephant Island. Their first two ships failed to get through the storms and ice. Shackleton then obtained a third ship and, on 30 August 1916, succeeded in reaching the island. The men had
65 been waiting for 128 days, hoping every day that Shackleton would return to save them. It had been 24 months since they had started out together on their expedition. Incredibly, every member of the expedition team survived.

Entry for 27 October in Shackleton's diary

The end came at last about 5 p.m. She was doomed, no ship built by human hands could have withstood the strain. I ordered all hands on to the floe, and as the floe near us was cracking, we started to sledge all the gear.

GLOSSARY

ice floe: large piece of floating sea ice

8 Comprehension check

1 What was the purpose of the expedition?

2 Why didn't they establish a base camp on land?

3 How long did it take for Shackleton to come back for his men?

4 What were the main difficulties they had to face on this expedition?

9 Making inferences

> Critical thinking

1 What do you think motivated the men to join this expedition?

2 What skills do you think helped the men to survive?

3 What kind of feelings do you think the men experienced on the Elephant Island?

4 Why do you think this expedition was more risky then than it would be today?

5 What is your opinion of Shackleton after reading this story? Was he foolish or heroic, or both?

6 Would you have joined this expedition? Why or why not?

10 Drawing a timeline

> Critical thinking Draw a timeline in your notebook showing the major events of the expedition. Remember to space the events along the timeline according to how much time elapsed between them.

11 Language study:
Narrative tenses

To help the reader follow a story and understand how the events are connected, we use narrative tenses. Useful narrative tenses are:

• the past simple (*became, intended, reached*)

• the past continuous (*was sinking*)

• the past perfect (*had imagined*).

1 Study the tenses in the story of the *Endurance* with a partner. Underline each verb and decide which tense it is.

2 Add an asterisk (*) if the verb is in the passive.

3 With your partner, discuss why each tense is used.

4 With your partner, make notes for each narrative tense, like this:

The past simple

• Typical examples in text:

• Formed by:

• Used in text because . . .

• Finally, check your notes with a grammar book.

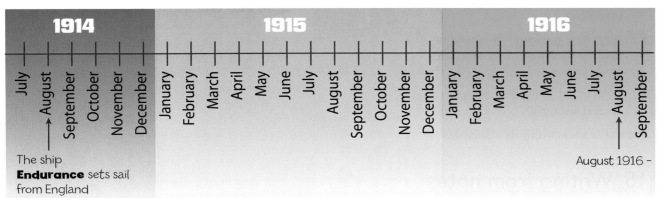

1914 — July, August, September, October, November, December

1915 — January, February, March, April, May, June, July, August, September, October, November, December

1916 — January, February, March, April, May, June, July, August, September

The ship **Endurance** sets sail from England

August 1916 –

12 Beginnings and endings

Beginnings and endings are important in a story. How interesting did you find the beginning of the story? How satisfying did you find the ending?

What tenses are used at the beginning and end of the story? Why?

13 Discussion: Heroism

1 > **Critical thinking** What do we mean when we say someone is a hero or heroine? In what way do you think Ernest Shackleton could be described as a heroic figure?

2 Can ordinary people living uneventful lives ever be called heroic? Why / Why not?

3 Who are your personal heroes or heroines? Share ideas in your group.

4 Shackleton's expedition failed to achieve its goal, but can nevertheless be seen as admirable and inspiring. Describe some ways in which failure can sometimes lead to a positive outcome.

14 Continuing a story creatively

Imagine you are a member of Shackleton's team on your way back to England. Use these questions to help you continue the story:

• What will you be most relieved about?

• What will you most miss about being on the expedition?

• What have you learnt from your experiences? How have the hardships of the expedition made you a better person?

• What might be the difficulties be of fitting into a normal life again?

Share your ideas with your classmates.

15 Writing from notes

Most narratives use a variety of past tenses. Imagine that you were a member of Shackleton's expedition trapped on the island and waiting for help. Write a paragraph about your experience using the notes below and past simple, past continuous and past perfect tenses.

We / wait / for over two months.

Some of us / give up hope / of rescue.

Every day / we scan the horizon / hope / for sign of a ship.

We / make a fire / to cook some meat / when we see a ship.

At last / help / arrive!

16 Comparing cultures

> **Critical thinking** What stories in your culture have a sea theme? Think carefully about a story you know well and like. Then retell it to your group.

17 Showing surprise: Stress and intonation

1   Listen to the stress and the intonation patterns in these *wh-* questions and answers. When does the intonation rise? When does it fall?

a   What was the goal of the expedition?
    To cross Antarctica.
    What was the goal?

b   How many men were on the ship?
    There were 27 men.
    How many men were there?

c   What destroyed the ship?
    It was crushed by ice.
    What destroyed it?

d   What did the men eat?
    They ate seal meat and penguins.
    What did they eat?

e   How long did the men wait to be rescued?
    One hundred and twenty eight days.
    How long did they wait?

2   Listen again and repeat the patterns.

Practice

Work in pairs. Ask each question with the falling intonation. Then repeat the question, showing surprise.

Continue with some questions and answers of your own about the story.

B Adrift on the Pacific

1 Pre-listening tasks

You are going to hear someone describing the story of a couple, Maurice and Maralyn, who were attempting to sail across the world when their boat sank. They survived on a life raft for four months before they were rescued. Afterwards, they wrote a book about their experiences.

Narrative questions

A narrative should answer these questions:

Who . . . ?	Why . . . ?	What . . . ?
How . . . ?	Where . . . ?	When . . . ?

Write a question about the story beginning with each word.

Example: *Where did the boat sink?*

Try to make your questions grammatically correct.

Vocabulary check

Match these words that you are going to hear with their definitions.

a	emigrate		1	extremely thin
b	adrift		2	floating without purpose
c	counter current		3	to make something using whatever materials are available
d	improvise			
e	emaciated		4	unaware of, not noticing
f	malnourished		5	a sea current running in the opposite direction
g	oblivious to			
			6	to go to another country to live there permanently
			7	unwell from lack of food

2 Detailed listening

Listen to a podcast interview with someone talking about Maurice and Maralyn's story. Note down answers to the questions you wrote.

 ## 3 Checking your answers

Did you find answers to your questions? With a partner, discuss which questions were or were not answered.

 ## 4 Listening and note-taking

Listen to the audio recording again and complete the notes below.

a Reason for the trip:

b Where and why the boat sank:

c Immediate reaction to the accident:

d Rowing towards the Galapagos Islands was a mistake because:

e What they ate:

f Problems with the raft:

g Length of time adrift on the raft:

h How they tried to attract attention:

i Length of time to recover:

j How they coped emotionally during their experience:

5 Discussion: Motivation and adventure

1 > **Critical thinking** What makes people want to become involved in risky projects, such as sailing across the world in a very small boat, climbing a dangerous mountain, trekking in polar regions or going into outer space? Discuss these ideas in your group:

• Are adventurers and explorers motivated by fame and money? Or a desire for risk and adventure? Or the competitive spirit?

• Is it a need to discover their potential and find out what they are capable of in the most challenging circumstances – a kind of 'spiritual quest'?

Do you think people who undertake this kind of thing have greater inner strength than others?

2 Is it right that each year large sums of money are spent rescuing people whose expeditions have gone wrong?

Could the desire for adventure be directed more constructively into doing voluntary work on projects such as helping refugees?

When conditions on a dangerous expedition become very difficult, is it braver to accept defeat than to risk everything for success?

6 Ordering events

1 Put the statements about the couple on the life raft into the correct order by numbering them 1–11.

a The yacht was damaged by a whale.

b They rowed towards the Galapagos Islands.

c They attempted to get to the Central American coast.

d The boat sank.

e A hostile current dragged them back out to sea.

f They tried to attract the attention of passing ships.

g They were rescued by South Korean fishermen.

h They were taken to Honolulu to receive medical care.

i They sailed by unaware of the couple's situation.

j They escaped onto a life raft.

k They left England for New Zealand.

2 Link the statements using time expressions and conjunctions where appropriate. Choose from:

first, then, when, eventually, finally, before, until, next, after that, after many days

and conjunctions like *and*, *but*, and so on.

For example: *First, they left England for New Zealand, but their yacht was . . .*

3 Check whether the order of events is correct by listening to the audio recording again.

7 Expressing emotions

In the interview, Yann says, 'Then, to their horror, a hostile current dragged them back out to the middle of the ocean.'

'To their horror' expresses the drama and emotion of the situation. Look at these similar expressions:

---

to our amazement	to her disappointment
to our (great) relief	to their alarm
to my astonishment	to her concern
to their joy	to our horror
to his annoyance	to our delight

These expressions highlight the responses of the people involved in the events.

1 Study the following situations. Use a suitable emotional phrase to add to each description.

Example: *We were waiting outside the operating theatre when, **to our great relief**, the surgeon came out and told us the operation had been a success.*

  a I was kayaking down the river when lightning ripped across the sky and heavy rain began to fall.

  b We feared the worst when our son disappeared driving in the desert, but yesterday he sent a text to say he was safe.

  c The racing driver was driving at top speed when he noticed his brakes were not working.

  d I was making dinner when the telephone rang and I learnt I had won first prize in a competition.

  e Joe was enjoying fishing for salmon when he saw a grizzly bear emerging from the forest.

  f We were waiting to go into the aquarium when we saw a large turtle crawling through the reception area.

2 Examine the uses of tenses in the sentences. What tenses are used and why? Some sentences use more than one tense. Why, do you think?

8 Dictionary work: Prefixes

The prefix *mal-*
Maurice and Maralyn didn't have enough food to eat so they became *malnourished*. The prefix *mal-* means 'badly' or 'wrongly'.

1 Replace the word(s) in italics in the sentences below with one of these words beginning with *mal-*. Work with a partner and use a dictionary to help you.

---

malfunctioning	malevolent
malpractice	malignant
malicious	malnutrition

---

  a The high-energy biscuits saved thousands of refugees who were suffering from *lack of food*.

  b The surgeon said the growth would have to be removed as it was *cancerous*.

  c To his horror, the pilot realised that one of the engines was *not working properly*.

  d The doctor was taken to court for *failing to care properly for his patients*.

  e Children's fairy stories often contain a character who is *very evil*.

  f This little boy is *deliberately hurtful* towards other children.

The prefix counter-

Maurice and Maralyn had hoped to get to the Equatorial *Counter Current*. The prefix *counter-* means 'opposite' or 'reverse'.

2 Complete each of the following sentences with one of these words beginning with *counter-*. Continue using your dictionary if you need to.

> counterbalance   counterpart
>
> counteract   counterargument
>
> counterproductive   counterattack

a Weights of the same size on this machine should be used to _____ each other.

b If our aim is to make the workers do a good job, paying them less would surely be _____.

c In spite of heavy casualties, the soldiers launched a determined _____ against the enemy forces.

d The doctor gave the child some medicine to _____ the poison she had swallowed.

e The Danish Prime Minister met his Swedish _____ in Stockholm today for urgent talks on the fishing crisis.

f The accountant came up with good reasons for selling the company, but the clients put forward equally strong _____ for keeping it.

9 Revision of reported speech

When we tell a story, we may change someone's actual words to reported speech.

For example, Maurice might have said to Maralyn, 'It's absolutely silent here. You can't have heard the engine of a boat. No one is coming to rescue us. You must be going mad.'

If this speech were reported, it would change to:

Maurice told Maralyn it was absolutely silent there, and she couldn't have heard the engine of a boat. No one was coming to rescue them. She must be going mad.

Study the example carefully, considering these questions.

- What has happened to the verbs? What is the rule for tenses when direct speech is reported?

- What has happened to *must*? Do other modals (*would, could, should, might, need, had better* and *ought to*) stay the same when speech is reported?

- How have the pronouns changed? What usually happens to pronouns in reported speech?

- What has happened to the infinitive? Do infinitives in direct speech change when the speech is reported?

10 Reporting verbs

Verbs such as *admit, promise, declare, invite, ask, explain, reflect, remind, mention, suggest, insist* and *refuse* are often used when we change direct speech into reported speech. Using them is a good idea because it brings breadth and variety into your writing.

Example: '*Remember to send your aunt a good luck message,' said their mother.*

Their mother reminded them to send their aunt a good luck message.

What other reporting verbs do you know?

The following comments were made by a young woman, Silvia, who is planning to sail around the world single-handedly.

Change her actual words to reported speech, using suitable reporting verbs from the box. Some of the verbs are similar in meaning, so decide which you prefer.

> acknowledge declare reveal add
>
> explain say admit insist
>
> confess mention

Example: *'I'm a yachtswoman and a loner. I would rather go sailing alone than in a group.'*

She declared (that) she was a yachtswoman and a loner. She insisted (that) she would rather go sailing alone than in a group.

a 'I'm attempting to break the world record for sailing non-stop around the world.'

b 'I'm being sponsored by several businesses.'

c 'I suppose my worst fear is personal failure.'

d 'I'm doing it because I'm hoping to beat the present world record of 161 days.'

e 'I'm taking food and drink to last me up to 200 days.'

f 'The food includes 500 dried meals, 150 apples, 144 bars of chocolate, 36 jars of jam and marmalade and 14 tubs of dried fruit and nuts.'

g 'When I'm thousands of miles from shore, and if I'm injured, then I'll be scared.'

h 'I've been taught to stitch my own flesh wounds in an emergency.'

i 'If there's a crisis, I think the answer is not instant action, but to think about it.'

j 'I know I can handle the boat, and I'll find out whether I have the strength to beat the world record.'

INTERNATIONAL OVERVIEW

An ocean of facts! Test your knowledge

1 The largest of the world's oceans covers more than a third of the Earth's surface. Which is it?

   A the Atlantic Ocean

   B the Pacific Ocean

   C the Arctic Ocean

   D the Indian Ocean

2 The Arctic Ocean is the world's smallest ocean.

   True or false?

3 The world's largest inland sea has an area of 371 000 square kilometres. Which is it?

   A the Baltic Sea

   B the Black Sea

   C the Caspian Sea

4 Which country of the world has the longest coastline? Choose from:

   A Australia

   B Canada

   C Russia

5 One country in the following list is the world's largest archipelago, with over 13 500 islands, of which about 6 000 are inhabited. Which is it?

   A Indonesia

   B the Philippines

   C the Seychelles

6 The world's oceans contain about ten billion tons of a precious metal, but nobody has worked out how to collect it. Which metal is it?

   A silver

   B gold

   C platinum

11 Writing a report of an interview

Imagine that you are a journalist. You have been asked to interview the yachtswoman. Write a report of the interview for your newspaper.

First make a plan.

- Select those sentences in Section B8 you would like to include in your report.

- Use a balance of reported speech and direct speech to make the report convincing.

- Invent other details readers might like to know. For example:

    - the place where you interviewed Silvia – on her yacht or in her house?

    - personal details about Silvia (e.g. her age, her appearance).

- Give your opinions of Silvia. Do you think she is brave? What do you think about her desire to test herself?

- Finally, decide on the correct order for the information and write your report.

C A remarkable rescue

1 Pre-reading tasks

1   Have you ever seen an animal or a bird that needed help? In pairs, ask each other questions using these prompts:

> Where / be you?

> Be you / alone?

> What / be you / do / when you realise / it needed help?

> What / you do / when you realise / what happen?

> How / you react?

> How / other people react?

> What / happen / in the end?

2   You are going to read a newspaper article about a whale. Look carefully at the headlines and photograph in the article. What do they tell you about the story you are going to read?

Do you think the story will have a happy ending? Why / Why not?

3   Do you expect the language to be chatty and colloquial? Or formal and serious? Why?

Who do you think would enjoy reading this story?

2 Reading for gist

Read the newspaper article carefully, trying to guess any unknown words from the context. Most of the story is told using past tenses. As you read, underline examples of different past tenses.

Flipping amazing . . . the moment a humpback whale 'thanks' rescuers who saved it from dying tangled in fishing nets

By: Daily Mail Reporter

A humpback whale which was freed from almost certain death by three men off the coast of California repaid the favour to its rescuers with a breathtaking display of breaches and dives. The amazing hour-long performance was caught on camera moments after the creature was cut free from fishing nets.

When the boat came across the whale it was trapped with its tail and flippers hopelessly entangled in the nets. The whale watchers first thought the humpback was already dead as it was floating on top of the water. But then it let out a loud breath through its blow hole.

Michael Fishbach decided the best thing to do was to get into the water and snorkel alongside the stricken whale.

He said: 'As I swam alongside the animal our eyes met. There were no words we could share but I wanted to let the whale know that we were there to help. It took some effort to stay focused given the great emotion of the moment. The sight of this large and beautiful creature trapped and so close to death was almost overwhelming. I must admit I was a bit scared because I knew the whale was frightened and fatigued but could still kill me with one panicked movement.'

He said the whale's tail was so entangled that it was weighed down by about 5 metres.

Michael got back on the boat and tried to cut the net off the whale with a small knife. The trio managed to free one of the fins but the whale sensed freedom and swam away, pulling the boat with it. But eventually it surfaced again and more net was cut away. After about an hour of working the whale was totally free.

They pulled the remaining fish net onto the boat and watched the whale give a dramatic show of freedom. For the next hour they watched the

whale **breach** around 40 times and then dive down waving its tail above the water.

Michael said: 'We all believed it was at least a show of pure joy, if not thanks. We were all proud and thrilled that we saved this fantastic young life. It was an incredible experience that none of us will ever forget.'

On the video a small girl can be heard saying: 'I know what she is doing. She is showing us that she is free.'

Her mother replies to her: 'I think she is showing us a thank you dance.'

Michael spends two months every winter photographing whales in the Sea of Cortez. He is the co-founder of the Great Whale Conservancy (GWC) Blue Whale Protection Program, set up to protect whales along the California coast from ship-strike caused injuries and death.

GLOSSARY

breach: to jump partly out of the water, head first, and land on the back or belly with a big splash

3 Multiple-choice questions

Answer the questions about the article.

1 Why did the humpback whale need help?

   A   It had been injured by a fishing boat.

   B   It was unable to escape from the nets.

   C   It was submerged in water below the boat.

2 When they found the whale, it was:

   A   struggling to get free.

   B   having difficulty breathing.

   C   exhausted from trying to escape.

3 How did Michael feel when he swam next to the whale?

   A   He was unable to express his emotions.

   B   He forced himself to concentrate.

   C   He was uncertain what to do.

4 In line 28, the writer mentions '5 metres' to illustrate:

   A   how heavy the nets were.

   B   how difficult it was to cut the nets.

   C   how deep they had to dive.

5 What does 'it' refer to in line 41?

   A   The whale's behaviour after being freed.

   B   The experience of helping the whale.

   C   The whale's feeling of happiness.

6 What did Michael find most memorable about this experience?

   A   Having the chance to see the whale close-up.

   B   Knowing that the whale is now free.

   C   Helping the whale get back to freedom.

4 Vocabulary check

Find words in the article and headlines to match the following definitions. To help you, the definitions are in the same order as the words appear in the article.

a   incredible

b   discovered

c   vulnerable

d   seriously affected

e   exhausted

f   scared

g   impressive

h   display

5 Narrative structure

› **Critical thinking** Like many newspaper accounts, the story is not reported in chronological order. It begins by explaining what happened at the end of the story. Then it goes back to the beginning, explaining why the whale was in trouble and needed to be rescued. Towards the end of the article, the ending is repeated with more details about the reactions of people on the boat.

Why do you think the story is told like this? Consider the following:

* to provide a dramatic opening, which is not slowed down by too much detail

* to enable us to hear actual spoken comments from the people who were involved

* to make the narrative as varied, moving and personal as possible

6 Writing a summary from notes

Write a summary of the story describing how the whale got trapped and how it was saved. Use these notes to help you:

humpback whale / trapped by fishing nets / off the coast of California

whale-watching boat / found the whale / the crew / decide / help the whale

one of them / decide / dive down / they / use / knife / cut nets / off

whale / put on a show / say thank you to its rescuers

7 Vocabulary practice: Adjectives

The whale is described as 'helpless and stricken'.

The following adjectives describe physical feelings and experiences. With a partner, rank each set of words in order from strong to weak. Use a dictionary if necessary. Start like this:

1 stricken, 2_____

1 breathtaking, 2_____

Physical condition
fatigued   frightened   hurt   injured   stricken

Experience
amazing   breathtaking   dramatic   impressive   interesting

8 Pre-listening exercise

> **Critical thinking** What do you know about the effect of human activities on the oceans? List four or five ways in which they may have a negative impact.

 ## 9 A lecture about the Earth's oceans

Listen to this introduction to a lecture and then answer the questions below about the speaker's views.

1   According to the speaker, _____ of the Earth's surface is covered by water.

   A   17 percent

   B   70 percent

   C   71 percent

2   The increase in temperature affects sea levels and . . .

   A   natural habitats

   B   fish supplies

   C   animal behaviour

3   The increase in carbon dioxide increases . . .

   A   greenhouse gases

   B   oxygen

   C   acidity

4   The speaker mentions chemicals as an example of . . .

   A   mining

   B   pollution

   C   dumping

5   The speaker mentions shipping as an example of . . .

   A   how habitats are destroyed

   B   how marine mammals are killed

   C   why fish are disappearing

10 Language study: Revision of defining relative clauses

Study this sentence from the article in Section C3:

'A humpback whale *which was freed from almost certain death* repaid the favour . . .'

The clause in italics is important to the meaning of the sentence. It is called a defining clause, because it defines or makes clear which person or thing is being talked about. Here are some more examples:

*   The sight of this large and beautiful creature *which was trapped and so close to death* was almost overwhelming.

*   They interviewed the captain *whose crew had found the whale.*

*   Those were the fishing nets *which / that had entrapped the whale.*

*   This is the part of the coast *where whales can be seen.*

A defining clause is essential to the meaning of the sentence. If it is left out, the sentence does not make complete sense or the meaning changes. No commas are used with defining clauses. Remember that the pronoun *that* can be used instead of *which* to refer to things in defining clauses.

Practice

Complete these sentences with suitable defining clauses.

a   They prefer stories _____ endings.

b   The man _____ has donated a lot of money to charity.

c   The student _____ received an award for bravery.

d   The shoes _____ last month have already fallen apart.

e   The factory _____ is now a tourist hotel.

f   The doctor _____ comes from Guatemala.

11 Language study: Revision of non-defining relative clauses

Non-defining relative clauses give extra information about something. They can be in the middle or at the end of a sentence. Commas are used to separate them from the rest of the sentence.

Study these examples:

- The amazing performance, *which was caught on camera*, continued for over an hour.

- Michael Fishbach, *who is co-founder of a whale protection programme*, helped to free the animal.

- The whale did lots of jumps and dives, *which they thought were her way of saying thank you.*

The pronoun *that* cannot be used in non-defining clauses.

Non-defining clauses expand your sentences and make them more complete. Try to use them, as they make your writing more interesting and complex.

Practice

1   Add suitable non-defining clauses to these sentences. You should use whose in at least one of the clauses.

   a   Rahmia Altat, _____, now does voluntary work.

   b   We heard about the heroic acts of the rescue workers, _____.

   c   Nurse Mara, _____, demonstrated the life-saving techniques.

   d   Drowning, _____, can usually be prevented.

   e   Smoke alarms, _____, should be fitted in every home.

   f   My cousin Gina, _____, is being brought up by her grandparents.

2   Expand these simple sentences into more complex ones, using non-defining clauses to add extra information.

   a   Mrs Nazir won a trip to the Caribbean.

   b   The new hospital is the biggest in the country.

   c   Our sailing teacher took us to an island.

3   Write some sentences of your own using non-defining clauses.

12 Consoling and sympathising

Working in pairs, decide which is the most appropriate way to respond to the following statements giving bad news. Select as many of the answers as you think are suitable.

1   I've just failed my driving test.

   A   What a shame.

   B   How horrific!

   C   That's a tragedy.

   D   You should have done better.

   E   Better luck next time.

2   My grandma just went into hospital.

   A   Oh, I am sorry. Is there anything I can do to help?

   B   You must be really fed up.

   C   How sad. Was it sudden?

   D   Don't get too worried about it.

   E   What bad luck!

3   I forgot my door key and had to wait outside for two hours until my father got back from work.

   A   How annoying!

   B   That was forgetful of you.

   C   My heart goes out to you.

   D   I'd just like to say how sad I am for you.

   E   You must remember to put it in your bag in future.

4 I thought I'd recorded 'Ocean of Adventure', but when I sat down to watch it, I discovered I'd recorded the wrong programme!

    A Never mind. I can lend you the DVD.

    B I bet you were furious.

    C I'd have been really annoyed.

    D You've got all my sympathy for what you're going through.

    E Remember to follow the instructions next time.

5 Study the following comments. Write down some appropriate responses, and then try them out on your partner.

    a I didn't get the job I applied for.

    b I'm really disappointed with my new haircut.

    c I broke my ankle on holiday.

13 Spelling and pronunciation: The suffix *-tion* or *-ion*

The suffix *-tion* or *-ion* is quite common in English. Examples in the article in Section C3 are *emotion* and *protection*. How is the final syllable pronounced in these words?

1 Listen carefully to the following words on the audio recording and mark the main stress in each word. Then practise saying them.

    a exhibition   **b** fashion

    c occupation   **d** demonstration

    e passion   **f** invention

    g qualification   **h** definition

    i recognition   **j** ignition

    k promotion

2 *Question* and *opinion* are exceptions to the rule. How are they pronounced?

3 Now match ten of the words from the list to these definitions:

    a will improve your chances of getting a job

    b another word for work

    c a machine or gadget that is original

    d strong emotion

    e a display of books or pictures

f the dictionary will give you this information about a word

g a better job with more money

h if this is turned off, the car will not start

i artists can work for 20 years without getting this

j the latest styles in clothes and shoes

14 Language study: Adverbs

Adverbs have a large number of different uses.

- They can tell us more about a verb.
  Example: She walked *slowly*.

- They can be used before an adjective.
  Example: It was *fairly* difficult.

- They can be used before another adverb.
  Example: He drove *terribly slowly*.

- They can tell us when or how often something happens.
  Examples: *occasionally, regularly, never*

- They can give information about how certain we are of something.
  Examples: *definitely, probably, perhaps*

- They can connect ideas.
  Examples: *firstly, however, lastly*

Formation of adverbs

Many adverbs are formed by adding *-ly* to adjectives. *Hopelessly* and *eventually* are examples from the article in Section C9 about the whale rescue.

Other examples are:

quick → quickly, cheap → cheaply

- If the adjective ends in *-y*, you change the *-y* to *-i* before adding *-ly*.
  Example: *angry → angrily*

- If the adjective ends in *-ic*, you add *-ally*.
  Example: *heroic → heroically*

- If the adjective ends in *-le*, you drop the *-e* and add *-y*.
  Example: *reasonable → reasonably*

- Remember that some adjectives look like adverbs.
  Examples: *lovely, elderly, friendly*

- Notice also: *early → early, fast → fast, good → well*

Practice

Read the web page about careers in marine science. Some of the words in italics need to be changed into adverbs. When you have finished, ask your partner to check that your spelling is correct.

Careers in Marine Science

Do you love the ocean? Do you enjoy learning about life underwater? Then a career in marine science might be for you! It's not all about analysing samples in a laboratory. There is
5 a *surprising* wide range of careers in marine science, and it's worth spending some time to explore the different career choices before *final* making a decision.

Marine biologist

10 Do you love watching ocean animals like dolphins or whales? Do you enjoy learning about seaweed and

15 other sea plants? A marine biologist studies the ocean and all kinds of marine life. They collect samples from the oceans and seas and analyse them *careful* to learn about patterns of change in the marine environment.
20 *Eventual,* this information will be used to help protect and preserve ocean life.

Marine archaeologist

Do you enjoy solving mysteries and making
25 *new* discoveries? Marine archaeology is all about finding and saving

underwater discoveries. You'll need to be good at operating *technical* sophisticated
30 equipment such as video cameras and remote robots. You'll need to be able to think *quick* in case you meet *unexpected* obstacles. You'll be spending a lot of time underwater, so a diving qualification is
35 *normal* required.

Marine toxicologist

40 Do you have a passion to protect our oceans and make them *safe* for marine life and for humans? A career in marine toxicology

45 means that you will collect and study water samples from a *wide* range of sources to identify *possible* sources of contamination and pollution. The work enables marine wildlife to continue living *safe* in their natural habitats.

Marine conservationist

50 Marine conservationists monitor marine life and underwater ecosystems. For example, you might

55 record numbers of fish species which could help limit *destructive* overfishing. Or you could be monitoring coral reef damage or the effects of plastic in
60 our oceans. Marine conservationists play a *crucial* role in keeping our oceans *healthy.*

Skills and qualities needed for a career in marine science

You must:

65 - Have a *suitable* degree in oceanography or marine science.

- Be able to work *independent* and as part of a team.

- *Clear* communicate your ideas *verbal*
70 and in writing.

- Follow instructions *safe* when underwater.

- Act *responsible* in *critical* situations.

- Observe and collect data *patient*
75 and *accurate.*

15 Look, say, cover, write, check

The article about the whale included the words *caught* and *thought*. The letters aught and *ought* are common combinations in many words. The phonetic spelling is /ɔːt/.

1 Learn these commonly misspelt words using the 'look, say, cover, write, check' method (see Unit 1, Section B12 if you need a reminder).

distraught	caught	naughty
thought	fought	taught
bought	sought	brought

2 Ask a partner to test you when you are confident you have learnt them correctly.

3 Choose six of the words and put each one into a sentence to show its meaning.

D Reacting to the unexpected

1 Pre-reading task: Making notes

Read about these unexpected events that happened to various people.

> I was walking home when a passer-by collapsed in the street.

> We had just gone to bed when the smoke alarms went off.

> My neighbour knocked on the door. She was sure her little girl had swallowed some poisonous berries.

> I was doing my homework when water started pouring through the ceiling.

> I was chatting to my best friend when one of the party guests insisted I tried the dancing competition, and I won first prize!

Have you ever had to cope with something, pleasant or unpleasant, that was completely unexpected? Think carefully about the event and then make notes under these headings.

The background to the event

- Where were you?

- What were you doing?

- Who was with you and what were they doing?

The event itself

- What happened?

- How did you react?

- What did other people do?

- What happened then?

The outcome

- What happened in the end?

- What do you feel you have learnt from the experience?

- How has the experience affected other people?

- Has the event had any other effects?

Compare your notes with your partner's. Look after them as you will need them later.

2 Reading an example narrative

Naila Khan Afza is a journalist. This summer, an extraordinary thing happened to her while she was on holiday. She posted the following story to her newspaper's blog. Do you think you would have reacted in the same way she did?

As you read, underline and identify examples of different past tenses.

Underline the tenses and examples of non-defining relative clauses.

The biggest event of my summer

By Naila Khan Afza,
The Online Journal

Naila Khan Afza, blogging since 2012

It seemed like another ordinary day. My family and I had decided to spend the day on the beach. I sat in the sun watching the children throwing pebbles into the sea or paddling.
5 I was thinking about having a swim when I noticed a strange object bobbing about in the sea. To my horror, I realised the 'object' was a child drowning. Without stopping to think, I plunged into the water and grabbed
10 the child. With my free arm, I swam back to the shore. The child, who was a boy of about five, was like a dead weight but I felt powered by a superhuman strength.

I laid the boy, who appeared to be
15 unconscious, gently on the ground and gave him mouth-to-mouth resuscitation, which revived him immediately. I was dimly aware that a large crowd had gathered and someone was telling me an ambulance was
20 on its way. By the time the ambulance arrived, to my great relief, the boy was sitting up and talking.

Dale's parents were delighted with his quick recovery. They rang me later to thank me, and
25 we had a long discussion about the dangers of playing near water. They have arranged for him to have swimming lessons, which I think is a very good idea. I would definitely recommend that everyone learn to swim –
30 young or old. I'd also like to remind everyone to take care near the sea, rivers or swimming pools. You can drown much more easily than you think!

3 Comprehension check

1 What was Naila doing when the incident happened?

2 Did she have time to tell anyone else what was happening?

3 What helped the boy regain consciousness?

4 What suggests that Naila was fully concentrating on mouth-to-mouth resuscitation?

5 How do we know that Dale's parents want him to be safe in the water?

4 Analysing the narrative

1 > Critical thinking Openings are important in narratives. Does the story interest you immediately? Why / Why not?

2 In the first paragraph, a number of different tenses are used. What are they, how are they formed and what are their functions?

3 'To my horror', 'Without stopping to think' and 'To my great relief' are used for effect. What other phrases could be used?

4 Endings are important in a narrative. The reader should not feel there are unanswered questions. Do you think the story is brought to a satisfactory conclusion? Why / Why not?

5 Remember, a narrative should answer these questions:

Who . . . ?	Why . . . ?	What . . . ?
How . . . ?	Where . . . ?	When . . . ?

How does Naila's narrative do this? For example:

a Who is involved in Naila's story?

b What happened?

c Where did the event take place?

5 Dramatic expressions

Your sentences can be made more dramatic by starting them with this kind of expression:

My hair stood on end . . .

My heart missed a beat . . .

1 Make complete sentences by matching the following openings a–f with the endings 1–6. More than one option may be possible, so decide which you prefer.

a With my heart in my mouth . . .

b A piercing scream cut through the air . . .

c I froze to the spot . . .

d Panic mounted . . .

e With trembling fingers . . .

f Sweat poured from us . . .

1 . . . as we fought to rescue the children trapped by the earthquake.

2 . . . when flames appeared at the side of the plane.

3 . . . as the hijacker produced a gun!

4 . . . when the hooded figure appeared in the graveyard.

5 . . . I tiptoed past the sleeping kidnappers.

6 . . . he struggled to open his parachute.

2 Now write four sentences of your own using dramatic expressions.

6 Pre-writing discussion

1 What does windsurfing involve?

2 What do you think is exciting about this sport?

3 Could it ever be dangerous? Why / Why not?

4 Does this hobby appeal to you? Why / Why not?

7 Ways of developing an outline

The following list of sentences is an outline of a story. It describes how a windsurfer was swept out to sea and what happened in the end. Read the sentences carefully. Make sure you understand all the points clearly.

I Fought To Stay Alive

- I was windsurfing off the Pacific coast.
- It was a calm sunny day.
- I'm a very experienced windsurfer.
- Everything was going well.
- The wind turned, forcing me offshore.
- I tried for an hour to get back to the shore.
- I began to feel weaker.
- The wind started coming in gusts.
- The sea was rough.
- I clung to the board.
- A helicopter flew over.
- I thought it was coming to rescue me.
- I waved and shouted.
- It flew over me to the other side of the bay.
- I was wearing a dark wetsuit on a blue and white board.
- I was part of the sea and no one could see me.
- When night fell, I lay down on the board, wrapped in my sail.
- I was in my own little world.
- Then I heard a helicopter.
- I waved.
- They saw me.
- They rescued me.

Obviously, a list of events does not make a complete narrative. In fact, the pleasure of reading a good story often lies not in the plot, but in the details.

What details could you add to the outline above to produce an exciting, well-written story? In small groups, consider the following techniques, which could make your story come alive.

- Begin the story with some interesting details that set the scene (e.g. *It was a beautiful, sunny day and I was doing what I like best – windsurfing.*)

- Describe the weather and the sea in a vivid way (e.g. *The wind was howling. / The waves were crashing.*)

- Use dramatic expressions (e.g. *My heart sank as the board was carried far out to sea.*)

- Use emotional expressions to add drama (e.g. *to my horror / to my intense relief* – See the exercise in Section B7).

- Write a clear conclusion to the story that expresses the feelings of the writer about the experience (e.g. *I am so grateful to the people who rescued me. I was not ready to die at sea!*)

Don't forget!

- Time expressions make the sequence of events clear (e.g. *Many hours passed, some time later, until, when, then, while, next, finally*).

- Conjunctions connect clauses or show connections between sentences (e.g. *however, although*).

- Non-defining relative clauses round out sentences and make them more interesting to read.

8 Building a story from a dialogue

In pairs, read this conversation about what happened during a school trip to the seaside.

Aisha: Where did you go for your school trip this year?

Firuza: We went to the coast. It was so hot that we all wanted to get out of the city.

Aisha: How did it go?

Firuza: Well, we had a great day, apart from one incident.

Aisha: Oh, what was that?

Firuza: Well, we all got to the beach without any trouble. We'd finished putting on sun cream and were just going for a swim when Mrs Kazan noticed that her purse, which had all our return train tickets in it, was missing.

Aisha: Oh no!

Firuza: Yes, she was really upset. She decided that the purse must have dropped out of her bag on the walk to the beach from the station. You see, Ethan had offered to carry the bag for her, and she thought maybe it had fallen out then – but she wasn't really sure.

Aisha: So, did you all go back to look for it or what?

Firuza: Well, I offered to go with her, but in the end, she said she'd retrace her steps with Ethan and see if they could see any sign of it.

Aisha: Poor Ethan. He must have felt awful.

Firuza: I think he did. I mean, he was just about to have a swim when he had to put his clothes back on and go back to the station with Mrs Kazan.

Aisha: And did they find it?

Firuza: Well, they walked right back to the station without seeing it. At the station, they asked at the information desk but it hadn't been handed in.

Aisha: Oh dear.

Firuza: On the way back to the beach, they stopped at a café for a drink. They were talking about the purse and wondering what to do next when the owner came over. He asked if they'd lost anything. They mentioned her purse, and the man produced it from under the counter.

> A passer-by had spotted it on the pavement outside and had handed it in at the café.

Aisha: Well, that was lucky! And was everything still inside?

Firuza: Yes, it was, thank goodness.

Writing the story

You are Ethan. Write an account of the incident for the class newsletter. Before you begin writing, plan what you will say. Use these notes to help you.

- Give the story a clear shape: background details, main events and the outcome should be clear.

- Tenses and pronouns should be appropriate.

- Write vividly, using a range of vocabulary and expressions.

- Use clearly defined paragraphs.

9 Post discussion task: Correcting and writing a report

> **Critical thinking** Each year, Cheng's school raises funds for worthwhile projects. This year the headteacher is thinking about giving the funds to help an expedition of young explorers going to Antarctica. The headteacher has asked Cheng, who is a student representative, to write a report saying whether he thinks this would be the best way to use the funds.

1 In Cheng's report below, there is one extra word in each sentence that should not be there. First, read the report to get the sense. Then read it again and delete the extra word in each sentence. The extra word in the first sentence has been done for you.

2 Finally, show where this missing sentence should go. It also contains an extra word that you need to delete.

In fact, a some member of the expedition previously attended our school.

Report for the headteacher

This report will consider at the pros and cons of supporting the young explorers going to Antarctica. I have spoken to other students in my year to find out of their views and these are given in the report.

The positive points of supporting to the expedition are that, firstly, the people taking part are from our town, so we would be helping local people. In addition, many of us admire the explorers because they are prepared to take risks and are testing in themselves to the limits. Their courage is a shining example and for encourages us to think about the importance of having challenging projects ourselves.

On the other hand, a few students have said it would be better to give the money to the Town Emergency Services rather than a group of teenagers who they want to have fun. Also, the trip might it end in disaster. While it is true that exploring the coast of Antarctica is dangerous, in my view, the people going on if the expedition are taking the project seriously and are well-prepared. They have spent a long time learning how survival skills. They are also going to do some research there in Antarctica, which will increase scientists' knowledge of climate change.

To sum up, I believe that we should support our the expedition. The explorers who deserve our help. The project is a worthwhile and inspiring one challenge. At school, we are all looking forward to reading on the Antarctica Expedition blog.

Cheng Fu

Student representative

GRAMMAR SPOTLIGHT

The interrupted past continuous

The interrupted past continuous is used to show that an action stopped at a specific point when something else happened:

I was packing for my trip when the police knocked at the door.

We use when to link the two tenses. If we want to emphasise two things happening at just the same time, we can also choose as:

It was snowing as/when he climbed higher up the mountain.

The interrupted past continuous is often used to set the scene and to make the beginning of a story more dramatic or interesting – for example, in the text in Section D2:

I was thinking about having a swim when I noticed a strange object bobbing about in the sea.

Practice

1   Look back at the speech bubbles in Section D1 and underline any examples of the interrupted past continuous. Which actions were interrupted, and by what event?

2   Now complete these sentences that set the scene for exciting stories:

   a   Tomaz was _____ on his life raft _____ hungry and scared when, to his relief, a rescue ship _____ on the horizon.

   b   The shipwrecked couple were_____ a conversation about what to do next when they_____ a rowing boat _____ towards them.

   c   Alan was alone on the desert island _____ to make a fire without matches when, to his amazement, he _____ some children _____ along the beach.

   d   Maha _____ home one evening when to her surprise several bright white circular objects suddenly _____ in the sky.

   e   The class were _____ quietly to Mr Hamsun's Science lecture and _____ notes when the teacher suddenly _____ his hand in his pocket and _____ a fistful of fabulous diamonds onto the desk.

   f   Anton _____ with his children in the woods when, to his amazement, he _____ a mysterious, veiled woman dressed in golden robes.

Complete the practice activities in your Workbook.

READING

Reading and writing: multiple matching

Read the article in which four record-breaking young explorers (**A–D**) share their views on adventure. Then answer the question.

Young explorers

A Carl

People ask me what special quality I have that makes my achievements possible. I don't know the answer, but I think everyone can do something amazing. You just have to keep trying to make your dreams a reality, no matter what the effort. As a teenager, I wasn't inspired by school, but I loved the freedom of the outdoors and I volunteered to help at an adventure club in the holidays where I learnt survival techniques, such as rope tying. I also got really good training and advice about how to prepare for expeditions. Amazingly, the club asked me to accompany a group kayaking on Lake Malawi, which was so amazing. It's not about breaking records or winning medals, but more about proving myself and being able to rise to a challenge. At the moment, I have all sorts of ideas about my next expedition, although I never like saying too much in advance.

B Grace

As a child, I was fascinated by explorers who had been to the North Pole. I wrote to them asking how they had accomplished their goals. They wrote back, telling me how they had coped in freezing temperatures and survived the unexpected. Determination isn't enough, you also have to be well organised. On my first solo expedition, I spent hours frantically searching for matches to melt ice for drinking. I was about to collapse from cold and exhaustion when I found the matches inside my sleeping bag! Now, when I'm on an expedition, I store all my equipment in its proper place. I have to pull my equipment along on a sled, so I have to make sure it's not too heavy. In my blog, I write about how I even cut off clothing labels and the metal tags from zips. My team laugh at my obsessions, and they gave me a prize on the last trip for always having the lightest equipment.

C Adam

When I got my first bicycle, a whole new world opened up for me. My bike gave me the freedom to explore the beaches and forests around my home. I came across a blog by an explorer who had cycled from Dublin to Islamabad. When I left school, I set off, determined to do something different and explore the world. As regards the costs of the trip, I was incredibly lucky as, by chance, a health organisation had heard of my expedition. They were studying the physiological effects of activity and diet and, to my astonishment, they offered to pay for my trip if I agreed to eat over 5,000 calories per day, twice the average intake. Despite consuming so much, I didn't put on weight – I lost it! Overall, I think my most memorable journey was cycling alone through Asia. In contrast to what I had heard, I felt safe and the hospitality was like no other. I would love to go back there.

CONTINUED

D   Zuleeka

When I was growing up, we spent family holidays exploring the Greek islands. My parents always involved us in the preparation for the trips, including how to pack lightly and how to read a compass. But I never considered myself adventurous. I certainly never thought I would sail solo around the world when I was 17! Although I have travelled the world, I think there are lots of adventures, big and small, waiting to happen on our own doorstep. In my work as an ambassador for a young people's organisation (which I was asked to do because I broke a world record), I encourage curiosity. To be an explorer, you need an open mind and an urge to find things out. Everyone can try out new things, even just getting off the bus earlier than usual and walking a different route home can teach you something new.

For each statement, write the correct letter A, B, C or D on the line.

Which person gives the following information?

1	The fact that they received public recognition for achievement	_____	[1]
2	An indication that they take preparing for an expedition to an extreme	_____	[1]
3	A preference not to talk about future plans	_____	[1]
4	A description of a time when they made a mistake	_____	[1]
5	A suggestion that a change in routine is helpful	_____	[1]
6	A belief that determination is the most important factor in success	_____	[1]
7	Something they were pleasantly surprised by in a place they visited	_____	[1]
8	A suggestion for how to ask for advice	_____	[1]
9	A description of how they assisted scientific research	_____	[1]

[Total: 9]

Reading and writing: informal

You and your family recently went on a sailing trip.

Write an email to a friend describing what happened.

In your email, you should:

- describe how it felt to be on board the ship
- describe some unusual and exciting things you saw
- say if you would like to go sailing again and explain why or why not.

Write about 120 to 160 words.   [15]

[Total: 15]

CONTINUED

Reading and writing: formal

Your school plans to organise an adventure holiday for next summer for your year group. Your headteacher wants students' views on possible destinations, and you have been asked to write a report.

In your report, suggest places to go and say which one might be best for your age group and why.

Here are some comments from students in your year group:

I think we should go sailing. Imagine learning how to sail on the Atlantic!

Could we go as far as South America? It would be great to travel into the Amazon Rainforest.

Let's go somewhere we can learn a sport like snowboarding or skiing.

Why don't we go camping in the forest and try to survive without electricity or internet?

Now write a report for the headteacher.

The comments above may give you some ideas, and you can also use some ideas of your own.

Write about 120 to 160 words. [15]

[Total: 15]

Reading and writing: formal

Your school year group recently went on a visit to explore some underground caves. Your headteacher wants students' opinions about the visit, and you have been asked to write a report.

In your report, say what was enjoyable about the trip, and suggest how it could be improved.

Here are some comments from students in your year group:

We loved exploring a place that so few people had seen before.

It was exciting to see so many different rock formations.

The caves were too dark and silent.

We needed better torches and climbing gear.

Now write a report for the headteacher.

The comments above may give you some ideas, and you should also use some ideas of your own.

Write about 120 to 160 words. [15]

[Total: 15]

CONTINUED

Reading and writing: formal

Your class recently attended a special course in survival skills. Your headteacher wants students' opinions about the course, and you have been asked to write a report.

In your report, say what students thought of the course, and suggest ways it could be improved.

Here are some comments from students in your class:

> We learnt useful skills such as how to build shelters and catch fish.

> The course was quite interesting, but it was a bit too long.

> The survival skills were difficult to learn.

> The course taught us all a lot about how to survive in really difficult situations.

Now write a report for the headteacher.

The comments above may give you some ideas, and you should also use some ideas of your own.

Write about 120 to 160 words. [15]

[Total: 15]

LISTENING

Listening: short extracts

You will hear five short recordings. For each question, choose the correct answer, **A**, **B** or **C**, and put a tick (✓) in the appropriate box.

You will hear each recording twice.

You will hear a camp leader giving some information about an adventure trail camp.

1   What should students have brought with them?

   A   Food for the weekend   ☐

   B   Camping gear   ☐

   C   Sports equipment   ☐   [1]

2   What will the students do first?

   A   Learn about safety rules   ☐

   B   Choose their activities   ☐

   C   Meet the team leaders   ☐   [1]

CONTINUED

You will hear two classmates talking about a presentation they are preparing for school.

3 Why might the boy choose Arctic Explorers for his topic?

    A It is more interesting than Space Travel ☐

    B He doesn't like the topic of Space Travel ☐

    C He thinks it's easier to research ☐ [1]

4 What will the girl do first?

    A Look for some websites ☐

    B Write a description ☐

    C Select some pictures ☐ [1]

You will hear part of a radio interview with an open water swimmer.

5 The woman decided to try open water swimming because:

    A she wanted to swim every day. ☐

    B she joined a swimming club. ☐

    C pool swimming was too easy. ☐ [1]

6 What does she expect to find challenging about her next swim?

    A Water temperature ☐

    B Movement of water ☐

    C The distance she'll swim ☐ [1]

You will hear a boy leaving a voicemail message for a friend about a sailing club.

7 Why does the boy want to go to the sailing club on Saturday?

    A The friends won't have to pay ☐

    B It's open all day ☐

    C It won't be too crowded ☐ [1]

8 The boy suggests meeting his friend near:

    A the playground. ☐

    B the water fountain. ☐

    C the café. ☐ [1]

You will hear a boy talking to friend about a trip he made to the coast.

9 What did the boy do on his trip to the coast?

    A He found some fossils ☐

    B He collected some shells ☐

    C He went for a swim ☐ [1]

CONTINUED

10 What happened to one of his friends on the trip?

    A He lost his way   ☐

    B He found some rocks   ☐

    C He missed the bus   ☐   [1]

[Total: 10]

SPEAKING

Warm-up questions

Warm-up questions help you feel more relaxed before you move on to answering assessed questions.

Take turns asking and answering the questions. Speak for 1–2 minutes.

- How often do you listen to music?
- Who is your favourite singer or musician?
- What kind of music do you like?

Interview

Read the questions. In pairs, decide who will play the interviewer and who will play the student. Then role-play the interview. Speak for about 2–3 minutes. Change roles and role-play the interview again.

Coping with challenges

- What kind of challenges have you faced recently?
- How do you prepare for a challenge such as a race or a competition?
- Do you think it is important to challenge yourself? Why or why not?

Short talk

Read the options and compare them. You have one minute to prepare your talk. Now give a short talk to your partner. Speak for about 2 minutes. Change roles and listen to your partner's talk.

Choosing a challenge

You are planning an expedition with a group of friends. Consider the following options:

- a weekend climbing trip in mountains that are steep and rocky
- a five-hour cross-country run across fields and hills.

Discuss the advantages and disadvantages of each option. Say which option you would prefer, and why.

Discussion

Read the discussion questions. In pairs, decide who will play the interviewer and who will play the student. Then role-play the discussion. Speak for about 3 minutes. Change roles and role-play the interview again.

- Many people climb mountains even though it can be very dangerous. Is this a good idea?
- Do you think physical challenges such as running a marathon are good for your mental health?
- Some people think that there is too much pressure on teenagers to be successful all the time. What do you think?

SELF-ASSESSMENT CHECKLIST

Reflect on what you have learnt in this unit. For each area listed, decide whether you feel confident or need more practice. If you feel you need more practice, you will find some ideas to help you in Advice for Success. Come back to your self-assessment scores later in your course and see if your confidence has improved.

I can ...	Need more practice	Fairly confident
explore the topic of adventure, exploration and the sea, using appropriate vocabulary		
identify the sequence of events in a story and a newspaper article		
write a narrative with effective use of tenses and engaging opening and closing paragraphs		
listen and identify key points in an interview and a lecture		
express surprise, console someone and sympathise with someone		

ADVICE FOR SUCCESS

This section is to help you help yourself. Choose the suggestions you like and adapt them if you want to. Make notes about what you do and how it helped you.

Extending your skills

1   When asked to write a narrative, students sometimes say they don't know what to write about. The ingredients for stories are all around us: in the incidents that happen in everyday life; in the stories your friends tell you about things that have happened to them; in news articles; in the letters read out on radio talk shows, and so on. Be creative and rework ideas into your own writing.

2   The plot isn't everything. Many wonderful stories do not have particularly original plots.

The main interest in a story often lies in the beauty of the writing. Giving attention to detail in your writing is as important as having an original plot.

3   If you enjoy reading and have any favourite authors, try to work out what you particularly like about their books. Study their style. What techniques do they use to help you 'picture' the story in your mind? Could you adopt any of these techniques in your own work?

4   Get into the habit of punctuating as you go along by 'hearing' the prose in your mind. Read your work aloud to hear what it sounds like. Imagine that you are reading it to another person. What will it sound like to them?

CONTINUED

Showcasing your skills

5   Aim to make your writing interesting so the reader really wants to read on and find out what happened next. Here are some ways you can do this:

- Use a mixture of short sentences and longer, more complex sentences.

- Use vivid language and a range of emotional and dramatic expressions.

- Set the scene at the beginning in a powerful, unusual way.

- Endings are important, too. Try to make the ending satisfying and logical.

6   Planning your composition before you start writing will help you structure it. Narratives usually start with background information. The story then develops and you explain what happened. Finally, there should be a definite conclusion so the reader isn't left wondering what happened in the end.

> # Unit 9
> # Animals and our world

LEARNING INTENTIONS

In this unit you will:

- Explore the topic of animals in zoos, farms, the wild and medical research

- Skim for general ideas and identify bias in an article about animal research

- Write a blog post using examples and explanations to develop your argument

- Identify key details and understand what is implied in an interview

- Use appropriate register and intonation for expressing disappointment and disagreement

 Watch the video about animals and our world in the digital coursebook.

BEFORE YOU START

Look at the photo on this page.

a   Choose three adjectives to describe the animal in the photo.

b   Why do you think this animal might be endangered?

c   Why is it important to protect endangered species of wild animals?

d   What do we learn from studying wild animals and their habitats?

A A fresh look at zoos

1 Animal vocabulary

1 › **Critical thinking** Working with a partner, match six of the words in the box with the pictures.

2 Make sure you know the meaning of all of the words. Then decide whether each creature is a mammal, reptile, fish or bird.

bear	lion	parrot	rhino	snake
camel	crocodile	elephant		salmon
lizard	penguin	dolphin		vulture
leopard	monkey	gorilla		shark
wolf	cheetah	eagle		kangaroo

2 Definitions

Choose the correct word or phrase to match these definitions. Work with a partner and consult a dictionary if necessary.

1 A person in a zoo who looks after animals is known as:

A a carer   C a warder

B a keeper   D a poacher

2 The natural surroundings of an animal are called its:

A habitat   C home

B location   D enclosure

3 Animals that hunt and kill other animals for food are known as:

A scavengers   C predators

B beasts   D prey

4 Animals that may die out altogether are known as:

A endangered species

B indigenous wildlife

C animals in captivity

D migrating herds

5 Animals that once lived but have now died out are known as:

A domesticated   C fossils

B extinct   D amphibians

3 Pre-reading discussion

1 › **Critical thinking** How do you feel about zoos? If you have been to a zoo, talk to your partner about one you have visited. Which aspects did you find particularly interesting?

Think about:

• the range of animals and birds

• the conditions under which they were kept

• whether they seemed contented

• the atmosphere of the zoo in general.

2   Was there anything about the zoo that you did not enjoy?

3   If you have never been to a zoo, would you like to visit one? Why / why not?

Keep a record of your views to use later in the unit.

4   Reading an article for the school website

Hammerton High School paid a visit to a zoo. After the visit, Michael wrote about the trip for his school website. Read his article below. How does his impression of the zoo compare with your own experiences of zoos?

As you read, underline the opinion words and phrases he uses.

| About | Curriculum | News | **Student articles** | Contact |

Can zoos ever be animal friendly?

1   The theme of our last class discussion was 'How can zoos provide animals with a decent life?' Everyone except me (I just wasn't sure) believed it was impossible for zoos to give animals the environment they need. Mr Hennessy suggested that, now the exams are over, actually visiting a modern zoo might give us a wider perspective.

2   I went to the zoo with an open mind and was pleasantly surprised by what I found. In our debate, many people had said that zoos are full of smelly cages containing animals with miserable, hunted-looking expressions. Metro Park Zoo, however, was set in an attractive, open environment. Trees and bushes had been planted around the enclosures. Small ponds had been dug out so the animals had access to water. In my opinion, the animals were peaceful rather than depressed.

3   As we entered, we were given information packs about the origins and habits of the animals. The zoo takes a lot of trouble to keep the animals' diet, living quarters and social groupings as natural as possible. Vets are on hand if they become ill.

4   At school, some people had accused zoos of exploiting animals for profit but at Metro Park, as I see it, nothing could be further from the truth. Most of the profits are used to improve conditions at the zoo or donated to charities for endangered species.

5   Before I visited Metro Park Zoo, I wasn't sure about the rights and wrongs of zoos. I can't deny that zoos take the freedom of animals away. On balance, I feel that, although zoos can't provide the freedom of the wild, they can give animals a safe, secure environment where they are well fed and protected from predators. As long as they do this well, to my mind, they make a positive contribution to animal welfare. They also play an important part in educating us about wildlife. I think lots of my friends changed their minds too.

6   On the bus back to school, we all agreed that what we liked most was the zoo's atmosphere and we would definitely recommend it for next year's trip.

By Michael Foley

5 Comprehension check

1   Why did Michael's class visit the zoo?

2   What was his first impression of the zoo?

3   What did he find out from the zoo's publicity?

4   What kind of role does he think zoos have in modern society?

5   What do you think are the bad points about zoos that Michael has not mentioned?

6 Analysing the article

1   > Critical thinking Does the first paragraph form a good opening to the article? Do you feel you want to read on? Why / Why not? How do we know that it is intended for an audience of students?

2   Paragraph 2 questions the attitudes many people have towards zoos by contrasting their opinion with the reality (as Michael sees it) of Metro Park Zoo. Find the words and phrases that do this.

3   Paragraphs 3 and 4 continue the theme of disagreeing with other people's opinions about zoos. Underline the phrase that expresses disagreement.

4   Paragraph 5 sums up Michael's view of zoos. Which phrase tells us that he has thought about both sides of the argument before coming to a decision? Which connector is used to develop his argument and link his ideas together?

5   Does the final paragraph round off the article effectively? How do we know that the writer is aware of his audience?

7 Typical opinion language

> Critical thinking In paragraph 2, Michael introduces an opinion with *In my opinion . . .*

1   What other opinion words and phrases does he use? Make a list.

2   What other opinion words and phrases do you know? Add them to your list.

Disagreeing with other people's views

In explaining his views, Michael thinks about and rejects the ideas other people have about zoos.

3   Study the list and select the phrases Michael used. Add any other similar phrases you know to the list.

Contrary to popular belief, . . .

It is believed that . . . , yet . . .

People think . . . but . . .

Some people accuse them of . . . but nothing could be further from the truth.

Many people say that . . . . However, . . .

It's unfair for people to say that . . .

People make the absurd/ridiculous claim that . . .

Despite claims that . . . ,

8 Making your mind up

> Critical thinking You can show that you have considered different ideas before making up your mind by using one of the following phrases. Which do you prefer? Do you recognise the one Michael used?

Now that I have considered both sides, I feel . . .

After weighing up the pros and cons, I would say that . . .

On balance, I feel that . . .

There are points in favour of each argument, but overall I believe . . .

I tend to come down on the side of . . .

9 Writing a paragraph

Choose one of the following topics and write a short paragraph giving your own opinions on the subject. Don't forget that you need reasons to back up your views. Use appropriate phrases from Section A7.

- Animals – better living in the wild or in the zoo?

- Pets – perfect companions or dirty nuisances?

- Eating meat – vital for health or unnecessary and unfair to animals?

10 Reading aloud

When you are ready, take turns reading your paragraphs aloud. This will give you a chance to get an overview of your classmates' opinions. Does hearing other students' paragraphs make a difference to your own views? If so, choose a 'making your mind up' phrase to express your feelings.

11 Expressions of contrasting meaning

In his article, Michael says that the animals in the zoo he visited were kept in 'an attractive, open environment', which was very different from the 'smelly cages' people might have expected to find animals living in.

1   For each of the following ideas, try to develop an expression that conveys a contrasting meaning. Work in pairs or small groups, and take time to check words in a dictionary when you need to.

Example: ***a bare, cramped room***
          a comfortably furnished, spacious room

a   a dull lesson

b   a worn-out pair of shoes

c   a poorly child

d   a tasteless meal

e   an awkward dance

f   an untidy, neglected garden

g   ugly, illegible handwriting

h   a rusty, bent bicycle

i   a loud, aggressive person

j   a hard, lumpy bed

2   When you have finished, compare your answers with the other groups. Which expressions do you think were most effective?

12 Before you listen

You are going to listen to an interview with a zookeeper. Write down three things you expect her to say about her job.

13 Vocabulary check

Make sure you know the meaning of the words and phrases in the box.

> animal welfare   conservation   enclosures
>
> enrichment   virtual tour

14 Listening for gist

Now listen to the interview. Does the speaker mention the topics you predicted?

15 Multiple-choice questions

Listen again and choose the correct option (A–C) for each question.

1 What was Jo's first experience of working in a zoo?

   A She went to a zoo to study wild animals.

   B She got a part-time job in a local zoo.

   C She spent a day with a real zookeeper.

2 What is Jo's main task at the zoo?

   A Feeding and exercising the animals.

   B Making sure the animals are healthy.

   C Keeping careful records on each animal.

3 Jo says that cleaning out the animal enclosures is:

   A something she doesn't mind doing.

   B something that isn't always popular.

   C something that everyone has to do.

4 Jo says that enrichment activities:

   A help to develop food hunting skills.

   B make animals feel more at home.

   C keep animals active and engaged.

5 Jo enjoys talking to people about animals because:

   A she is proud of the work they do.

   B she likes meeting people.

   C she wants to encourage people to work at the zoo.

6 Visitors to the zoo website can:

   A see live videos of some animals.

   B get a personal tour of the whole zoo.

   C watch educational videos about wildlife.

16 Post-listening discussion

1 〉 **Critical thinking** What do you think about a zookeeper's job? Would you enjoy it? What would you like or dislike about it?

2 If you could choose between a visit to a real zoo and a virtual zoo, which would you prefer? Explain your reasons.

3 How do you think technology will change the way we think about zoos in the future?

17 Expressing disappointment and disagreement, and making your opinions clear

1 Have you ever been to a circus? Tell your partner what you thought of it.

2 Now listen to the following dialogue. Silvia is expressing disappointment. Does her voice go up or down?

Malik: What did you think of the circus?

Silvia: Well, to be honest, I was just a bit disappointed.

Malik: Why was that?

Silvia: The trapeze artists weren't very exciting, and I didn't like seeing large animals performing tricks.

Malik: Surely the jugglers were good fun to watch?

Silvia: As a matter of fact, they weren't as skilful as I thought they'd be.

Malik: But wasn't seeing a real live fire-eater amazing?

Silvia: To be frank, I've seen better things on television.

Malik: Sounds like a waste of money, then.

Silvia: It was! In fact, we left before the end.

Expressing disappointment

I was just a bit disappointed.

It didn't come up to my expectations.

It wasn't as interesting / enjoyable / well done / polished as I thought it would be.

I've seen better things on television.

It was a let-down.

Expressing disagreement informally

Surely the clowns/costumes/performances/songs were amusing/spectacular?

But wasn't a real live fire-eater / film star / pop singer / famous athlete amazing/superb/unforgettable to watch?

Wasn't it wonderful to see the real thing?

Introducing personal opinion

As a matter of fact, . . . / In fact, . . .

To be honest, . . . / If you want my honest opinion, . . .

To be frank, . . . / Frankly, . . .

Actually, . . .

Commenting

It sounds like a waste of money, then.

It sounds as if it wasn't worth going to.

It sounds as if you'd have been better off at home.

18 Practice dialogues

1. Make a complete dialogue from the prompts. Make sure the person expressing disappointment sounds disappointed!

   A: What / you think / class visit / virtual zoo?

   B: Frank / just bit / disappointed.

   A: Why / that?

   B: Most of the animals / asleep / not do very much.

   A: Surely / elephants and giraffes / fascinating?

   B: Actually / not be / interesting / thought / it be.

   A: But / not be / livecam / baby panda / fantastic?

   B: Matter / fact / be / let down.

   A: It / sound / waste of time.

   B: honest / better / watch a wildlife documentary.

2. Create similar dialogues around the following situations:

   - A disappointing visit to an animal sanctuary where injured animals are cared for before being returned to the wild.

   - A disappointing visit to a theatre or concert to see well-known performers.

   - Some other disappointing event you have personally experienced.

B Animal experimentation

1 Pre-reading discussion

> **Critical thinking** Experiments on animals play a large part in medical research. Scientists say they hope to find cures for many human diseases by finding out how animals react to specific drugs or medical operations.

However, animals are living beings and experimenting on them raises ethical questions. Discuss the ethical questions below, which will help you explore the rights or wrongs of this issue.

1   Discuss these ethical questions with your partner. Use a dictionary to check unfamiliar language. Back up your answers with reasons and opinions.

- Is it ethical to experiment on animals without painkillers or anaesthetics?

- Is it acceptable to give a laboratory animal a human ear or heart?

- Minor illnesses like colds and sore throats usually get better by themselves. Should animals be subjected to experiments to find cures for unimportant illnesses like these?

- Genetic engineering can mean that laboratory animals are given genes that cause birth defects. When they reproduce, their young will be born with genetic problems. How justifiable is this?

- Some serious illnesses can be caused by too much sugar and salt in our diet. Should animals suffer because of our bad habits?

- Laboratory animals are used for non-medical experiments too. Is it fair to use animals to test the safety of luxury products, such as perfume and aftershave?

2   Overall, what is your view of animal experimentation?

- *It doesn't trouble me at all.*

- *It's cruel and unjustifiable. I am totally opposed to it.*

- *It's a necessary evil – alright so long as animals are not exposed to unnecessary suffering.*

3   It has been said that the average pet has more stress from living with its owner than the laboratory animal ever suffers. Do you think that's a reasonable view? Why / Why not?

2 Predicting content

You are going to read an article written by a medical research scientist who is in favour of medical experiments on animals. Would you expect the opinions expressed in the article to be:

a   balanced?

b   a bit extreme?

c   undecided?

3 Vocabulary check

Make sure you understand the meanings of these phrases:

> an emotive issue   a controversial issue

4 Reading for gist

⟩ Critical thinking The writer answers five myths about animal research. Skim the article and match paragraphs 2–6 with the myth it challenges.

☐ A   Animals are used unnecessarily in experiments.

☐ B   It is unethical to use animals for research.

☐ C   Research animals suffer unnecessary pain and cruelty.

☐ D   Animal research has not resulted in significant scientific benefits.

☐ E   Results of animal research are not comparable in humans.

Fact or myth?

Animal research explained

1 The use of animals in medical research is a controversial and emotive issue. Let's take a look at the myths versus the facts.

2 Many major cornerstones of medical science have been achieved with the help of animal research, including antibiotics, anti-cancer drugs, artificial joint replacements, high blood pressure medication, and vaccines for smallpox, polio and Covid-19. These and many other medical advances would not have been possible without the help of animal research.

3 While concern for the inhumane treatment of living creatures is undeniably valid, it is important to remember that medical research today is governed by strict regulations. In the USA, for example, there is a federal law called the Animal Welfare Act (AWA). Researchers are required to justify why they need animals for their research and use only the most appropriate species and the fewest possible number of subjects.

4 Medical research using animals is conducted according to ethical guidelines. These are known as the three Rs. First, scientists must try to **replace** animals with alternative methods of testing. Some tests, for example, can be carried out with cells in test tubes or using computer models. Secondly, they must aim to **reduce** the numbers of animals in their studies, using only the minimum number necessary. Finally, they must try to **refine** their experiments in order to minimise pain and distress as far as possible. They must also ensure that animals are kept in clean, healthy living conditions with adequate food, light and ventilation.

5 In fact, there are many similarities between humans and animals that makes their data scientifically valid. Vaccines such as the Covid-19 mRNA vaccine could not have been developed without the use of animals in clinical trials. Researchers were able to prove that the synthetically manufactured vaccine produced a strong immune response in living creatures by injecting it into mice. This was an important step before trialling the vaccines on human volunteers.

6 There are many life-threatening diseases such as malaria, Ebola and HIV for which we do not yet have a cure or a vaccine. Animal testing is a crucial element in the vaccine and drug development process, one with potential benefits for generations of humans to come. The long-term benefits for humans outweigh any moral misgivings concerning the carefully controlled use of animals in medical research.

5 Vocabulary practice

Match these words and phrases from the text with their definitions.

a	cornerstones	1	worthwhile or reliable
b	inhumane		
c	refine	2	reduce to the smallest amount
d	minimise	3	improve
e	scientifically valid	4	the most important elements of something
f	crucial		
		5	extremely important, vital
		6	cruel

6 Post-reading discussion

> Critical thinking The writer believes that medical experiments on animals are both humane and necessary. What do you think of this point of view? Explain your opinions to your classmates.

7 Note-taking

Read the article again in more detail. Make notes from the text about:

a   the reasons for carrying out medical experiments on animals.

b   the achievements that have come about through animal research.

c   the steps that are taken to make medical experimentation as humane as possible.

8 How the writer achieves an objective tone

1   > Critical thinking The writer achieves a calm, objective-sounding tone and style. How do you think she achieves this? Write down your ideas. Compare your ideas in your group.

2   The following list shows techniques the writer uses to achieve the impression of being fair. How do the points compare with your list?

One of these techniques is not used. Identify which one.

• She gives examples of medical advances.

• She uses emotive language.

• She mentions arguments against animal research.

• She describes how animal welfare has improved.

• She explains how animals have helped medical research.

• She acknowledges opposing views of animal research.

3   Find examples of the above points in the text. Compare your findings with the other groups. Is there anything you disagree about?

9 Finding the right angle

The writer suggests that the real issue is not *whether* you should be for or against animal experiments but *how* animal research can be as kind as possible to animals, so as to minimise any suffering to them. This is an important change in the angle of the usual argument. Why?

10 Understanding bias in an argument

1   > Critical thinking Not everyone would say that the writer is completely fair or unbiased. What points against animal experiments did the writer, as you see it, choose not to include? Write down some ideas.

2   Study the opinions below, which view animal experiments from a different perspective. Make sure you understand each one. Compare them with your own ideas and select any points that appeared on your list. Are there any ideas that you did not note but which you think are important points to consider? Select them too.

Animals are physically different from people so they react differently to drugs and medical experiments. You can't always make predictions on how people might react based on what you know about animals. As a result, many animal experiments are a waste of time.

Research studies using human volunteers have been responsible for major advances in medical understanding. For example, the development of a vaccine for Covid-19 could not have been achieved without the help of human volunteers.

Many members of the public think of medical research scientists as torturers and murderers.

Advanced technology, such as lasers and ultrasound, is improving our understanding of the causes of disease. We could make more use of advanced technology and less use of living creatures in research.

Not all laboratories are wonderful. A laboratory was taken to court recently for its disgraceful treatment of animals.

It's difficult for the public to see behind the closed doors of a laboratory. So scientists have a lot of freedom in the way they work and what they say they do.

Great improvements in health and life expectancy have come since the development of clean water systems and sanitation. This had nothing to do with laboratory animals.

Health education has helped people avoid disease. People have learnt about a good diet, being hygienic and taking exercise. We don't need to experiment on animals.

11 Writing an article for the school blog

Your class has been discussing the rights and wrongs of animal experimentation. You feel that medical experiments on animals are useful and necessary, but it is important to consider alternative techniques, too.

Write an article entitled 'Is animal experimentation really worth it?' to post on your school blog. It should explain:

- how animal experimentation has contributed to medical understanding

- why animal experiments do not always give useful results

- the alternatives to medical experiments on animals.

The angle of the argument

Get the angle clear. You are not writing a composition that is totally against animal experimentation because you accept the need for it. Your aim is to show that medical experiments on animals, while sometimes helpful, do not always produce useful results. You want to explain how our health can often be improved using alternative methods.

Plan the content

What points do you want to include? Can you give any explanations or examples to develop your points? How can you relate your content to the interests of the readers of the newsletter?

Structure and language

Use a strong opening for your article: get the reader's attention and keep it. Finish the article with a paragraph that leaves your reader in no doubt about what you really believe.

Structure your composition so the argument you are presenting is clear and easy to follow. Using opinion language and linking words will help you do this. Some of the expressions in Sections A7 and A8 will be helpful.

12 Prepositions after verbs

There are many examples of prepositions following verbs in the article about animal experiments:

Hundreds of children are *born with* cystic fibrosis.

Let's *start with* the most obvious facts.

Blood *circulates through* our veins.

You *replace* animal experiments *with* alternatives.

People who *experiment on* animals are just the same as the rest of us.

Practice

1 Fill the gaps in the following sentences. Choose from these prepositions.

about	at	from	of
on	to	with	

a Is it right to experiment _____ animals?

b Why bother _____ animal suffering when children are dying _____ incurable diseases?

c I am surprised _____ you.

d I object _____ all this animal rights propaganda.

e Alan decided to contribute _____ an animal charity.

f I won't quarrel _____ them.

g Elephants depend _____ their keepers.

h He died _____ a broken heart, so they say.

i Can you provide him _____ an information pack?

j Baby rhinos respond well _____ human contact.

2 What other verbs do you know followed by these prepositions? Discuss with a partner and make a list.

13 Spelling and pronunciation: Regular plurals

Most regular plurals in English simply add -*s*.

1 Look at this list of regular plurals. Check the meaning of each word and write a translation if necessary.

a	cats	g	spiders	m	houses
b	hens	h	faces	n	monkeys
c	insects	i	horses	o	bees
d	cages	j	goats	p	roses
e	wasps	k	birds		
f	donkeys	l	cows		

2 The -s at the end of the noun plural can be pronounced /s/ or /z/ or /ɪz/. Copy out the table below. Listen to the list of words and write each word in the correct column, according to the sound of its ending.

/s/	/z/	/ɪz/
cats	hens	faces

3 Now say the words aloud to your partner. Do they think the sound of each ending is clear?

14 Spelling and pronunciation: Irregular plurals

The following rules show how irregular plurals are formed. Say the examples aloud clearly, checking your pronunciation with a partner.

1   Nouns that end in *-ch, -s, -sh, -ss* or *-x*: add *-es* to form the plural. The *-es* ending is pronounced /ɪz/.

Examples: ben*ch* – *benches*   *bus* – *buses*   *rash* – *rashes*   *pass* – *passes*   *box* – *boxes*

2   Nouns ending in *-f* or *-fe*: replace the ending with *-ves* to form the plural. The *-s* is pronounced /z/.

Examples: *calf* – *calves*   *leaf* – *leaves* *wife* – *wives*

3   Some nouns form the plural simply by changing the vowel. The pronunciation changes too.

Examples: *goose* – *geese*   *mouse* – *mice*   *tooth* – *teeth*   *man* – *men*

4   Nouns that end in *-o* usually form the plural by adding *-es*, which is pronounced /z/.

Example: *tomato* – *tomatoes*
Common exceptions: *photos*   *pianos*   *rhinos*

5   Nouns ending in a consonant and *-y*: form the plural by changing the *-y* to *-ies*. The *-s* is pronounced /z/.

Examples: *fly* – *flies*   *lady* – *ladies*

Nouns ending in a vowel and *-y* just add *-s*, which is pronounced /z/.

Example: *donkey* – *donkeys*

6   Some nouns are always plural.

Examples: *trousers*   *scissors*   *glasses*

7   Some nouns are the same in the singular and the plural.

Examples: *sheep*   *deer*   *fish*   *salmon*   *bison*

15 Vocabulary practice

Work with a partner to fill the gaps with the plural forms of the nouns in brackets. Make sure you understand the meaning of each sentence. Check your pronunciation, too!

a   The _____ have just given birth to several _____. (*sheep, lamb*)

b   Watch out for _____, _____ and _____ if you go camping in the wild.   (*bear, wolf, wildcat*)

c   If you're lucky, you'll be able to see _____, _____ and _____ in the park.   (*deer, goose, fox*)

d   A pet mouse needs a friend. The problem is you might soon have lots of baby _____.   (*mouse*)

e   _____ and _____ have the most amazing _____. (*crocodile, rhino, tooth*)

f   Tropical _____ need special care, but make interesting pets. (*fish*)

g   It's strange to think that ugly _____ can turn into lovely _____. (*caterpillar, butterfly*)

16 Look, say, cover, write, check

1   Learn these commonly misspelt words using the 'look, say, cover, write, check' method (see Unit 1, Section B12 if you need a reminder).

potato	anaesthetic	potatoes
elephant	clothes	leopard calf
laboratory	calves	innocent leaf
benefit leaves	terrible	vaccine
veterinary	scissors	rhino

2   Ask a partner to test you when you are confident you have learnt them correctly.

3   Choose six of the words and put each one into a sentence to show its meaning.

C Animals in sport and entertainment

1 Discussion

Discuss these questions with a partner. Make notes of your ideas to tell the class.

1 Horse racing and camel racing are popular sports for many people. Circuses that use performing animals draw large crowds. Do you feel it's fair to animals to involve them in human leisure activities in this way?

2 How are animals used for sport or entertainment in your country?

3 Sports in which animals are hunted are called *field sports*. Are these sports popular in your country? Have you ever seen or taken part in this form of sport? How did you feel about it?

2 People's opinions

Here are some reasons why people say they like animals to be involved in human activities. Discuss them with your partner and tick any that reflect your own views.

☐ 'I admire the skills and bravery of performers at the circus who ride on horses or control wild animals.'

☐ 'What I find so impressive about bullfighting is the total concentration needed by the matador – without it, he'd be dead or injured.'

☐ 'Shooting birds demands a steady aim and perfect hand–eye coordination. What makes me cross is people who criticise me for shooting but think nothing of eating meat.'

☐ 'What I love about horse racing is the thrilling atmosphere as the horses approach the finishing line.'

3 Letter completion: My views on animal charities

The following text is a letter written by a student to a newspaper giving the reasons why she is against giving money to an animal charity.

1 Work in pairs or groups of three to fill in the words and phrases that link the writer's ideas and show her opinions and attitudes. Choose from the suggestions in italics. Then compare your answers to those of other groups.

Dear Editor,

I read in your newspaper that there are plans to give a large amount of money raised through our town's annual charity appeal to the Green Pastures Horses' Home. The home is a place where racehorses can live in comfort when they retire from racing. I am writing to say that (a) _____ (*for instance / naturally / I think this is a very*) (b) _____ (*unhealthy/ cruel/foolish*) idea.

I am not against spending on animal welfare, but what makes me really angry is the thought of money being spent on giving animals a happy retirement when many old people in our country are neglected and live in poverty.

It is (c) _____ (*argued/denied/appealed*) that racehorses have provided people with sport and entertainment, (d) _____ (*definitely / but / of course*) I can't see how this justifies spending so much on them. After all, they are only animals, and humans should come first.

People (e) _____ (*shout/demand/insist*) that animal cruelty is wrong, (f) _____ (*on balance / in other words / yet*) they ignore the cruel treatment the elderly receive. I think money raised through charity should benefit human beings. The care of aged animals is the responsibility of those who own them, and it is (g) _____ (*unfair/ confusing/depressing*) to expect us to support them. (h) _____ (*It's all very well / As I see it/ Nevertheless*), people who own racehorses are rich and have the resources to fund a good retirement for their animals. Wouldn't it be more sensible for the owners to save a percentage of the big profits they have made (i) _____ (*also / and / as well*) use that for their animals' welfare in old age?

Our senior citizens have worked hard in their lives. People say their **pensions** are adequate but (j) _____ (*nothing could be further from the truth / on the contrary / nonsense*). In fact, many old people have hardly enough money for food and bills, let alone luxuries such as horse racing.

At my school, I am starting a campaign to increase young people's awareness of the purpose of charity fundraising. I know we will not be in time to stop the funds from going to the horses' home this year. (k) _____ (*Despite / In addition / Nevertheless*), we shall do all we can to ensure charitable funds are not wasted on useless projects in future.

Yours faithfully,

Bella Balkano

GLOSSARY

pensions: money paid to elderly people who have retired from work

2   Re-read the letter to get a sense of the flow of the argument. Do you think that the opening gets straight to the point? What do you think of the end of the letter?

4 Vocabulary check: Words for feelings

Bella expresses her feelings and attitudes in a forceful, impassioned way. The following exercise shows how adjectives of similar meaning can be used to describe feelings and attitudes.

Complete each group of synonyms with an appropriate word from the box.

a   I am *disgusted* / _____ by your actions.

b   He is *worried* / _____ about the lack of clean water for the farm animals.

c   It is *wrong* / _____ to use animals in medical experiments.

d   He is *sorry* / _____ about the trouble he has caused.

e   It is *ridiculous* / _____ to say animal are as important as people.

f   I feel *distressed* / _____ when I hear about children being unable to get proper medical care.

absurd	uneasy	horrified
apologetic	saddened	immoral

5 Language study: Adding emphasis

What . . . clauses

We can use a clause beginning with *what* to sound more emphatic. For example, Bella says:

What makes me really angry is the thought of money being spent on giving animals a happy retirement.

This is another way of saying:

The thought of money being spent on giving animals a happy retirement makes me really angry.

Restructuring the sentence, using what, makes Bella sound more emphatic.

Contrast the structure of these pairs of sentences. Which one is more emphatic? Why? How has the structure been changed to achieve this?

She loves the idea that the safari park will provide jobs for people.

***What** she loves is the idea that the safari park will provide jobs for people.*

We doubted that the water was clean enough to drink.

***What** we doubted was that the water was clean enough to drink.*

I respect organisations that campaign to raise awareness of animal welfare.

***What** I respect are organisations that campaign to raise awareness of animal welfare.*

The person who . . . , the place where . . .

Consider these two similar constructions for adding emphasis.

The keeper understands the animals best.

***The person who** understands the animals best is the keeper.*

Polar bears thrive best in their natural habitat.

***The place where** polar bears thrive best is (in) their natural habitat.*

So + adjective

Consider the use of *so* before an adjective:

Their attitudes were caring.

*Their attitudes were **so** caring.*

He was thoughtful.

*He was **so** thoughtful.*

Do + main verb

Consider the use of *do* before a main verb. Are any other changes necessary?

I like your project work.

*I **do** like your project work.*

We're late. Hurry up!

*We're late. **Do** hurry up!*

Take a seat.

***Do** take a seat.*

He enjoys his work with orphaned elephants.

*He **does** enjoy his work with orphaned elephants.*

Look back at the opinions in Section C2 and underline any examples of emphatic forms. Why are they effective in that context?

Practice

1   Rewrite these sentences beginning with the word(s) in brackets to make them more emphatic.

   a   She admires attempts to reduce animal suffering. (*What . . .*)

   b   We need better fences to stop animals wandering onto the road. (*What . . .*)

   c   The safari park wardens worry about animals escaping. (*What . . .*)

   d   You can see owls, eagles and hawks in a falconry centre. (*The place where . . .*)

   e   We didn't understand that animals have adapted to live in certain habitats. (*What . . .*)

   f   I didn't realise how animals depend on each other. (*What . . .*)

   g   Hunters are responsible for the reduction in rhino numbers. (*The people who . . .*)

   h   The golden eagle prefers to nest in treeless, mountainous country. (*The place where . . .*)

   i   Endangered species in our own country ought to concern us. (*What . . .*)

   j   I want the right to object to things I think are wrong. (*What . . .*)

2   Add *so* or *do* to these sentences for greater emphasis. Make any changes to the sentences that you need to.

   a   Having a purpose in life has made her happy.

   b   We all shouted, 'Tell us more about your adventures.'

c   Take lots of photos when you visit the wildlife park.

d   I never realised that baby rhinos were affectionate.

e   Raising funds for charity is worthwhile.

f   Your granny enjoys her garden, doesn't she?

g   You look tired today.

h   Thirsty animals are miserable.

i   Gordon felt sorry for the animals he saw at the circus.

j   I worry about you, you know.

k   Turn off the tap properly when you have finished washing.

l   Come in, Sophie. I'm pleased to see you.

6 Comparing languages

How do you add emphasis in your own language? Share words or structures you use with your group.

7 Writing sentences

Make up some sentences of your own using emphatic forms.

D Animals at work

1 Thinking about working animals

1   In what ways do animals 'work' in your country?

For example:

☐ on farms, producing milk

☐ being raised for meat

☐ being raised to provide skins, leather and wool

☐ as guard dogs, customs dogs or police dogs

☐ as rescue dogs

☐ being used for transport

☐ as dogs for the blind or hard of hearing

2   Are animals used for work in any other ways?

3   People who keep animals have a responsibility to feed them. What other responsibilities do they have?

2 Discussing ethical issues

> Critical thinking Work in groups of three to discuss these questions.

1   Generally speaking, do you feel working animals in your country have a decent life? Explain your opinions.

2   People who are cruel to their animals may be prevented by law from keeping them. This might mean the loss of a business or family income. Do you think this is right? Why / Why not?

3 Building an email from prompts

Using the following prompts, build up a complete email to the editor of a national newspaper.

> Dear Sir,
>
> Why it is wrong to accuse farmers of cruelty?
>
> I write / response / recent articles / say / people / keep / animals for profit / be 'cruel and heartless'. My family make / living from / keep / sheep. In my view / our life / be harder / the animals'!
>
> In lambing time / example / there be / no day off / no rest. My father get up / as soon as it / be light / and hurry out / to first task / of day / without even bothering / to have / drink. He work / for several hours / without break. He check / lambs that / be born / in night / or attend / ewes that have difficulty / give birth. He bring / poorly lambs indoors / be bottle-fed.
>
> He try / get round the flock / four or five times / day / often in snow / cruel winds. If there be / specific problem / he have to / go out several times / night / with flashlight. Although / expensive / vet / always call / when he be / needed.
>
> It be / true that every ewe or lamb that / die / be a financial loss / us / so it be / in own interest / care for / sheep. Sheep / eventually be sold / at market. How / we can live / any other way? But we be / certainly not / 'ruthless exploiters' / of your article. In fact, nothing be / further from truth.
>
> Yours faithfully,
>
> Orla O'Connor

4 Assessing the argument

When you have written the complete email, re-read it to get a better sense of the argument. Has Orla convinced you that her family provides a high standard of care for animals?

5 The closing paragraph

Study the closing paragraph carefully. Closing paragraphs should bring an argument to a conclusion. The language you use to end an email or letter depends on what you said before.

Do you think Orla's final paragraph is effective?

6 Vocabulary check: Young animals

Humans have children; sheep have lambs. Choose a word from the box to match with each animal or bird. You will need to use some words more than once.

calf   foal   pup/puppy
kitten   kid   cygnet
cub   chick/chicken   duckling

a	bear	g	goat
b	duck	h	horse
c	hen	i	elephant
d	cow	j	whale
e	cat	k	swan
f	dog	l	lion

7 Comparing languages

Does your language have special words for young animals? Discuss the words or expressions you use.

8 Vocabulary check: Collective nouns

Decide which of the words in the box can follow the collective nouns. Sometimes more than one answer is possible.

> bees   elephants   ants   dogs
>
> wolves   goats   fish   sheep   deer
>
> cows   locusts

a   A herd of _____

b   A flock of _____

c   A shoal of _____

d   A pack of _____

e   A swarm of _____

9 Discussion: Intensive farming

› **Critical thinking** With your peers, consider the issues in the article below, which relates to food production using intensive animal farming.

What are your views? How do you think food should be produced? How can organic and sustainable farming methods be made more attractive to farmers? Work in groups and note down your ideas.

Intensive farming

What are the issues?

Many farmers use modern technology to rear their animals intensively. Some kinds of animals and birds (calves and hens, for example) can
5   be reared inside, in very small spaces. Feeding can be controlled very carefully. Some animals are given hormones to increase their growth and antibiotics to prevent disease. This is sometimes called factory farming.

10 **Why people object**

Some people object to modern farming methods because they think they are cruel to animals. Also, people are increasingly worried about the effect of hormones and antibiotics in the
15 food chain. There are environmental concerns that factory farming uses up natural resources without replacing them and causes water and air pollution. Factory farms damage the local economy, putting small farms out of business
20 and paying low wages to workers who often work in a dangerous work environment.

What the farmers think

Farmers using intensive systems argue that they are an efficient method of producing food
25 cheaply. Large scale farming can lead to bigger profits. They also argue that there are now so many people in the population that they cannot all be fed using more environment-friendly and humane farming methods.

30 Some farmers are reluctant to change their farming methods because they have invested a lot in new technology. Also, they feel more environment-friendly and humane farming methods will be less reliable, will involve higher
35 costs and might lead to higher food prices for the consumer.

10 Punctuation

The following letter was written to a farming magazine. When you feel you have understood it, rewrite it with punctuation and paragraphs. Remember to use a comma after an introductory linking word or phrase such as *Nevertheless, . . . , In fact, . . . , Despite claims to the contrary, ...*

Dear Sir

Fair methods of food production

like many of your readers i want to buy healthy food which is produced in a way which is fair to farm workers and animals furthermore i don't believe food production should damage the environment many farmers in our area say that it is cheaper to rear animals under intensive conditions than it is to give them a decent life however if farmers were given subsidies they would be able to afford more space and comfort for animals farmers get subsidies for intensive methods so why not pay them for a kinder approach similarly many of the farms around here use hormones and antibiotics which can get into the food chain farmers say it is less expensive to add growth hormones to animals food than it is to use more natural or 'organic' methods which require a bigger labour force and so would be more expensive what is more expensive in the end subsidies to the farmers for organic farming or a damaged environment in my view we have a right to know what is in our food tins packets and fresh food should be labelled by food companies as free-range or factory farmed or if antibiotics were used so that we know exactly what we are eating i realise my ideas might lead to higher food prices but i have no doubt at all it would be worth it

Yours faithfully

Shahar Rishani

---

11 Checking the text flow

When you have punctuated the letter correctly, read it through to get a sense of the way the text flows. Is the letter clear? Does it begin and end well?

12 Discussion

〉 **Critical thinking** How far do you agree with Shahar's view that it's worth paying more for food that is produced using more humane and sustainable methods?

In what ways do you think intensive methods of food production could be harmful to animals and humans? Try to give some specific examples.

Here are some helpful expressions similar to those you have seen earlier in the unit:

Shahar says . . . and in my view,

Shahar thinks . . . but . . .

Now that I have considered Shahar's opinions, I feel . . .

After weighing up the pros and cons of paying more for food, I would say that . . .

13 Rhetorical questions

A rhetorical question is a question to which you do not expect an answer. It's a device to get more attention for your opinions when presenting an argument.

1   Study the following rhetorical questions. What is the opinion of each speaker?

    a   'Don't you think it's about time people showed more sympathy to farmers?'

    b   'Who can honestly say they would enjoy eating a battery hen?'

    c   'Which is worse: to pay a little bit more for food produced ethically or to make animals suffer terribly in factory farm conditions just so we can get cheaper prices in the supermarket?'

    d   'Wouldn't we all be happier knowing our food was ethically produced?'

    e   'Do we really need all this food from thousands of miles away?'

    f   'Who can worry about animals when little children are starving?'

    g   'The theory is that pets are safe and happy with their owners, but is it the whole truth?'

    h   'How can you put a price on a child's life?'

2 Rewrite the following statements in the form of rhetorical questions.

a A vegetarian meal is not always healthy.

Is _____ ?

b No one can say the farmers are wrong.

Who _____ ?

c We can save an animal or save someone's life.

Which is _____ ?

d No one knows the extent of the problem.

Who _____ ?

e I think we would all be happier knowing that our food was free of chemicals.

Wouldn't _____ ?

f I think it's about time we remembered endangered species at home.

Isn't _____ ?

g I think we should consider farm workers before worrying about animals.

Shouldn't _____ ?

3 Look back at the email in Section D3 and the letter in Section D10. Underline the examples of rhetorical questions.

You may like to use the rhetorical question device in your own arguments. One or two are usually enough.

E Helping animals in danger

1 Discussion: Could you help animals?

> **Critical thinking** Many species are being endangered by human activity. Hunting, overfishing and poaching, for example, reduce animal numbers. In addition, forests are cut down for agricultural or commercial purposes, and wildlife loses its habitat as a result. Similarly, when cities expand, new roads and buildings mean wild animals and birds lose their homes and sources of food.

Work in pairs to discuss these questions. Write down your ideas to tell the class.

1 Do you know of any examples in your own country of wildlife being affected in this way?

2 Which endangered species in the world do you know about? Which do you care most about? How could you help endangered species in your own country or overseas?

INTERNATIONAL OVERVIEW

The chart below shows the approximate numbers of selected big cats still in existence in the wild. Which three species on the chart are the most endangered?

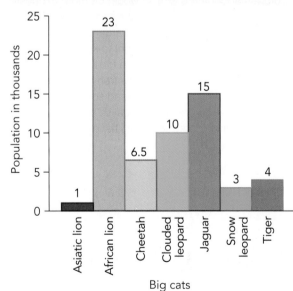

Approximate populations of seven 'big cat' species in the wild, 2020

2 Reading for gist

Skim-read the following leaflet, which gives information about two ways of helping to protect endangered animals. Try to work out the meaning of unfamiliar words from the context.

Wild action appeal

The adoption scheme

Woodland Zoo, as well as being a very special place to visit, plays an important part in protecting endangered species. The Zoo is often
5 the last breeding ground for these animals. We have 160 different species of animals, birds and reptiles, many of which are endangered in the wild. We need your support to help these animals win their battle against possible extinction
10 with breeding programmes funded by the adoption scheme.

Most animals in the Zoo are available for adoption. Many individuals and families, as well as groups, take great pleasure in adopting their
15 favourite animal. Companies, too, can benefit from the scheme. Our website has thousands of weekly visitors, so it is a worthwhile and cost-effective form of advertising.

What do adopters receive?

20 All adopters will receive an adoption certificate and regular copies of 'Zoo Update', the Zoo's exciting newsletter. For a donation of $50, you will receive four free entry tickets; for a donation of $100 or more, you will receive eight free
25 entry tickets and a personalised plaque on the animal's enclosure.

What happens to your donations?

Our Wild Action appeal was launched in 2016 to support work with endangered species in their
30 threatened natural habitats. Donations to the appeal will go directly towards the following conservation projects.

Rainforest Action Costa Rica

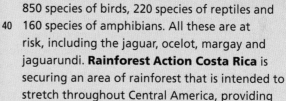

35 Costa Rica's tropical forests contain a wealth of wildlife – 200 species of mammals, 850 species of birds, 220 species of reptiles and
40 160 species of amphibians. All these are at risk, including the jaguar, ocelot, margay and jaguarundi. **Rainforest Action Costa Rica** is securing an area of rainforest that is intended to stretch throughout Central America, providing
45 a sanctuary for indigenous wildlife. Just $30 will save half an acre of Costa Rican rainforest.

The Tiger Trust

The Tiger Trust is creating two natural
50 habitat sanctuaries in Thailand for the Indo-Chinese tiger, which is facing the threat of extinction. Tiger Mountains I and II provide a near-natural
55 existence for tigers orphaned by poaching.

Only around 3000 tigers remain in the wild and hundreds are being trapped and shot by poachers for an appalling trade in tiger bones and body parts. A donation of $40 will go towards looking
60 after Sheba, a two-year-old Indo-Chinese tiger, who was found next to the body of her mother. She now lives with other rescued tigers on Tiger Mountain II in Thailand. You will receive a colour photo of Sheba and a tiger T-shirt.

3 Comprehension check

Now answer the following questions.

1   Which animals are available for adoption?

2   How does the zoo use the adoption money it raises?

3   What does a $50 donation to the adoption scheme give you?

4   What is the aim of Rainforest Action Costa Rica?

5   Where are Tiger Mountains I and II, and what is special about them?

4 Writing a report from notes

Each year, Ken's school raises funds for charity. This year, the headteacher is considering using the funds raised to adopt a zoo animal. Ken is a student organiser of the school Wildlife Club, and the headteacher has asked him to write a report saying whether adopting a zoo animal is the best way for the school to help wildlife.

Rewrite Ken's rough draft of main points in the form of a finished report, following the advice below.

Structure

Structure the report into paragraphs. Use strong opening and final paragraphs. Use clauses to make sentences more complex. Link ideas with linking words and expressions.

Tone and register

Your report is for the headteacher. It should sound calm and fair. You should use opinion language to introduce your views, but be careful to provide clear evidence for your opinions.

Content

Ken makes several very interesting points. Try to provide a few details, facts, statistics and examples. Look back at previous exercises for information if you need to.

Making the report suitable for the audience

The headteacher is the audience for this report, so try to link the report to their concerns and priorities. If money is to be given to a zoo, the headteacher will want it to

Points in favour of using our funds to adopt a zoo animal

• it provides an opportunity to adopt from a wide range of animals

• we would get:

  • a plaque at the zoo with the school's name on it

  • discounts on zoo entrance tickets

  • gift shop discounts

  • invitations to special events (e.g. see newborn animals)

• the zoo uses donations to support breeding programmes for endangered species, which are returned to wild when ready.

Points against

Adopting a zoo animal means we cannot help other conservation projects such as:

• projects that create a safe haven for wildlife when rainforest is destroyed

• projects that care for animals threatened by poachers who / kill animals and sell skins / organs / bones / for commercial products (e.g. tiger sanctuaries in Thailand).

Conclusion

Wildlife Club – special meeting. Result: in favour of adopting a zoo animal, possibly a tiger or a tamarin monkey. Younger children love seeing/learning about a real live wild animal. Older students gain more information for science projects; benefits those wanting careers in science / with animals. Breeding in captivity scheme – long-term benefits.

be worthwhile for the animals and educational for the students. It should be of interest to everyone, not just a few students. Example points you could include are: 'How might adopting a zoo animal educate younger pupils about endangered species?', 'Why might a zoo visit be better for younger students than reading about a conservation project or watching a wildlife film?'

Making the report sound like it comes from the organiser of the Wildlife Club

Ken is the Wildlife Club organiser, so think about how you can link his comments to his role at the club. Would he discuss the idea and report their views?

Proofreading

Proofread your work for punctuation and spelling errors.

Feedback

When you feel you have produced a reasonable draft, show your work to a partner and listen carefully to their comments. Would you like to add or change anything?

5 Improving paragraphing and punctuation in a report

Read the following report for a headteacher about a school trip to meet a wildlife expert.

1   When you understand the report, add capital letters and full stops in the correct places.

2   Then decide where new paragraphs should start.

mr bavsar's talk about his work in southern india was so inspirational mr bavsar explained why he started his special project, the elephant information service one night a child woke up to see a small elephant calf standing by his bed somehow, the elephant had got into the house and gone into the bedroom without disturbing the boy's parents the elephant made a strange noise and then turned around and left the way he had come, without causing trouble as chief wildlife officer, mr bavsar was asked to investigate the incident when he visited the family, they said they were not worried but they were shocked they said that if they had known wild elephants were so near, they would have been better prepared for potentially dangerous situations this made mr bavsar realise that animals and humans could co-exist peacefully, as long as they took sensible precautions to avoid conflict mr bavsar set up the elephant information service and now there are early warning systems in the area the service alerts families when animals are nearby by sending texts, flashing warning lights and making phone calls the whole class loved mr bavsar's talk he was so knowledgeable and showed us his personal photo collection of the rare and beautiful animals he has cared for including elephants elephants sadly are often orphaned when their parents are killed by hunters and have to be cared for in an elephant sanctuary before being returned to the wild mr bavsar even brought in a large toy elephant, a blanket and feeding bottle, and encouraged the little children to practise the right way of feeding a baby elephant who has lost its mother as a result, they understood as much as the older ones about the needs of infant elephants overall, we felt extremely lucky that we had been given the chance to meet a true wildlife pioneer and we all learnt so much i would certainly recommend it for next year's group, if the opportunity is still available

GRAMMAR SPOTLIGHT

The past perfect passive

The passive form of the past perfect is used to describe something that was completed in an earlier past, when the action is more important than who or what did it, for example:

Trees and bushes had been planted around the enclosures. (We do not need to know who planted the trees and bushes.)

The past perfect passive is formed with *had + been + past participle*.

The negative is *had not been* (or *hadn't been* in informal English); for example:

In spite of the methods the farmers had introduced, the wolves **had not been driven** *away.*

Practice

1   Find another example of the past perfect passive in paragraph 2 of the article in Section A4.

2   Write the following notes as full sentences:

   a   If the Siberian tiger cub not / be / find in time, it would have died in the snow outside its den.

   b   The tiger cub's tail be / badly / damage by severe frost.

   c   A leg / be / bit / badly.

   d   The wildlife officials who found the cub said they / be / shock by the cub's condition. 'We believe the poor little thing be / attack by a predator and the severe temperatures made everything worse.'

   e   After a year, the tiger cub had made a full recovery and be / return to the wild.

Complete the practice activities in your Workbook.

EXAM-STYLE QUESTIONS

READING AND WRITING

Reading and writing: multiple choice

Read the blog written by someone who went on a whale-watching trip, and then answer the questions.

The thrill of watching whales

When I volunteered to spend a summer on a land-based whale-watching project in the west of Scotland, the project secretary warned me, 'You have to be able to detect the whales from the shore — it's not as easy as you think.' Although I assumed I was well qualified for the job, at the start of the
5   project I often imagined I could see dorsal fins in the dark tip of every wave and dolphins leaping in the wake-tracks on the water made by passing boats. I had a few embarrassing moments, screaming 'Whale!' before realising that what I was pointing out were only waves breaking over submerged rocks, not sea creatures at all!

10   After a while, I trained my eyes to 'see' — to distinguish between waves splashing over rocks and the rolling movement of whales underwater. I spent a lot of time just watching the sea through my binoculars, looking

CONTINUED

actively for anything that indicated sea life below. Learning more about the marine environment increased my ability to differentiate, especially in regard to the tides and currents, as these draw whales to certain areas. My binoculars enabled me to spot the fins of a porpoise against the darkness of the sea, and without a good pair of
15   binoculars, I definitely would have missed out on lots of stunning marine life.

In addition, I eventually realised that the birds provide us with signals that cetaceans – whales, dolphins and porpoises – may be in the area. Where there is a flock of feeding seabirds such as seagulls or gannets, there is often a whale feeding beneath them. Gannets are really easy to spot from a distance – they drop out of the sky at speeds of up to 100 kilometres per hour, spearing the surface and sending bursts of water up behind them.
20   I also learnt how to take my time, to be patient, peaceful and quiet so that the whales were undisturbed by my presence. One of my favourite moments occurred when I was sitting quietly by the seashore and a group of porpoises came in so close to the shoreline that I could hear the gentle puffs of their breath.

Land-based whale watching is so much more environment-friendly than watching whales from a boat or a ship. The presence of humans and the noise of ship motors can cause stress to all kinds of marine life. It can disturb
25   them while they are feeding or resting. There is also the danger of colliding with whales or dolphins and causing them injuries.

If you want to try this activity, it is worth organising and planning carefully for your whale-watching trip. I recommend getting some good polarised sunglasses. They reduce glare which makes it much easier to spot wildlife activity underwater. Also be sure to take a sun hat and sunscreen to avoid sunburn on your face. I
30   recommend using a notebook to record details of what you've seen and the environmental conditions at the time. You can also log details and photos of your sightings on a whale and dolphin tracking app. Your contributions will be added to a global database that helps researchers monitor cetaceans and find out more about their numbers and their migration patterns. This will help us to protect these valuable species and their habitats.

Despite the early disappointments I had, I think there is undoubtedly something very special about watching
35   whales. Nothing can compare with the secret thrill and the tranquillity of seeing a wild animal just doing its own thing.

1   How did the writer feel at the beginning of her project?

    A   Unsure about how to get started   ☐

    B   Worried that it might be too difficult   ☐

    C   Confident that she was able to succeed   ☐   [1]

2   At first, she felt embarrassed because:

    A   she couldn't see any whales.   ☐

    B   she made a few mistakes.   ☐

    C   she misunderstood her task.   ☐   [1]

3   In paragraph 3, the writer mentions gannets to illustrate how:

    A   she developed better observation skills.   ☐

    B   she discovered more about whales.   ☐

    C   she learnt to be more patient.   ☐   [1]

CONTINUED

4   The writer says that watching whales from land is better than from a boat because it is:

    A more interesting.   ☐

    B less harmful.   ☐

    C easier and quieter.   ☐   [1]

5   What does 'This' refer to in line 33?

    A Uploading data   ☐

    B Taking photos   ☐

    C Studying cetaceans   ☐   [1]

6   What was the writer's main reason for writing this blog?

    A To encourage people to try this activity   ☐

    B To give an account of her experience   ☐

    C To explain how whales are endangered   ☐   [1]

[Total: 6]

Reading and writing: informal

You are planning to visit an aquarium in your town.

Write an email to a friend inviting him/her to join you.

In your email, you should:

- explain why you think the trip will be fun
- describe what you can learn at the aquarium
- say when and where you can meet to go on the trip.

Write about 120 to 160 words.   [15]

[Total: 15]

Reading and writing: formal

There are plans to build a small safari park close to your town. Visitors will be able to see animals from all over the world. You want to write an article for your local newspaper on what people think about the idea.

In your article, give the arguments for and against this idea, and suggest a way to move forward.

Here are some comments in local newspapers on the topic:

I would love to see how animals look and behave in real life.

The animals will be unhappy and stressed.

It will be so exciting and attract tourists, too.

Wild animals should stay in their natural habitat.

CONTINUED

Now write an article for the local newspaper.

The comments above may give you some ideas, and you should also use some ideas of your own.

Write about 120 to 160 words.   [15]

[Total: 15]

Reading and writing: formal

Your school ecology club is trying to persuade students not to use products that have been tested on animals. The club committee wants to know what students' opinions are and you have volunteered to write an article.

In your article, give the arguments for and against this idea, and say which side of the argument you agree with.

Here are some comments from students in your class:

We need to ensure human safety before selling any products.

Products like shampoo and soap don't need to be tested if they are made with natural ingredients.

Testing on animals is cruel and unnecessary.

Products should be tested in the laboratory, but not on animals.

Now write an article for your school magazine.

The comments above may give you some ideas, and you should also use some ideas of your own.

Write about 120 to 160 words.   [15]

[Total: 15]

Reading and writing: formal

Your school would like to start supporting a charity and is considering a charity that does research into animal diseases. Your headteacher wants students' opinions about the idea, and has asked you to write an article.

In your article, give the arguments for and against this idea, and conclude with your own opinion

Here are some comments from students in your class:

How wonderful! Animals deserve to be healthy and happy.

Sometimes research on animal diseases can help humans too.

I would prefer to support a charity that helps fight human diseases.

We need to save and protect all animal species in the world.

CONTINUED

Now write an article for your school magazine.

The comments above may give you some ideas, and you should also use some ideas of your own.

Write about 120 to 160 words.   [15]

[Total: 15]

LISTENING

Listening: multiple matching

You will hear six people talking about wildlife.

For questions **1–6**, choose from the list (**A–H**) which idea each speaker expresses. For each speaker, write the correct letter (**A–H**) on the answer line. Use each letter only once. There are two extra letters, which you do not need to use.

You will hear the recordings twice.

Now look at the information **A–H**.

Information

A	I am keen to help people in my area live with wildlife.	**1**	Speaker 1 _____	[1]
B	We no longer worry about having dangerous wildlife nearby.	**2**	Speaker 2 _____	[1]
C	When I was camping, I met a grizzly bear near the campsite.	**3**	Speaker 3 _____	[1]
D	Human food attracts wild animals.	**4**	Speaker 4 _____	[1]
E	Wild animals can give people financial problems.	**5**	Speaker 5 _____	[1]
F	Safe crossings to protect wildlife from traffic are unlikely to be a success.	**6**	Speaker 6 _____	[1]
G	Human activities have had a negative impact on wildlife.			
H	Wild animals can sometimes spread harmful diseases.			

[Total: 6]

SPEAKING

Warm-up questions

Warm-up questions help you feel more relaxed before you move on to answering assessed questions.

Take turns asking and answering the questions. Speak for 1–2 minutes.

- Can you tell me about your friends?
- What do you do in your free time?
- What kind of hobbies do you have?

CONTINUED

Interview

Read the questions. In pairs, decide who will play the interviewer and who will play the student. Then role-play the interview. Speak for about 2–3 minutes. Change roles and role-play the interview again.

Keeping a pet

- Can you tell me which kind of animal you like best?
- Do you think it's a good idea to have a pet animal at home?
- Have you ever been to a zoo or an aquarium? Did you enjoy it?

Short talk

Read the options and compare them. You have one minute to prepare your talk. Now give a short talk to your partner. Speak for about 2 minutes. Change roles and listen to your partner's talk.

Learning about wildlife

Your teacher is planning a school visit to learn about wildlife and has given your class the following two options:

- a visit to the local zoo
- a visit to a safari park.

Compare the two options and say which option you would prefer, and why.

Discussion

Read the discussion questions. In pairs, decide who will play the interviewer and who will play the student. Then role-play the discussion. Speak for about 3 minutes. Change roles and role-play the interview again.

- Do you think it is good to keep wild animals in zoos?
- Some people think it is wrong to eat meat. What do you think?
- Many animals are endangered because of climate change. What do you think we can do about it?

SELF-ASSESSMENT CHECKLIST

Reflect on what you have learnt in this unit. For each area listed, decide whether you feel confident or need more practice. If you feel you need more practice, you will find some ideas to help you in Advice for Success. Come back to your self-assessment scores later in your course and see if your confidence has improved.

I can ...	Need more practice	Fairly confident
discuss issues related to animals in zoos, farms, the wild and medical research, using appropriate vocabulary		
skim for general ideas and identify bias in an article		
write a blog post using examples and explanations to develop an argument		
identify key details and understand what is implied in an interview		
express disappointment and disagreement		

ADVICE FOR SUCCESS

This section is to help you help yourself. Choose the suggestions you like and adapt them if you want to. Make notes about what you do and how it helped you.

Extending your skills

1   Plan your opinion essay or report carefully. Think about content. Try to have enough interesting ideas to expand fully: don't run out of ideas halfway through. Engage with the subject and try to make the argument sound serious and important. Sound convincing and you will convince other people.

2   Structure your essay so that it is clear and logical. Use paragraphs and linking words.

3   Use an appropriate tone. Opinions should sound reasonable and be supported with examples where appropriate. If you are writing a report for someone important, you should sound polite, objective and avoid bias.

4   Devices such as rhetorical questions or restructuring sentences for greater emphasis will make your writing stronger and more persuasive, but don't overdo it.

5   Use a mature and varied vocabulary that is appropriate to the topic.

Showcasing your skills

6   Get used to seeing what 150 words, for example, looks like in your handwriting. You will then be able to see whether you are writing to the right length.

7   The word limit is a guide to the required length. Don't worry if you write a few words more or less than this.

8   Punctuate carefully, using commas, full stops, question marks and so on. Proofread your work for punctuation errors.

9   Check your spelling carefully, especially words you know you usually misspell or words that present special problems, such as plural forms, silent letters and suffixes.

10 If you are writing by hand, pay attention to your handwriting. If your composition is interesting and well-structured, and your handwriting is attractive, your work will be a pleasure to read. Find a pen that helps you to write better, and practise writing any letters that can cause problems.

> ## Unit 10
The world of work

LEARNING INTENTIONS

In this unit you will:

- Explore the topic of work and employment

- Identify connections between ideas, opinions and attitudes in an article about work

- Write a formal letter and an article using appropriate style and register

- Understand key points and bias in a lecture about marketing strategies

- Take part in a role-play discussion for developing a new product using a range of interactive skills

 Watch the video about the world of work in the digital coursebook.

Look at the photo on this page.

a   What kind of job do you think this person has?

b   How do you think they feel about their job and their workplace?

c   Would you enjoy working in this setting?

d   What do you think are some advantages and disadvantages of working here?

A The rewards of work

1 Discussion

Why do people work? Earning money is one reason. What other reasons are there? With a partner, add four or five more ideas to the list.

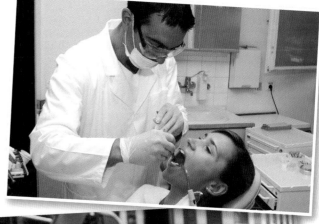

Reasons why people work

They get a sense of achievement.

They feel good about themselves.

2 Skills and qualities for work

1 Look at the photos. What kinds of skills do you think are needed in these jobs?

2 Match the following skills and qualities to the occupations you think they are essential for.

a	patience	1	software engineer
b	good communication skills	2	dentist
		3	nursery teacher
c	artistic flair	4	firefighter
d	an ear for languages	5	interior designer
e	business sense	6	cellist
f	physical stamina	7	labourer
g	courage	8	company director
h	musical talent		
i	dexterity	9	interpreter
j	coding skills	10	journalist

3 Pre-listening task

What aspects of a job do you think might be most important when choosing a job? For example, you might think salary, career prospects or opportunities to travel are important. Work in a group to make a list of ten things you might look for. Number them in order of importance.

4 Why I like my job

1 You are going to hear six people talking about their jobs. Choose the most likely opinion (A–G) for each speaker. There is one opinion you do not need to use.

Speaker 1 ☐

Speaker 2 ☐

Speaker 3 ☐

Speaker 4 ☐

Speaker 5 ☐

Speaker 6 ☐

A My favourite part of the job is talking to customers.

B I enjoy working under pressure.

C I'm happy if I can help people find what they want.

D Dealing with unexpected problems is a challenge I enjoy.

E I prefer working in a team to working alone.

F I feel that I have contributed to scientific progress.

G I like fixing things and making them work again.

2 Listen again and guess what each person's job is. Which job would you find most interesting?

5 Predicting

You are going to read about two people who have chosen to work as freelancers. Why do you think they made this decision?

6 Reading for gist

Now read the text for general meaning. Try to work out the meanings of any unfamiliar words from the context. Decide if the unfamiliar word is a noun, verb or adjective. What words do you already know that might be similar to the difficult word? Sometimes the general meaning becomes clearer as you read further through the text.

Remember, you do not have to understand every word to understand a text well.

Young people who do not want to be tied down are turning to freelance work

An accidental freelancer

Melody Chong, 38, is a freelancer in not one, but two industries – public
5 relations and health coaching. She does **PR** for mainly health- and fitness-related companies, such as PanAsia Surgery. Her other
10 job involves giving advice on nutrition, sleep and training to individuals and organisations. She earns between $3 000 and $10 000 a month. Her father is a
15 retired businessman and her mother a housewife.

Ms Chong never set out to be a freelancer. She says her younger self would have laughed at the idea. She used to work full-time for restaurant group Tung Lok and was its advertising and promotions manager.
20 But as her colleagues left one after the other, her workload grew.

I was still happy about getting the work done, but I started to feel something wasn't right,' she says, recalling how she would get tightness in her chest
25 and shortness of breath. She went for a full health screening, but doctors told her the results showed she was healthy and physically fit.

They asked me questions like 'Are you suffering from depression?' It was a wake-up call. It made me sit up
30 and re-think what I really wanted to do in life.'

She left her job in 2007 and searched for an MBA programme in the United States, but requests from former work contacts to help with short-term public relations work derailed those plans. She says: I started
35 with two, then three, then more, and realised, with so many projects lined up, I could be a full-time freelancer – and that was it.'

After entering a make-your-own-ice-cream-flavour contest with Ben & Jerry's, she got in touch with the company. In 2010, it offered her a job and she moved to San Francisco to work as a sales and marketing manager. She was exposed to Californian-style health-consciousness there and, after two years with Ben & Jerry's, took up a one-year degree course with the Institute for Integrative Nutrition.

In 2013, she returned to Singapore a qualified health coach. Now she conducts health talks and programmes at schools and wellness events, as well as cooking demonstrations, while juggling her PR work. She says: I feel really blessed. I am doing what I love, loving what I do and that means I don't have to work a day in my life.'

He works five hours a day – at home or in cafés

At 19, Temasek Polytechnic graduate Kelvin Lim decided a nine-to-five job was not for him. He did not want to be stuck sitting in a cubicle or trapped in an office hierarchy. So he dived straight into the world of freelancing, despite not having any work experience.

Mr Lim, who is now 24, has a diploma in interactive media informatics. He taught himself web design so that he could set up a website to showcase his works. To boost his credentials, he enrolled in the Lasalle College of the Arts, taking up a degree in design communications and juggling work and study.

His portfolio as a freelancer includes an app for Digital Fashion Week, whose design he was in charge of, and a site for the Hong Kong Tennis Open. He usually sets aside up to five hours a day, working from home or from cafés in town.

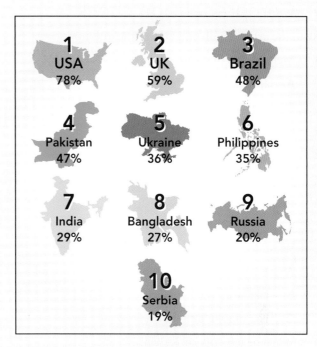

Top ten countries, ranked by the percentage income generated by freelance workers

In October, he took up a full-time job as a graphic designer at an events management company, but this is only a temporary stint for him. He says: The only reason I'd put myself on a nine-to-five job would be for the experience, to handle bigger projects and, of course, to learn how to run a business so I can start my own company one day.'

Freelancing can be a constant struggle with irregular income, he admits. He once went for three months without a project and had to dip into his savings. But he adds: I don't think I would give up my carefree lifestyle in exchange for a fixed and routine lifestyle, even if it means having a stable income with **CPF contributions** and benefits.'

GLOSSARY

PR: Public relations: helping a company to maintain a positive image with the public

CPF contributions: compulsory payments by both employer and employee into a central fund used to pay for employee health insurance and pensions

7 Comprehension check

Read the article again and answer the questions.

1   Melody says that she:

   A   always wanted to be a freelancer.

   B   used to work as an employee.

   C   changed her job a few times.

2   Melody left her job because:

   A   she wasn't enjoying it.

   B   she needed more challenge.

   C   it was affecting her health.

3   What does 'it' refer to in line 29?

   A   Her doctor's evaluation.

   B   Her work performance.

   C   Her aim in life.

4   When he left college, Kelvin:

   A   couldn't decide what to do.

   B   had difficulty finding a job.

   C   decided to take a risk.

5   Kelvin says that he would consider a full-time employee position:

   A   to have more responsibility.

   B   to earn more money.

   C   to make useful contacts.

6   In the last paragraph, Kelvin mentions his savings to illustrate:

   A   how much money he has been able to make.

   B   how unreliable freelance work can be.

   C   the extra expenses that freelance workers have.

8 Note-taking and discussion

1   > Critical thinking Read the article again and make notes on the following:

   a   three benefits and one drawback of freelance work.

   b   three drawbacks and one benefit of being an employee.

2   What other advantages and disadvantages of each type of working can you think of? Which type of working would you choose? Discuss in a group.

9 Vocabulary check

1   Find words in the article that match these meanings.

   a   No longer working and receiving a pension.

   b   Working in the same job the whole working week.

   c   People who work with you in the same company.

   d   People who are in your work network of work acquaintances.

   e   Trying to balance two or three different activities.

   f   A small square-shaped office space, smaller than an office.

   g   The rank of people in the company structure.

   h   Qualifications and achievements that make you suitable for a task.

   i   A collection of documents that illustrate your achievements.

   j   A fixed amount of money every month or every year.

2   Make a list of any other work-related vocabulary you can find in the article. Put a question mark against words you don't understand, then look these up in a dictionary.

10 Idioms

1   What do you think these expressions mean in the context of the article? Paraphrase them in your own words.

   a   Her *younger self* would have laughed.

   b   It was a *wake-up call*.

   c   It is only a *temporary stint*.

   d   He had to *dip into* his savings.

11 Look, say, cover, write, check

1   Learn these commonly misspelt words using the 'look, say, cover, write, check' method (see Unit 1, Section B12 if you need a reminder).

accessible	achievement	application
appointment	apprentice	capable
career	entrepreneur	independent
personnel	professional	qualification
responsibility	successful	temporary

2   Ask a partner to test you when you are confident you have learnt them correctly.

3   Choose six of the words and put each one into a sentence to show its meaning.

12 Is freelance work for everyone?

> Critical thinking Work in pairs or groups of three.

1   What skills and qualities do you feel would be necessary for working as a freelancer? How are they different from working as an employee?

Examples: *motivation, time management*

2   What types of work do you think are more likely to be available to freelance workers?

13 Understanding visual data

> Critical thinking Visual data, graphs and charts are often included in newspaper and magazine articles and web pages, especially those of a factual type.

Study the visual data that accompanies the article. What information does it convey? How does it reflect or extend the information in the article? Why do you think freelance work is more popular in some countries than others? What do you think would encourage or deter people in your country from being a freelance worker?

14 Pre-role-play discussion

1   The article mentions a 'make-your-own-ice-cream-flavour contest' organised by an ice-cream company. Why do you think the company runs this contest? Why is it important for a company to develop new flavours and new products?

2   Brainstorm some ideas for a new ice-cream flavour. List at least six ideas.

15 Product development meeting and role play

Four executives of the Deliciously Healthy Ice Cream company are meeting to discuss the production of a new ice-cream flavour.

1   First, scan the questions, which will give you an idea of what the following texts are about. Then read the texts carefully to find the answer to each question.

a   Which person thinks producing a new ice-cream flavour may not be a good idea?

b Which person thinks that the ice-cream name doesn't need to mention the ingredients?

c Which person wants to produce an ice cream aimed at the narrowest age range of customers?

d Which person seems the most interested in the appearance of the product?

e Which person is concerned about the nutritional value of the product?

f Which person is concerned about the cost of producing the new product?

Public relations manager

Your job is to manage the media messaging surrounding the launch of any new products. You aim to promote the image of the company as a producer of healthy delicious ice-cream desserts. The name of the ice cream and the packaging should reflect this message. You prefer flavours that sound natural and organic, such as Fresh Fruity Mango or Organic Orange.

You are a good listener. You do your best to get on with everyone, but are also keen to stand up for company principles.

Marketing manager

Your job is to make sure that the new product will produce good sales for the company. Your market research with customers shows that there is a need for an ice-cream flavour that will appeal to older teenagers and young adults. You think the packaging is very important to appeal to this audience and should not look too childish or cartoonish. You prefer flavours that sound up-to-date and trendy, such as Cool Coco Almond or Crisp Coffee Nut.

You are quite critical of other people's ideas and always try to find negative points in their suggestions.

Food tester

Your job is to create recipes that taste good, have easily sourced ingredients and are within the production budget.

You think there are already enough ice-cream flavours and it would be better to develop and improve the most popular flavours, which are chocolate and vanilla. You prefer ice creams that have only two flavour combinations, such as Chocolate Mint or Coconut Almond. You are a bit cautious about ice-cream names that sound too unusual or mysterious.

You are willing to discuss new ideas, but prefer to stick with ideas that have been tried and proven to be successful.

Advertising executive

Your job is to create an advertising campaign that will make the new product attractive to new customers and expand the customer base.

You are convinced there is a need for a new ice cream aimed at adults who want some variety from traditional ice-cream flavours and aren't afraid to try something new. You think current product names aren't interesting enough and prefer product names that suggest something surprising or unusual, such as Mystery Train or Midnight Moon. You are going to suggest that the product is advertised on the internet and through social media campaigns; these are cheaper than traditional TV or magazine advertising, which is extremely expensive.

You are rather forceful in meetings and give your opinions firmly and clearly. (You may want to look back at the opinion language in Unit 9.) You also hate to be interrupted.

2   Use the texts to do a role play of the meeting. Work in a group of four and each choose a role. Your meeting needs to decide:

- who the ice-cream flavour will be aimed at

- the name of the flavour and the main ingredients

- the type of packaging and your advertising strategies.

B Facts and figures

1 Approximations

Study the following exact amounts.

1   Where does the stress fall in the word 'percent'?

2   Say the amounts aloud carefully, checking the pronunciation with a partner. Then match the exact amounts to the approximations 1–8.

a	4.9 percent	1	nearly three-quarters
b	10.4 percent	2	just over a half
c	52.3 percent	3	just over one in ten
d	74.7 percent	4	just under one in five
e	98.8 percent	5	almost a quarter
f	19.2 percent	6	practically all
g	23.8 percent	7	nearly a third
h	32.9 percent	8	about one in twenty

3   When facts and figures are presented, both exact amounts and approximations might be used. For example, you may hear '*19.8 percent of the town's population, that's getting on for one in five men and women of working age, are unemployed.*'

What are the advantages of using approximations to present information? Are there any disadvantages?

2 Questioning statistics

1   ⟩ **Critical thinking** Statistical information looks authoritative but you need to treat it with caution. Pressure groups, for example, may use statistics to influence public opinion.

What has the following survey found out? How does it compare with your own experience?

A recent survey found that children who come from homes where the mother works have half as many absences from school as the children of non-working mothers. Working mothers seem quite prepared to send their children to school when they are unwell.

2   Before deciding whether the above conclusion is valid, you need to ask more questions. For example:

- Who asked for the survey to be carried out?

- Why was it carried out?

- Who took part in the survey?

- What was the size of the sample?

- Exactly what kind of questions were asked?

- Were the groups of children closely matched in terms of age, background and social class?

Why are these questions important? What kind of answers do you think you might get?

3   With your partner, make notes on the questions you would want to ask before accepting the validity of the following 'facts and figures':

a   The majority of the population thought that young people under the age of 18 should not be allowed out after 9 p.m.

b   A survey found that the Rio School was much better than the other schools. It had by far the best exam results.

3 Criticising statistics

> **Critical thinking** Study the following statement and then read the reactions to it. Make sure you understand the expressions in **bold** type.

A survey of young people found that the majority were not going to bother to get a decent job when they left school or college.

> It's a **total distortion of the truth**. The teenagers I know would do anything to get on a good training scheme.

> They're **fudging the facts.** We all want a good job.

> I can't stand surveys that **bend the truth.** I'd like to know exactly who they asked and what questions they used.

> **Who dreamt that up?** It's rubbish!

Look back at the statistics mentioned in Section B2. Practise criticising the statements with your partner. Do you both sound annoyed enough?

4 Young lives: Good or bad?

> **Critical thinking** A survey of young people produced the results a–j below:

1   Read each statement carefully and decide with a partner whether it gives a good or bad impression of teenagers. Mark each statement P if a positive impression is being given, and N if the impression is negative. Underline the words that help you decide.

   a   Twenty-three percent valued spare-time jobs more highly than their school studies.

   b   Over three-quarters were concerned the schools did not arrange work experience.

   c   Over a fifth said that having part-time jobs was the only way they could pay for ordinary things they needed, or buy treats such as sweets.

   d   Eighteen percent objected to the amount of pocket money they received but were not prepared to work to earn extra spending money.

   e   Over a quarter of teenagers were dissatisfied with the amount of freedom their parents allowed.

   f   Seventy-four percent were happy with the amount of freedom they were allowed.

   g   Reading was a popular activity for two out of three of those interviewed.

   h   A third never pick up a book outside school.

   i   The majority do nothing to help their community.

   j   One in three teenagers do voluntary work for their community.

2   Decide which statistics you would choose to present if you were:

   a   an employer who feels teenagers are a bad employment risk.

   b   a youth leader encouraging firms to develop training schemes for young people.

INTERNATIONAL OVERVIEW

World population by level of education

The graph shows the number of people in the world who have completed different levels of education.

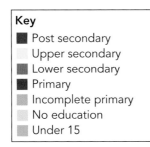

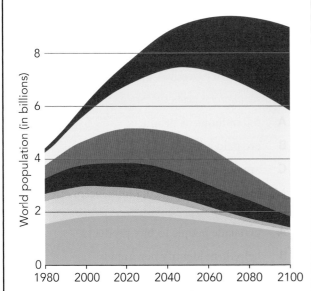

Projected world population by level of education (data from outworldindata.org)

1   Which level of education shows the largest increase over time?

2   About how many people will have completed post-secondary education by 2100?

3   What general global trends does the graph indicate? What do you think may be the causes of these trends? Discuss your ideas in a group.

5 Rewriting in a more formal style

The following letter was written to a newspaper by a teenager who disagreed with a report it had published.

1   Discuss the letter with your partner and decide whether it is written in an appropriate tone and register for its target audience.

Consider the use of:

•   slang

•   colloquialisms

•   contractions

•   rhetorical questions, question forms and question tags.

Underline those aspects of the letter both you and your partner are unhappy with.

Hi, you guys at the newspaper,

Hi! It's me again! Ollie Debeer from your go-ahead high school just outside town. Your report 'Young Lives Shock!' just got me mad! I mean, the report says, 'We are unconcerned about employment'. Talk about fudging the facts, eh? All my mates are totally worried about getting a decent job. I also read 'teenagers value their spare-time jobs more than their studies'. Who dreamt that up? There's no way my parents can afford to buy me the trainers or the kind of phone I want. No way! So I work for them, right? I work in a café twice a week after school and, yeah, I do find it hard to concentrate the next day, but I do extra homework to catch up. That stuff about teenage entertainment was kind of distorted, too, wasn't it? 'The youth of today show a strong preference for the company of their peer group over spending time with their parents.' I mean, who wouldn't rather be out with their mates than stuck at home? But it didn't say we dislike our parents, did it? Anyway, write me back, will you? It's gonna be great hearing your views!

Bye for now,

Ollie

2   Rewrite the letter in a more formal style and divide it into suitable paragraphs. Remember, a letter to a newspaper can include some aspects of informal style, such as the occasional idiom or colloquialism. However, the general impression should be formal.

Show your finished letter to your partner. Do they think that the balance of your style (neither too formal nor too informal) is about right?

C Internet marketing

1 Pre-listening discussion

If you want to buy a new laptop or printer, for example, where do you go to get advice on the best brands? Do you go to the company website? Ask your friends? Or something else?

Work with a partner to brainstorm six different ways you could get advice on brand recommendations and rank them in order of reliability.

2 Predicting content

You are going to listen to the beginning of a lecture about internet marketing. What aspects of internet marketing do you think will be mentioned? Write four ideas.

3 Vocabulary check

Before you listen, make sure you understand the meaning of these words and phrases. How do you think they relate to marketing?

> endorsement   engagement   credibility
>
> followers   niche market   target audience

4 Listening for gist

Listen to the audio recording. Which of the ideas that you thought of in Section C2 are mentioned?

5 Detailed listening

Now listen for detail and complete each of the following statements correctly.

1   The main topic of the lecture is:

    A   how to reach the right audience.

    B   how to improve your website.

    C   how to use a range of social media.

2   The main problem with email marketing is:

    A   it's difficult to build up an address list.

    B   there are too many emails.

    C   people don't read the emails.

3   An instruction video is suggested as a way to:

    A   demonstrate a new product.

    B   review the pros and cons of a product.

    C   compare a product with other similar products.

4   The speaker suggests that mega influencers:

    A   sell millions of products.

    B   are paid a lot for their endorsements.

    C   are not popular with social media users.

5   Marketers like social media influencers because they:

    A   persuade people to buy products.

    B   help them identify new trends.

    C   are enthusiastic about their work.

6   When deciding to work with an influencer, it is most useful to look at:

    A   how many people follow them.

    B   which social media platforms they use.

    C   how they interact with their audience.

6 Post-listening discussion

1   > Critical thinking The lecturer says that social media influencers 'are always passionate about something'. Do you think this statement is true about all influencers? What kind of stereotype do you think it conveys? Is it positive or negative? What other stereotypes might people have about social media influencers?

b   The new assistant is hard-working and enthusiastic – *a real go-getter*.

c   He got a *golden handshake* worth $20 000 when he retired from his job.

d   Although the policeman was *off-duty*, he arrested the thief.

e   I'm called an 'office assistant', but really I'm just a general *dogsbody*.

f   Not liking the structure of big companies, I got work where I could *be my own boss*.

g   He's not *a high flyer*; he doesn't have any brilliant ideas, but you can depend on him.

h   Because of their working conditions, *blue-collar workers* are more likely to have accidents at work than *white-collar workers*.

8 Pronunciation: Linking sounds

1   Practise reading this advert aloud, checking your pronunciation with a partner. Does your partner feel you are reading naturally? Notice that if a word ends with a consonant and the next word begins with a vowel, the sounds are linked.

2   Stereotypes often form around particular occupations. What would you expect a 'typical' person doing each of the following jobs to be like?

- Sales person
- Prison governor
- Pop star
- Scientist

3   Do you think the stereotype of an occupation helps you when you are choosing which career to follow? Why / Why not?

4   Can you think of someone who doesn't fit the norm for their job? Explain your views.

7 Common work-related expressions

1   The lecturer suggests 'thinking outside the box' as a way to come up with ideas. What do you think she means?

2   Work out the meaning of the following expressions from the context:

a   I meet friends from work socially, but we always relax completely and no one *talks shop*.

BRIGHTEN UP YOUR SUMMER
– GET A JOB WITH US!

If you need extra cash and are 16+

WE NEED YOU!

There are lots of vacancies in our seafront restaurant.

It's fun, it's easy and hours to suit!

Apply to:
Ian.Valentine@mymail.com

2 Now mark the linked sounds in this advert and practise reading it aloud to your partner:

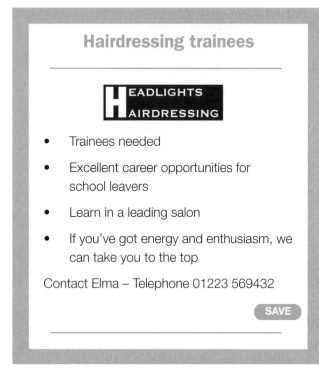

Hairdressing trainees

HEADLIGHTS
HAIRDRESSING

- Trainees needed

- Excellent career opportunities for school leavers

- Learn in a leading salon

- If you've got energy and enthusiasm, we can take you to the top

Contact Elma – Telephone 01223 569432

SAVE

9 Writing a job advert

You work in a laboratory. One morning you find this email from your boss.

Hendrik,

The lab is getting so messy that I've decided to advertise for someone to come in on Saturdays to wash up, sweep up and keep the area tidy. We can pay $8.00 per hour and travel expenses as well. It might interest a student. Can you draft an advert to put on our website? Use the lab office email and telephone number. Amy Jones will take the calls.

Thanks.

Joanna

1 Write a suitable advert based on the note.

2 Mark the linking sounds and show it to a partner. Does your partner agree with the word that you have chosen for linking?

3 Ask your partner to read the advert aloud. Correct the pronunciation if necessary (tactfully, of course).

D Recruitment with a difference

1 Pre-reading task

1 Do you enjoy 'fast food'? When (if ever) do you visit fast-food restaurants? What do you think are the strong points of these restaurants?

2 You are going to read an article about a fast-food restaurant that is run by deaf staff. Write down four questions you would like to see answered in the article.

Example: *How do customers communicate with the staff?*

2 Vocabulary check

Make sure you understand the meaning of these words and phrases, which you will meet in the article.

hearing impairment	recruiting
agile criteria	mentor

3 Reading for gist

Now read the article. Are any of the questions you wrote down in Section D1 answered?

Work without limits

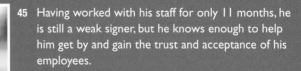

When Aly Sarhan, 28, was asked to head a new branch of the Kentucky Fried Chicken restaurant chain in Egypt, run
5 by deaf people, he didn't know what to expect.

'Working with 30 deaf young people is like working in a foreign land,' says Sarhan, who
10 took a crash course in Arabic sign language.

For Sarhan, however, the experience has been an eye-opening one, and has changed his attitudes towards
15 people with disabilities. 'My staff's hearing impairment does not stop them from doing anything a hearing person can do. They certainly have a whole load of determination in them,' he says.

The idea for a deaf-run KFC – the first in the Middle
20 East – was born when KFC's top management decided to 'fulfil their obligations towards society,' according to Sarhan. 'We found that deaf people existed in large numbers in Egypt, so we decided to do something for them,' he explains.

25 The obvious place to start recruiting from was the Deaf Society in Heliopolis. The KFC board used the same criteria they apply when choosing hearing applicants. Successful candidates had to be tactful, presentable, agile, and no older than 25 years of age. 'It was very
30 difficult turning people down, so we decided to pick the most eligible applicants, in addition to drawing up a long waiting list,' Sarhan says. For KFC, this was groundbreaking work.

Sarhan, one of the youngest store managers working at
35 KFC worldwide, says his biggest concern in the beginning was how to communicate with his employees. 'I did not know a single sign, so I had to use an interpreter. Whether the kids got to like or dislike me depended on the interpreter. I was determined, however, to learn the
40 language and remove any barriers between us,' he says.

That was easier said than done, he remembers. 'Arabic sign language is one of the most difficult languages you can learn, because it is mainly composed of gentle hand movements rather than distinct signs,' Sarhan explains.

45 Having worked with his staff for only 11 months, he is still a weak signer, but he knows enough to help him get by and gain the trust and acceptance of his employees.

So far, the restaurant has been a big success and
50 has helped create a supportive environment for the employees. 'What made the kids so enthusiastic about our new project was the fact that they get to be in a place where being deaf is the norm. Most of them have been through bad work experiences in which they
55 were the only person with hearing impairment in the place, which made them feel lonely and left out.'

This supportive environment, Sarhan says, has made many of the deaf employees depend on themselves more. 'Many of the employees had been spoilt and
60 pampered all their lives by their parents, out of pity, which made them rather bad-tempered and lazy. Once they began to like us, it was as if we found previously undiscovered energy.'

At the branch in Dokki, pictures on the menu
65 and light signals compensate for the lack of verbal communication. Customers simply have to point to the picture of the food item they want on the picture-menu. 'Despite that, lots of people come in with the feeling of not knowing what to do written all over
70 their faces. They start making signs, and are relieved to find out I can talk. I start carrying out the customer's role without signing, to show them how easy it all is,' Sarhan says.

The newly married Sarhan says that he considers his
75 staff part of his family now. He has become something of a mentor for them and has helped to create a friendly environment. 'This place has helped the deaf
80 employees psychologically, not just financially. I hope more companies will think of embarking on similar adventures. It's great to
85 help make a difference to people's lives,' he says.

by Manal el-Jesri

4 Comprehension check

1 Why did the restaurant choose to employ deaf people?

2 How did the management decide what would be the right criteria for selecting applicants?

3 Contrast the way employees felt about work before they began their jobs at the restaurant with their feelings about work now.

4 Describe the personality changes the employees undergo.

5 What does Sarhan feel he has gained from this work? Name two things.

5 Post-reading discussion

1 > Critical thinking Sarhan hopes other companies will follow the example of his restaurant and employ staff with disabilities. How can companies be encouraged to recruit a wider range of types of people? Share your ideas.

2 Sarhan says, 'It's great to help make a difference to people's lives.'

Jobs that are 'people-orientated', such as nursing and teaching, or in human resources and the hotel trade, bring different rewards and stresses from 'product-orientated jobs', such as those in engineering, carpentry or design.

Which kind of work would you find rewarding, and why?

3 Sarhan is described as being a 'mentor'. He supports and inspires his employees.

Many schools and colleges have 'mentoring schemes', whereby students are matched with successful adults of a similar background. The mentors give encouragement and practical advice to their students. Sometimes students spend time at the mentor's workplace, 'shadowing' them or doing some work experience.

a Do you think this is a good idea? Why / Why not?

b Who would you choose for your mentor and why?

6 Vocabulary practice

1 Put these adjectives into order, from most active to least active. Use a dictionary to check unfamiliar words.

lazy	hyperactive	energetic
	indolent	

2 Now put these adjectives into order, from most positive to most negative:

friendly	affectionate	indifferent
loving	supportive	critical	cold

3 Which word is the odd one out?

bad-tempered	cross	irritable
moody	placid	irate	grumpy

7 Language study: Similes

Similes are descriptive forms of comparison that enrich your writing. Study these examples:

'(It) is **like working** in a foreign land.'

Notice that like is followed by a noun or gerund:

It's **like a fridge** in here – let's turn the heating on.

It was **like being** on holiday.

As if / as though are followed by a verb clause, for example:

He felt **as though** his heart would burst.

Similes also include traditional expressions, such as: *as good as gold, as thin as a rake, as flat as a pancake, as white as snow, like talking to a brick wall* and many more.

Complete the following sentences with suitable similes.

a The room was so hot. It felt like _____.

b Her hands were as cold as _____.

c The house was so dirty. It looked as if

_____.

d Samira was thrilled with the news. She reacted as though _____.

e We're not allowed any freedom. It's like _____.

f I was so depressed when I couldn't get a job. It was as if _____.

8 Spelling: -able or -ible?

1 In the article, you met the adjectives *presentable* (line 28) and *eligible* (line 31). The adjective endings -*able* and -*ible* are often confused. From the word *depend*, we get *dependable*, but *convert* gives us *convertible*.

Complete the adjectives in these sentences, using a dictionary if necessary. Then learn by heart the spellings you find most difficult.

a I'm afraid I won't be avail_____ until after the 14th.

b The house was almost invis_____ in the fog.

c Fortunately, the disease was cur_____.

d I'm sure she'll make a respons_____ parent.

e I found Ken's story absolutely incred_____.

f That is a sens_____ idea.

g Let's take your car – it's more reli_____ than mine.

h Cheating in exams is not advis_____.

i Heavy snow made the house inaccess_____.

j Tiredness tends to make him irrit_____.

2 Now complete these adjectives with the endings -*able* or -*ible*. Then use each one in a sentence of your own:

a wash _____

b ined _____

c digest _____

d desir _____

e approach _____

f excit _____

g bear _____

h incomprehens _____

9 Phrasal verbs

1 Notice how these phrasal verbs are used in the article in Section D3.

turn down (line 30)

leave out (line 56)

draw up (lines 32–33)

carry out (line 71)

get by (line 47)

2 Use these phrasal verbs in a suitable form in sentences a–e.

a Gavin earns so little money, I don't know how he _____.

b She was careful to _____ all the instructions exactly.

c We're going on holiday next week, so I'm afraid I shall have to _____ your invitation.

d All the children in my son's class were invited to the party as we did not want to _____ anyone _____.

e The management have _____ new guidelines for staff interviews.

10 'Eye' idioms

1 Sarhan says the experience of working with people with disabilities has been 'an *eye-opening one*' (lines 13–14). What do you think he means by this?

2 Match the first parts of these sentences (a–h) with their endings (1–8).

a   Jim wanted to paint the room green, but Vera wanted blue, . . .

b   As she had to do the ironing, . . .

c   After a 12-hour flight, seeing my family at the airport . . .

d   When I first saw the Pyramids, I thought they were so amazing that . . .

e   Although it was very late, we walked home, . . .

f   The children weren't supposed to be eating sweets . . .

g   Visiting a foreign country for the first time . . .

h   The new manager was so much more astute than the old one that it was impossible . . .

1   I couldn't keep my eyes off them.

2   is quite an eye-opener.

3   keeping an eye out for a taxi all the way.

4   to pull the wool over his eyes.

5   but I decided to turn a blind eye to it.

6   was a sight for sore eyes.

7   I kept an eye on the baby.

8   so I'm afraid they didn't see eye to eye.

E   Preparing for work

1   How well does school prepare you for work?

1   What kind of career would you like to have when you leave school or college? What general things do you feel you have learnt at school that will help you?

Write down any ideas that seem relevant, even if you don't have a clear picture in your mind of the exact career you want to follow.

Examples:

I've learnt how to use my initiative when I do projects.

I've learnt foreign languages, which will give me international opportunities.

I've learnt to be more punctual, which is essential in most jobs.

I want to be an engineer, and my school arranged some work experience for me.

2   Have you held any positions of responsibility at school (e.g. helped run a club or society) that might be useful when you apply for college or work? What have you learnt from 'working' at school? Note down your ideas.

Examples:

I've learnt how to get on with different kinds of people.

I've become more mature.

Keep your notes, as you'll need them later.

2 Before you read

Many schools have a prefect system. Students who are prefects help the school run smoothly by keeping a check on other students' behaviour, doing litter patrols, helping in the dining room, and so on.

Do you think this is a good idea? Could there possibly be any drawbacks?

Students who show special abilities are chosen as head boy or head girl. In many schools, one of their main tasks is to represent the opinions of the students to the teachers.

Do you have a head girl or boy in your school? What are their duties? How are they chosen?

3 Reading, analysing and writing

Read this article from a school newsletter. What is its purpose?

1 Read the article again and underline examples of:

- complex sentence constructions, including defining and non-defining relative clauses (see Unit 8, Sections C10 and C11)

- comparisons, including comparative/ superlative constructions

- collocations describing qualities and skills

- idioms

- audience awareness.

2 Now write an appropriate closing paragraph to Luke's article, trying to use the same style:

Matthew is . . .

4 Comparing two styles

Now read this second newsletter article. What are the main differences between this article and Luke's? Make a list.

Example: *There are no paragraphs.*

HEAD BOY ELECTIONS

by Luke Adams

I know you all have your own ideas about the best candidate for head boy, but if you can spare a minute to read this, I'll explain why Matthew Okoro is the strongest and most experienced candidate.

Matthew, who is the youngest senior prefect in his year, has shown the most fantastic negotiating skills. Do you remember when we were banned from the swimming pool at lunchtime? Matthew was the one who persuaded the teachers to let us use it by offering to supervise it himself. The fact that we can go on school trips is due to Matthew's hard work, too. He worked round the clock to raise funds for a reliable minibus to take us on trips. He might not be as keen as some of us on playing team sports, but he is a regular supporter at all our matches.

Outside school, Matthew helps at a home for disabled teenagers. His experience has made him much more understanding of people's problems, which makes all the difference in a large, mixed school like ours.

HEAD GIRL ELECTIONS

by Leila Masoon

You've got to vote for Mira Patel. It's not fair if she isn't made head girl. She set up a social club. She worked after school every day. She worked on Saturdays as well. Before that, we didn't have a club. Now we have a club. Everyone goes to the club. It is good. She has stopped the bullying. The bullying was happening a lot. She spoke to the bullies. She made them stop. Now everyone is nice to each other.

She started a 'Welcome Day' for new students. Now new students are happy. They are not lonely. We had to wear skirts in winter. It was horrible. We were cold. Mira explained we wanted to wear trousers. Now we can. That was because of Mira.

The other prefects talk about themselves. They say how good they are. But Mira doesn't. She works in a hospital on Saturdays. She visits patients. They are patients who have no visitors. She knows more about people now. You must vote for Mira

5 Developing your writing style

Rewrite Leila's article so that it includes a wider range of structures and uses a more formal style. Use Luke's article to help you.

When you've finished, show your article to a partner. Listen carefully to their comments. How far do you agree with them? Will you change anything?

6 Brainstorming

1 > **Critical thinking** Work in small groups. Make notes about unemployment under the headings below, using the prompts to give you ideas. Remember, brainstorming allows you to write down anything you think of at the time. Don't worry about relevance at this stage.

Think about your own country. Note examples of problems and remedies that are relevant to your own situation.

Why are people unemployed?

- Industries such as . . . have closed down because . . . and so . . . .

- We import goods such as . . . and people prefer to buy these rather than the similar products we make at home, because . . . . This results in . . . in our own industries.

- Modern technology has . . . .

- The level of education and training is . . . .

- Industries have moved out of city centres because . . . and now city centres are . . . .

- People are leaving their farms in the countryside, which means . . . and going to the towns, which results in . . . .

What would help people get jobs?

- Government money could be given to . . . .

- Industries such as . . . could be encouraged to set up in our area.

- Training schemes such as . . . could be organised.

- Industries that use old, out-of-date *equipment* could . . . .

Other ideas

- The school-leaving age is now . . . and it could be changed to . . . which might help . . . .

- Colleges should offer more courses in . . . because . . . .

- Unemployed people could visit advice centres to find out . . . .

- Schools should arrange work experience in . . . .

- Careers guidance at school could . . . .

2 When you have finished, compare your notes with those of other groups and add any useful ideas. Keep your notes carefully, as you will use them later.

7 Reading an email to a newspaper

Study this email, which was written to a local newspaper. The writer makes four separate points. What are they?

Dear Editor,

Unhappy to be jobless

I do not usually write to newspapers but when I read your report, which suggested that young people were happy to be unemployed, I felt I had to respond.

I am a school leaver and, in my opinion, school leavers need much more detailed careers guidance. Moreover, I think schools should start a mentoring scheme, which would match pupils with successful career people. Spending one day a week with a mentor would be a real eye-opener and provide us with the work experience companies say they want but which students find so hard to get!

Furthermore, the majority of firms in our area are 'hi-tech', whereas some school leavers around here are not computer-literate. Firms should form a partnership with schools to develop training schemes that would enable us to learn the relevant skills.

I would also like to add that the statistic in your report '85 percent of pupils had no idea what life without a job is like' is a complete distortion of the truth. Many of us have parents who are out of work and we definitely do not want to be in that position.

When you are at school, getting a good job is like a high wall you have to climb. Young people need all the help they can get, not criticism.

Yours faithfully,

Fatima Aziz

8 Analysing the email

When you write formally, you should aim to use certain structures and phrases. The following list shows what you might include in a formal email. Re-read Fatima's email and find examples for each item on the list.

a   defining clauses

b   comparative structures

c   idioms

d   similes

e   linking devices

f   opening sentence

g   conclusion

h   style and register

9 Writing an email of reply

Write an email to Fatima describing the employment situation in your country and explaining what you think would help people in your country to get jobs.

Remember to:

*   keep to the topic
*   start a new paragraph for each new topic
*   begin and end the email with an appropriate phrase.

10 Correcting a report for the headteacher

Huan's class recently attended a careers talk given by a business owner about the skills he looks for in recruiting new employees. Huan is head boy and the headteacher asked him to write a report saying whether the talk was worthwhile or not.

Each sentence in the report has an extra word that should not be there. Read the report carefully, deleting the unnecessary words. The first one has been done for you.

Mr Chen's talk was the most interesting careers ~~the~~ event we have attended. He began by explaining how he had built up with his factory, 'Chen's Engineering,' from a small company to a large business. He explained that, when he was growing up, he helped them in the family engineering business. Mr Chen most enjoyed it repairing motorcycle engines. At a young age, he realised he liked working with machines, and got a lot of satisfaction from making a damaged engine to work well again. Most of all though, he learnt him about giving good customer service. He saw that his parents they were always patient and pleasant to customers, no matter what the effort. His father he would say, 'A man without a smiling face should not open a shop.' Mr Chen says he has never forgotten of those words, as they have been essential to the success of his business.

Mr Chen then told us what he looks for in when he recruits new employees. He said that job applicants think high exam grades are everything, but they are in wrong. He chooses people, including school leavers, because they are polite, enthusiastic and willing them to learn. He expects it employees to speak in a professional way to customers, and not to say, for instance, 'Hi you guys, wanna have a coffee?' He said everyone can you learn to be respectful, talk confidently on the phone, take notes and ask for help when necessary.

We appreciated and Mr Chen's careers talk very much, especially the emphasis on good communication skills at work. As a result of the talk, some of us now want to get wider our experience. We are thinking of doing voluntary work or getting us a part-time job in the holidays.

Huan Lee, Head Boy

11 Choosing appropriate vocabulary

When you read an exam question, you need to identify the topic and think of language connected to it. This also helps you to avoid answering the question in a way that is not relevant to the topic. For example, a question about medical experiments on animals should not include reasons why vaccines are necessary.

Read the following example questions and the vocabulary that follows. Working in small groups and using dictionaries, decide what vocabulary is unlikely to be connected to each question. Make sure you all agree. (Note: You are not being asked to answer the example questions.)

1   You had an important test and left home in very good time. However, something very unexpected happened on your journey. You arrived at the test only just before it was due to begin. Write

an account of what happened for your school newsletter.

decide my future   emergency services

decide my future   emergency services

with seconds to spare

not a moment to lose   panicked

indifferent   yelled   alarmed

shoved   strolled   anxious

broke out in a sweat   grabbed

announcements   absolutely desperate

share prices   snatched   despair

sales figures

2 You have been selected for a special training scheme that will help you get the job of your dreams. Explain the way you felt when you heard the news and how this training scheme will help bring you closer to your chosen career.

---

disappointed   over the moon

relieved   challenge

thrilled   develop new skills

isolated   practical experience

delighted   saddened

amazed   worthwhile

many benefits   colleagues

irritated   breathed a sigh of relief

golden opportunity

---

12 Timed writing

1 Choose one of the example questions that you find appealing from the previous exercise. Write about 150–200 words in response to the question. Allow yourself 15–20 minutes to write the composition.

2 Read your composition aloud to your group and pay close attention to the feedback. How far do you agree with the comments, and what would you change?

13 Listening: Four work scenarios

You will hear four short audio recordings. Answer each question using no more than three words for each detail. You will hear each recording twice.

1 **a** Maria is ringing up to change the time and date of a job interview. What alternative is she offered?

   b What is Maria doing on Tuesday?

2 **a** According to the careers talk, what special qualifications are needed to enter training schemes for the police force?

   b What two personal qualities are needed?

3 **a** What did the headteacher think about your friend's idea of helping at the children's clinic?

   b When does your friend want to visit the clinic?

4 **a** Has the speaker received good news or bad news?

   b What job does he want to train to do?

GRAMMAR SPOTLIGHT

Superlatives of long and short adjectives

Superlatives of short adjectives are made by adding *-(e)st*.

> Examples: *the oldest*   *the cleverest* *the largest*

With some words, there are also spelling changes.

> Examples: *lazy – laziest*   *big – biggest*
>
> She had **the happiest** *smile of anyone I had ever met.*

For superlatives of longer adjectives, we use *the most* before the adjective.

Example: *I thought Mel's presentation was* **the most interesting**.

Note these irregular superlatives: *the best, the worst, the furthest.*

Adverbs of degree

We can use adverbs of degree to modify or intensify an adjective. In Section A12, two of the participants' opinions were:

The packaging . . . should not look too childish.

The current names aren't . . . .interesting enough.

Notice that *too* goes before the adjective but *enough* goes after it.

Other adverbs of degree include *very, extremely, rather, quite, a little, a bit* (informal). These all go before the adjective.

> Example: *Don't you think it's* **a bit late** *to start watching a film?*

Practice

1 The article in Section E3 contained this example of superlatives:

   Matthew Okoro is the strongest and most experienced candidate.

   Skim-read the article and underline other examples of superlatives.

2 Skim-read the role-play descriptions in Section A12 and underline examples of adverbs of degree.

Complete the practice activities in your Workbook.

EXAM-STYLE QUESTIONS

READING AND WRITING

Reading and writing: multiple choice

Read the blog written by someone who is a freelance travel photographer, and then answer the questions.

A day in the life of a travel photographer

Alicia Stefanario offers some advice on what to expect in this career

Travel to exotic destinations, take photos of amazing places – and get paid for it! Sounds like a dream job, doesn't it? The career of a travel photographer can be exciting, glamorous and fun, but it's not always easy!

CONTINUED

Travel photography is one the most competitive fields you can be in. Years ago, photographers were commissioned by magazines
5 or companies to take pictures to illustrate a magazine story or advertise a resort or a hotel. They received a salary for the period of their contract and all their expenses, such as accommodation and travel, were paid for. Nowadays, that's very rare. Most photographers like myself are freelancers.
10 That means we pay our own expenses and take photos that we later try to sell, competing with thousands of other photographers doing the same thing. It's challenging, but on the other hand you also have more creative freedom and can follow your own path wherever it leads.

15 If you love travel and have a good technical knowledge of photography, this is definitely a career path for you to consider. But you also need to have patience, enthusiasm and stamina. Waiting hours for the perfect light. Getting up at 4 a.m. to climb a mountain so you can catch that perfect sunrise. Coping with hectic schedules and tight deadlines. This is all part of the job. Above all, you need the skill to take photos that are creative and unusual. Taking a picture of a mountain at sunrise isn't enough. It has to convey the magnificence, the
20 solemnity, the majesty of the scene, so that the viewer can really feel what it's like to be there.

Travelling around the world sounds fun, but also has its downside. I spend a lot of time in airports and train stations, waiting for transport to arrive or pushing luggage and equipment from one place to another. I'm frequently away from home and family. It can be really upsetting to miss someone's birthday or anniversary because a photo shoot got delayed. You'll often come up against unpredictable situations, requiring a sudden
25 change of plans; a flood that makes it impossible to drive somewhere, a rainstorm that knocks out the electricity. It's important to be flexible and not get too disappointed when your plans don't work out.

Marketing your work may not seem like an obvious part of the job, but in today's competitive market it is vital. To be successful, photographers have to build up their online profile. Having a website with an online portfolio is an essential way to showcase your work and you need to dedicate time to keeping it fresh and up-to-date.
30 Developing a niche market for a specific kind of photo, for example underwater caves or tropical plants, can also help to attract a strong customer base. Selling to online libraries is another way to earn money, but again you have to have photos that stand out from the crowd. It's worth looking through the libraries to see what kinds of photos are missing or could be improved upon.

This all makes it seem as if it will take a long time to develop a career in this field. And it's true, it takes time
35 to build a name for yourself, but with dedication and determination, it will be worth it and, as you follow your path, you'll find so many amazing places to visit and so many exciting stories to tell.

CONTINUED

1 How was travel photography different in the past?

A Photographers were employed full-time. ☐

B Companies didn't pay for train tickets or hotels. ☐

C Photographers had to do several jobs at one time. ☐ [1]

2 What does 'it' refer to in line 10?

A Paying expenses ☐

B Taking photos ☐

C Selling photos ☐ [1]

3 In paragraph 3, Alicia mentions a sunrise to illustrate:

A that you need to be patient. ☐

B how difficult the job is. ☐

C an exciting moment in her career. ☐ [1]

4 Alicia suggests that the job suits people who:

A like getting up early. ☐

B like everything to be on time ☐

C adapt easily to new situations. ☐ [1]

5 Alicia advises looking through online libraries in order to:

A get ideas for what kinds of photos to take. ☐

B find photos that are similar to yours. ☐

C understand what photos are popular and why. ☐ [1]

6 What was Alicia's main reason for writing this article?

A To persuade people to take up this career ☐

B To warn readers about the negative aspects of this job ☐

C To describe why this is a dream job ☐ [1]

[Total: 6]

Reading and writing: informal

You recently spent the holidays working at an international holiday camp for children aged 11–12 years.

Write an email to tell a friend about the experience.

In your email, you should:

- describe the kind of work you did

- explain what you learnt from doing it

- say whether you think your friend would also enjoy an experience like this.

Write about 120 to 160 words. [15]

[Total: 15]

CONTINUED

Reading and writing: formal

There is a proposal at your school to offer students two weeks of local work experience after exams have finished. Your headteacher has asked you to write an article about the idea.

In your article, give the benefits and drawbacks of this idea, and suggest a compromise solution.

Here are some comments from other students about the idea:

> We will learn skills that will help us understand the working world.

> We would not benefit because work experience is not like doing a real job.

> It will be useful when we apply for a real job in the future.

> Holidays should be for relaxing and spending time with family and friends.

Now write an article for the school magazine.

The comments above may give you some ideas, and you should also use some ideas of your own.

Write about 120 to 160 words.   [15]

[Total: 15]

Reading and writing: formal

Your class recently went on a trip to a careers event. The organisers want students' opinions about the event, and you have been asked to write a report.

In your report, say what you learnt from the event, and suggest how it could be improved for next year.

Here are some comments from students in your class:

> We did not find out what training courses are available in our area.

> It made me much more aware of the jobs I can apply for.

> We were given helpful information about the skills employers look for.

> I still don't understand what I need to do in order to get a job.

Now write a report for the organisers of the careers event.

The comments above may give you some ideas, and you should also use some ideas of your own.

Write about 120 to 160 words.   [15]

[Total: 15]

CONTINUED

LISTENING

Listening: interview

You will hear an interview with a writer called Peter Robinson.

For each question, choose the correct answer, **A**, **B** or **C**, and put a tick (✓) In the appropriate box.

You will hear the interview twice.

Now look at questions 1–8.

1   Peter started writing seriously:

   A   while he was at school.   ☐

   B   after finishing his studies.   ☐

   C   when he had a full-time job.   ☐   [1]

2   How did Peter get his first book published?

   A   He found a literary agent.   ☐

   B   A friend of his worked in publishing.   ☐

   C   A publisher gave him some advice.   ☐   [1]

3   What inspires him to write?

   A   He visualises part of the story.   ☐

   B   He writes a list of people and places.   ☐

   C   He starts with an interesting storyline.   ☐   [1]

4   How does he deal with a mental block?

   A   He does some physical exercise.   ☐

   B   He listens to music.   ☐

   C   He works on a different project for a while.   ☐   [1]

5   What is Peter's daily routine like?

   A   He writes a fixed number of pages.   ☐

   B   He works for a target number of hours.   ☐

   C   He writes all day until dinner time.   ☐   [1]

6   What quality does Peter say is important for a writer?

   A   Accuracy   ☐

   B   Flexibility   ☐

   C   Independence   ☐   [1]

7   What does Peter say about book festivals?

   A   He doesn't like difficult questions from the audience.   ☐

   B   He enjoys meeting his readers.   ☐

   C   He prefers giving interviews on the radio.   ☐   [1]

CONTINUED

8   Peter says that reading novels is a way of:

   A   understanding ourselves.   ☐

   B   becoming a writer.   ☐

   C   telling your own story.   ☐   [1]

[Total: 8]

SPEAKING

Warm-up questions

Warm-up questions help you feel more relaxed before you move on to answering assessed questions.

Take turns asking and answering the questions. Speak for 1–2 minutes.

- Can you tell me about your favourite subject at school?
- What do you usually do at the weekend?
- What kind of outdoor activities do you like?

Interview

Read the questions. In pairs, decide who will play the interviewer and who will play the student. Then role-play the interview. Speak for about 2–3 minutes. Change roles and role-play the interview again.

Choosing a job

- What jobs are the most important and worthwhile in the world today?
- What kind of skills and qualities are important to get a good job?
- What kind of careers are you interested in, and why?

Short talk

Read the options and compare them. You have one minute to prepare your talk. Now give a short talk to your partner. Speak for about 2 minutes. Change roles and listen to your partner's talk.

Choosing a careers event

Your headteacher is considering careers events for your year group. There are two options:

- logging onto an online international careers event
- going out to a local careers event.

Discuss the advantages and disadvantages of each option. Say which option you would prefer, and why.

Discussion

Read the discussion questions. In pairs, decide who will play the interviewer and who will play the student. Then role-play the discussion. Speak for about 3 minutes. Change roles and role-play the interview again.

- What do you think is most important when choosing a job or a career?
- What aspects of a job would you find most motivating or rewarding?
- What kind of skills can you learn at school which will help you in a future job?

SELF-ASSESSMENT CHECKLIST

Reflect on what you have learnt in this unit. For each area listed, decide whether you feel confident or need more practice. If you feel you need more practice, you will find some ideas to help you in Advice for Success. Come back to your self-assessment scores later in your course and see if your confidence has improved.

I can ...	Need more practice	Fairly confident
discuss issues related to work and employment, using appropriate vocabulary		
identify connections between ideas, opinions and attitudes in an article		
write a formal letter and an article using appropriate style and register		
understand key points and bias in a lecture		
take part in a role-play discussion for developing a new product		

ADVICE FOR SUCCESS

This section is to help you help yourself. Choose the suggestions you like and adapt them if you want to. Make notes about what you do and how it helped you.

Extending your skills

1 Refresh your memory by studying your vocabulary records, reading through good examples of your own work and looking at the examples in your book. Take regular, short breaks and do something relaxing. You probably can't concentrate effectively for more than 20 or 30 minutes at a time.

2 Ask your teacher for practice papers. Time yourself answering the questions. Why not practise with a good friend?

3 Concentrate on staying relaxed and calm. Visualise yourself completing the paper well and in good time. Relax the night before your exam by doing something enjoyable such as watching a film.

Showcasing your skills

4 The order in which you tackle questions on reading and writing papers is a matter of personal preference, but it's generally a good

idea to answer those questions you feel most confident about first.

5 Make sure you don't run out of time because you have spent too long answering one section of the paper. The number of marks for each individual question is shown at the end of the question.

6 Always read the questions very carefully. Don't be tempted to answer comprehension questions without reading the passage first. You will probably miss important links in the text. For summaries and compositions, make sure you understand the 'angle' of the question.

7 Never try to twist a pre-prepared essay to fit the topic of the composition. It's far better to tackle the question confidently and write something fresh that answers the question set.

8 Try to stay calm and relaxed during your exam. Flex your fingers so they do not become stiff, and stretch from time to time. Make sure you are sitting comfortably and with the correct posture.

9 If you get really stuck on a question, leave it, move on to another, and go back to that question later.

> Acknowledgements

The authors and publishers acknowledge the following sources of copyright material and are grateful for the permissions granted. While every effort has been made, it has not always been possible to identify the sources of all the material used, or to trace all copyright holders. If any omissions are brought to our notice, we will be happy to include the appropriate acknowledgements on reprinting.

We would like to thank CATS Cambridge for their help with the videos; especially Mangy Greve and the students who featured in the videos.

'Facing the Fear' is adapted from 'A mother makes up for lost years' by Angela Neustatter for the Telegraph Magazine, 15 June 1996 © Telegraph Media Group Limited; Data on world literacy rates from UNESCO; OurWorldinData. org/world-population-growth (data source: UN World Populations Prospects, 2017); Extract adapted from 'Extreme conditions, loud birds and fresh food by boat – could you live on a remote island?' by Patrick Barkham 20 April 2019, Copyright Guardian News & Media Ltd 2021; Global greenhouse gas emissions data adapted from OurWorldinData. org (by Hannah Ritchie, 2020) Data Source: Climate Watch, the World Resources Institute, 2020; Extract from 'Meet the Cyclist Changing the Streets of Mexico City Into a Bike Lane for All' from theculturetrip.com, reproduced with the permission of Culture Trip; Extract adapted from 'Offshore Italy' in *Good Housekeeping* May 1996, reproduced with permission of Hearst; Extract adapted from 'Flipping amazing... the moment a humpback whale 'thanks' rescuers who saved it from dying tangled in fishing nets', Daily Mail, July 2011 reproduced with permission of dmg media licensing; Extracts from 'Young workers who do not want to be tied down turn to freelancing' by Nur Asyiqin Mohamad Salleh, December 2015, Straits Times, Straits Times, reproduced with permissions of Singapore Press Holdings Ltd; Projected world population by level of education from OurWorldinData.org/future-population-growth, Data source:Global Projection, Medium SSP2 - IIASA (2016); 'Work without limits' adapted from 'Faces – signs of concern' by Manal el-Jesri in Egypt Today; Extract adapted from 'Can you cure a phobia' by Richard Reid © Telegraph Media Group Limited 2009. Reproduced with permission of Telegraph; Excerpt from 'A life-saving stroll› © Telegraph Media Group Limited 2009. Reproduced with permission of Telegraph; 'The thrill of watching whales' adapted from 'Seeing cetaceans' by Anna Levin, reproduced with permission of Anna Levin www.anna.levinwriting.co.uk

Thank you for permission to use the following images

Cover Andriy Onufriyenko/Getty Images; *Inside* Unit 1 Shannon Fagan/GI; Chan Srithaweeporn/GI; Deimagine/ GI; JohnnyGreig/GI; Fotokostic/GI; SDI Productions/GI; Abstract Aerial Art/GI; Jose Luis Pelaez Inc/GI; Xijian/ GI; Kate_sept2004/GI; Johner Images/GI; John M Lund Photography Inc/GI; Drazen/GI; Ezra Bailey/GI; David Sacks/GI; Aleksandr Zubkov/GI; GuruXOOX/GI; JGI/Jamie Grill/GI; SOREN ANDERSSON/GI; Paul Harizan/ GI; MachineHeadz/GI; Rifka Hayati/GI; Kali9/GI; Unit 2 Heath Korvola/GI; JGI/Tom Grill/GI; Lane Oatey/ Blue Jean Images/GI; Delmaine Donson/GI; LaylaBird/GI; MEDITERRANEAN/GI; Mike Watson Images/GI; Hill Street Studios/GI; PhotosIndia.Com/GI; Eli_asenova/GI; Thomas Barwick/GI; ChrisBoswell/GI; Aynur_sib/ GI; LightFieldStudios/GI; Johner Images/GI; Matt McNulty - Manchester City/GI; Milanvirijevic/GI; Jasmin Merdan/GI; Blend Images - Rolf Bruderer/GI; SDI Productions/GI; monkeybusinessimages/GI; Victor Ling/GI; Ben Welsh/GI; SolStock/GI; Mayur Kakade/GI; Unit 3 Lindrik/GI; Henryk Sadura/GI; Motortion/GI; Maskot/ GI; Joe Alfano/GI; Tara Moore/GI; StefaNikolic/GI; fotoVoyager/GI; Naris Visitsin/GI; ralucahphotography.ro/ GI; Thomas Demarczyk/GI; coldsnowstorm/GI; MickyWiswedel/GI; Keith Kamiya/GI; Vincent Jary/GI; Heritage Images/GI; ViewStock/GI; Alistair Berg/GI; WhitcombeRD/GI; Nuzulu/GI; KatarzynaBialasiewicz/GI; Aleramo/ GI; Image Source/GI; AJ_Watt/GI; rudi_suardi/GI; Unit 4 Jorg Greuel/GI; Anton Petrus/GI; Nayan Kar/SOPA Images/GI; AleksandarGeorgiev/GI; coldsnowstorm/GI; Chris Gorman/GI; Yasser Chalid/GI; Magnus Larsson/ GI; SUJIT JAISWAL/AFP/GI; CSA Images/GI; Leonid Andronov/GI; Pavliha/GI; Rhoberazzi/GI; Tetra Images/ GI; SEBASTIAN KAULITZKI/SCIENCE PHOTO LIBRARY/GI; Canetti/GI; Simon McGill/GI; ©fitopardo/GI; bo1982/GI; Orbon Alija/GI; Massinissa Anki/GI; chictype/GI; narvikk/GI; Hill Street Studios/GI; miodrag ignjatovic/ GI; Alex Saurel/GI; Lisa Marie/GI; Unit 5 kali9/GI; cristianl/GI; Donald Iain Smith/GI; FG Trade/GI; David Wall/